GRAMMAR IS A DESTINATION

Third Edition

Dr. Bonnie Ronson
Hillsborough Community College

Kendall Hunt
publishing company

In Memory of
my father T. A. Whaley
and my sister Joy Hagy
whose stories about the Wild Man, Why Cross the Road, The Eggs and the Snake, The Light Changes
Everything, and The Race Horse are legacies from their gentle hearts.

Readings from Stories to inspire pgs. © by Bonnie Ronson

Cover image © Shutterstock, Inc.

Kendall Hunt
publishing company

www.kendallhunt.com
Send all inquiries to:
4050 Westmark Drive
Dubuque, IA 52004-1840

Copyright © 2010, 2012, 2014 by Kendall Hunt Publishing Company

ISBN 978-1-4652-3953-2

Printed in the United States of America
10 9 8 7 6 5 4 3 2 1

Contents

INTRODUCTION

Skillful writing can be an invaluable personal and professional tool. Skillful writing can give an applicant a winning edge in the competitive arena. Poor writing, however, constricts the writer, diminishing his or her qualifications and credibility. Writing conveys ideas, provides information, presents views and opinions, and identifies and even labels the writer. Writing is an essential component of every project and every idea. Writing provides verification and documentation from the conception of an idea to the completion of a project. If the details are ineffectively written or not recorded at all, an idea may never be actualized or a project may never be realized or its benefits justified or its possibilities visualized. Effective writing maximizes communication. Capable writing documents achievements, goals, and possibilities. Unquestionably, writing can represent a person's strengths and abilities or demonstrate a person's weaknesses and limitations. The written word can be used to persuade, to incite, and to motivate. The written word can be reviewed, revised, filed, recorded, and retrieved. It can serve as legal documentation or to record a person's most private thoughts. It can determine the fate of a nation and the direction of future generations.

The United States Constitution, the Magna Carta, the Bible, and the Koran are just a few examples of the power and permanence of the written word. Effective writing stimulates reflection and promotes change. It can elicit compelling emotions and leave lasting impressions. Novels are still read, poems are still recited, and songs are still sung even though their writers have long departed from the earth. The written word endures even after civilizations expire.

The written word can be altered, manipulated, controlled, and changed. The written word can also be stored or filed for thousands of years, or it can be erased and forgotten in a second. The written word can provide a voice for millions of people, and it can deliver a message to a million others. The written word can change the way people think. It can strengthen their beliefs or leave them confused and uncertain. Effective writing is a skill. Like any other skill or talent, effective writing can be developed and ultimately mastered.

Anyone can learn to write. There are writing rules and grammar mechanics that guide and direct the learning process. Effective writing is a powerful instrument to have at your command. Effective writing can improve your confidence and, ultimately, your quality of life.

SENTENCE PARTS

Writing is basically a simple and common means of expression. The process of writing involves grouping together a number of words to convey a meaning or a message that the reader can understand. There are accepted conventions or standards that are used to help the writer put thoughts into words.

EXAMPLE OF A CLEAR THOUGHT

The student earned an "A" on the essay exam because his responses were clearly stated and supported by examples from class discussions.

EXAMPLE OF AN UNCLEAR THOUGHT

Examples from class discussions on the essay exam earned the student an "A" because clearly stated and supported were his responses.

⚡ Exercise 1

Rewrite the following sentence so that the meaning is clearly understood.

for washing its food the raccoon is known because water increases the sensitivity in its paws to feel the food better

_____

_____

_____

Did you begin with a capital letter? Did you place a period at the end of your sentence? Did you add spaces between the words?

Starting a sentence with a capital letter and ending the sentence with the appropriate punctuation (either a period, a question mark, or an exclamation mark) are some of the standards that are used in writing to help the reader know when thoughts begin and end. Words are separated from one another to make them easier to recognize and their meanings easier to understand.

Does your sentence look something like this one?

The raccoon is known for washing its food in water because water increases the sensitivity in the paws, so the raccoon can feel the food better.

Did you move the word "raccoon" toward the front of the sentence? Did you follow "raccoon" with the words "is known"?

The word "raccoon" is the subject of the sentence. The subject is the person, place, or thing that the sentence is about. "Is known" is the verb of the sentence. Every sentence has a subject and a verb. Usually the verb follows the subject and describes what the subject is doing. You may have placed "is known" after "raccoon" without knowing why you did that. Word order, subject then verb, for instance, is considered one of the standard practices in the English language.

The example also has two sentences, so it has two subjects and two verbs. The word "so" connects the two sentences. "So" is called a coordinating conjunction. The coordinating conjunctions for, and, nor, but, or, yet, and so are used to connect sentences. "Raccoon" is the subject of the second sentence and "can feel" is the verb. Look at your rewrite again to see if you have two sentences. If you do, how did you connect them?

Every sentence has a **subject**. The subject is either a noun or a pronoun. A noun is a person (Alice Jones), a place (Tampa), a thing (book), an idea (freedom), or an emotion (love). A **noun** that is a person, place, or thing is easy to recognize. These nouns can be seen. Everything that can be seen or touched is a noun. There are trillions of nouns. A sentence may have more than one noun: The *dog* jumped over the *log*. Dog and log are both nouns. Dog is the subject of the sentence because it is the noun performing the action. The subject of a sentence is the noun or pronoun (he, she, it, they, I, we) that performs the action or that is the focus of the action.

⚡ Exercise 2

Look around you and write down twenty things that you see.

1. _____	6. _____	11. _____	16. _____
2. _____	7. _____	12. _____	17. _____
3. _____	8. _____	13. _____	18. _____
4. _____	9. _____	14. _____	19. _____
5. _____	10. _____	15. _____	20. _____

You may have had pencil, pen, hand, shoe, foot, head, hair, fingers, etc.

Nouns are generally male, female, or without gender (neither male nor female).

All of these things that you saw and wrote down are nouns.

Every sentence has a **verb**. The verb expresses what a noun is doing or what is being done to a noun. A verb can show action. The dog *is jumping* over the log. A verb can also connect a noun to its description. The dog *is* large. The dog *was* fat, but now the dog *is* skinny. A verb can also indicate a perception. The dog *looks* mean.

Exercise 3

Underline the verb in each sentence.

1. Birds sing.

2. Flowers smell sweet.

3. Toads are croaking.

4. The sun was hot.

5. Thunder is loud.

Exercise 4

Now that you have identified the verb, circle the subject in each of the sentences above.

Pronouns identify nouns as male, female, or it. Unlike the trillions of nouns, there are a limited number of pronouns. A pronoun that refers to a man or a boy, for instance, is *he* or *him*. A pronoun that refers to a woman or a girl is *she* or *her*.

A pronoun that refers to a tree or a desk is *it*. The pronouns that refer to a group of females or a group of males or a group of things are *they* or *them*. A pronoun can take the place of a noun in a sentence. The dog chased the cat and barked at *it*.

The pronoun it replaced the noun cat in the sentence.

Exercise 5

Write he, she, it, or they next to the appropriate noun.

1. bicycle _____   6. mother _____
2. uncle _____   7. brother _____
3. tree _____   8. John _____
4. tables _____   9. houses _____
5. Mary _____   10. girls _____

Adjectives describe nouns. Adjectives make it possible to differentiate similar nouns. The *tall* man. The *short* man. The *muscular* man. The writer can make the man any size or shape just by changing the adjective in front of man.

Adjectives are important because they bring nouns to life and give them particular characteristics. The *tall, funny* man made the children laugh. Tall and funny are both adjectives because they describe the man. Adjectives usually come in front of a noun.

Exercise 6

Underline the adjective in each set.

1. green leaves

2. blazing fire

3. hollow log

4. muddy water

5. ferocious storm

Adverbs describe verbs, adverbs, and adjectives. An easy way to remember adverbs is to think of an adverb as adding to a verb: **ad verb**.

Adverbs explain how an action is carried out: The dog *quickly* jumped over the log. Adverbs also explain when and where the action is carried out. Adverbs also describe adjectives and other adverbs.

The *very* large dog *loudly* barked at the intruder.

Exercise 7

Underline the adverb in each set.

1. slowly walked

2. talked yesterday

3. diligently studied

4. bright red wagon

5. awkwardly jumped

Prepositional phrases are groups of words within a sentence that describe where something is or where something occurs. Prepositional phrases begin with words like under and over. An easy way to identify prepositions is to think of what a mouse can do to a table. A mouse can run *over* a table, *under* a table, *below* a table, *above* a table, and so on. The subject and the verb of a sentence are easier to identify if the prepositional phrases are crossed out.

Exercise 8

Cross out the prepositional phrase in each sentence.

1. The turtle slowly walked across the busy street.

2. The students studied under the bright lights.

3. Boats can be seen in the distance.

4. A trail of ants traveled up the wall.

5. The motorcycle raced down the street.

Exercise 9

Now that you have crossed out the prepositional phrases, circle the subject and underline the verb in each sentence above.

Below is a list of commonly used prepositions:

above	between	toward
across	beyond	under
after	by	underneath
against	down	until
along	during	up
although	for	with
among	from	within
around	inside	without
at	into	of
because	near	
before	over	
behind	past	
below	since	
beneath	to	

A **noun** is a person, place, thing, idea, or emotion. **Proper nouns** are capitalized and name specific people, places, or things: *Aunt Mary, Lowry Park*, and *Hillsborough Community College* are proper nouns. **Common nouns** are not capitalized and do not name specific people, places, or things: *aunt, college*, and *park* are common nouns. Nouns that represent a unit or a group are called **collective nouns**: *class, jury*, and *committee* are collective nouns. Nouns can be **singular** or **plural**: *tree* is a singular noun while *trees* is a plural noun.

Exercise 10

Identify each of the following nouns by checking the appropriate column.

	PROPER	COMMON
1. ocean	_____	_____
2. Canada	_____	_____
3. Gulf of Mexico	_____	_____
4. national park	_____	_____
5. cats and dogs	_____	_____

Exercise 11

Identify each of the following nouns by checking the appropriate column.

	SINGULAR	PLURAL
1. lakes	_____	_____
2. pen and pencil	_____	_____
3. desks	_____	_____
4. a bird's nest	_____	_____
5. computer	_____	_____

To form the plural of a noun add **-s, -es, -ies**, or **-ves** according to how the singular noun is spelled.

Add **-s** to most nouns:

Singular	Plural
book	books
car	cars

Add **-es** to nouns ending in **-ch, -sh**, and **-x**.

Singular	Plural
ranch	ranches
crush	crushes

Drop the **-y** and add **-ies** to nouns ending in a **-y** preceded by a consonant.
Add only an **-s** if the **-y** is preceded by a vowel.

Singular	Plural
baby	babies
day	days

Add **-ves** to some nouns ending in **-f** or **-fe** and drop the **-f** or **-fe**.

Singular	Plural
wolf	wolves
knife	knives

Some nouns do not change spelling from singular to plural.

Singular	Plural
deer	deer
sheep	sheep

Some nouns change their spelling to form the plural

Singular	Plural
tooth	teeth
woman	women

Add **-s** to the root word of some compound nouns to form their plurals.

Singular	Plural
maid-of-honor	maids-of-honor
mother-in-law	mothers-in-law

Exercise 12

Change the following singular nouns to plural.

1. half _____
2. box _____
3. table _____
4. movie _____
5. brother-in-law _____

6. lady _____
7. printer _____
8. candy _____
9. foot _____
10. child _____

SUBJECT/OBJECT/VERB/AGREEMENT

A singular subject has a singular verb. The subject of a verb is always in the nominative case. The object of a verb must be in the objective case.

Examples

WRONG: John and her were in the front row.

RIGHT: John and she were in the front row.

   Note: You can hear the correct pronoun to use if you read the sentence without the noun that accompanies the pronoun: Her was in the front row. She was in the front row.

WRONG: John read the book to Jane and I.

RIGHT: John read the book to Jane and me.

   John read the book to I. John read the book to me.

WRONG: John is taller than me.

RIGHT: John is taller than I.

   John is taller than me is. John is taller than I am.

Exercise 13

Underline the nouns in each sentence.

1. The koala is a unique marsupial native to Australia.

2. Koalas are often called koala bears because of their close resemblance to teddy bears.

3. Koalas are also sometimes classified as wombats, but the main difference is that the koala has a bigger and longer body structure than a wombat.

4. A baby kangaroo is referred to as a "Joey."

5. Kangaroos are the only known large mammals that are mobile through hopping.

6. Another mammal that gets around by hopping is the lemur.

7. Emus and ostriches are the only birds that are unable to fly.

8. Ostriches lay the biggest eggs of any bird species.

9. The dingo is known as the feral dog of Australia.

10. Cold-blooded animals need warm climates to survive.

Exercise 14

Underline the subject and circle the verb in each sentence

1. Some scientists believe that an enormous asteroid collided with the Earth, killing most of the species, including dinosaurs.

2. Humankind has dumped at least 10,000 pieces of equipment in space that will forever revolve around the Earth.

3. The sun is continually growing and in five billion years will consume Venus.

4. The highest peak in our solar system exists on Mars.

5. The Olympus Mons on Mars is 2 ½ times taller than Mount Everest.

6. Humans see only a fraction of the trillions and trillions of stars in the universe.

7. The Milky Way Galaxy is only one of 100 billion galaxies.

8. Each galaxy consists of 100 billion stars.

9. Neil Armstrong was the first person to set foot on the moon.

10. The first moon landing occurred on July 21, 1969.

11. The moon is considered a natural satellite.

12. The moon orbits the Earth approximately every 27 days.

13. The universe was created nearly 14 billion years ago.

14. Some scientists believe that a single cosmic egg exploded, called the big bang, resulting in the creation of the universe.

15. The Earth is the third planet from the sun.

16. Life has not been determined to exist on any other planet than Earth.

17. The Earth's ozone layer blocks harmful radiation.

18. Nearly 75% of the Earth's surface is covered by water.

19. It takes one year for the Earth to rotate around the sun.

20. The moon is responsible for the oceans' tides.

Exercise 15

Underline the subject and circle the verb in each sentence

1. The hottest recorded temperature on Earth measured 136 degrees Fahrenheit.

2. The coldest recorded temperature on Earth measured minus 129 degrees Fahrenheit.

3. The world's tallest waterfall is in Venezuela.

4. The largest volcano is in Hawaii, and it is more than nine miles high; however, the Olympus Mons on Venus is 16 miles high.

5. The deadliest earthquake occurred in China, killing nearly 1 million people.

6. No one can dig to China from the opposite side of the Earth because the distance is 8,000 miles.

7. The moon used to orbit the Earth in 20 days, but now that the moon is farther away from the Earth, and it takes 27 days to complete its orbit.

8. Longer orbits mean longer days, so when the moon was closer to the Earth, a day was 18 hours long.

9. The Nile River is the longest river on Earth.

10. Lloro, Colombia, has nearly 40 feet of rain per year.

11. The largest canyon on Earth is the Grand Canyon.

12. The Atlantic Ocean is one-half the size of the Pacific Ocean.

13. The average depth of the Pacific Ocean is 2 ½ miles.

14. The deepest part of the Pacific Ocean is estimated to be nearly 7 miles.

15. The Pacific Ocean is the largest ocean.

16. The center of the Earth is estimated to be 7000 degrees Fahrenheit.

17. The strongest wind recorded on Earth, 318 mph, was generated by a tornado.

18. The planet Neptune has winds in excess of 900 mph.

19. Greenland is the largest Island.

20. The mountain range called the Mid-Atlantic Ridge is in the Atlantic Ocean.

Exercise 16

Underline the subject and circle the verb in each sentence

1. The Mid-Atlantic Ridge is the longest mountain range.

2. Approximately one-half trillion gallons of water are used each day!

3. Glaciers contain nearly 70% of the world's fresh water.

4. Antarctica is the coldest continent.

5. Diamonds are the hardest minerals.

6. Cows become agitated when they smell blood, so the smell of blood is minimized in slaughter houses.

7. Dolphins sleep with one eye open.

8. Crocodiles cannot see under water, but they have a keen sense of hearing.

9. Tarantulas can live two years without food.

10. The animal that makes the loudest noise is the Blue Whale.

11. The hummingbird is the smallest bird in the world, weighing only 1 ounce.

12. Reaching speeds of 124 mph the falcon is the world's fastest bird.

13. Tea has been a drink of choice for nearly 5000 years.

14. Britain's Royal Family is among the richest families on earth.

15. Marlon Brando refused to accept the Oscar for his role in the *Godfather* movie.

Exercise 17

Underline the subject and circle the verb in each sentence

1. The Gulf of Mexico touches Florida, Alabama, Mississippi, Louisiana, and Texas.

2. The mainland shores of the gulf stretch more than 4000 miles, and the total area of the gulf is 600,000 square miles.

3. The deepest part of the gulf is 12,000 feet.

4. Hundreds of artificial reefs line the Florida coasts.

5. These reefs are built from the remains of sunken ships, airplanes, and bridges.

6. Florida has more artificial reefs than any other state.

7. The Gulf of Mexico is home to the gentle manatee.

8. Alligators and crocodiles make the Gulf of Mexico their home, too.

9. The gulf is also home to mangrove jungles.

10. Mangroves are state-protected plants.

11. The mangroves are home to a myriad of aquatic life.

12. Fish lay their eggs in mangrove roots, birds nest in the limbs, oysters attach themselves to roots, fish feed off of the root algae, and larger fish feed on the smaller fish that feed on the root algae.

13. Raccoons eat the oysters that have attached themselves to the mangrove roots.

14. Mangrove roots allow land extensions because they trap debris.

15. Mangrove jungles help protect the coastline from erosion.

PRONOUN

A **pronoun** takes the place of a noun, represents a noun, or refers to a noun. There are trillions of nouns but only a small number of pronouns. Pronouns are helpful in identifying the gender of a person, place, or thing as male (**he, him, his**) or as female (**she, her**). **It** is used if the place or thing is neither male nor female. The pronouns **they** and **them** refer to a group of nouns regardless of gender. The noun the pronoun refers to is called an **antecedent**.

Pronoun and Antecedent Agreement

A pronoun must agree with its antecedent in number, gender, and person. The term *antecedent* means the noun or the pronoun to which another pronoun refers.

Examples

WRONG: The <u>company</u> honored <u>their</u> top producers at the banquet.
RIGHT: The <u>company</u> honored <u>its</u> top producers at the banquet.
    Note: The pronouns "everybody," "everyone," "someone," "somebody," and "nobody" are singular and take singular verbs. These pronouns mean each individual.
WRONG: <u>Everyone</u> <u>were</u> singing from <u>their</u> <u>books</u>.
RIGHT: <u>Everyone</u> <u>was</u> singing from <u>his or her</u> <u>book</u>.
WRONG: <u>Everybody</u> accepts <u>their</u> responsibilities.
RIGHT: <u>Everybody</u> accepts <u>his or her</u> responsibilities.

Example

   Dinosaurs became extinct 65 million years ago because <u>their</u> environment changed and <u>their</u> source of food was depleted.

Who and Whom: " Who" Is Subjective and "Whom" Is Objective

"Who" refers to people and to animals with names. "Who" is generally followed by a verb. "Whom" generally appears following "to" in a phrase, and it never has a verb.

Examples

It is the Robinsons <u>who</u> are coming to the party.
It is the Robinsons <u>who</u>, I feel certain, are coming to the party.
    Note: "I feel certain" is a nonrestrictive phrase and can be removed without changing the structure of the sentence.
To <u>whom</u> would you like the package sent?
    Note: "Whom" is followed by the verb "would," but "you" is the subject, and "would like" is its verb. "Whom" also appears in a phrase and follows "to."

Kinds of Pronouns

Personal Pronouns

I / me / you / your / him / his / he / she / her / they / them

Demonstrative Pronouns

These / those / this / that

Relative Pronouns

Who / whoever / whom / whomever / whatever / what

Indefinite Pronouns

Everybody / anybody / somebody / each / every / someone / everyone
    These indefinite pronouns are singular and refer to one thing, one person, or one place.

Intensive Pronouns

Myself / yourself / herself / ourselves / themselves / himself
    Intensive pronouns are used for emphasis.

Reflexive Pronouns

Myself / yourself / herself / ourselves / themselves / himself
    Reflexive pronouns reflect a specific noun.

Interrogative Pronouns

Who / which / that
    Interrogative pronouns introduce questions.

Exercise 18

Circle the pronouns in each paragraph.

1. Garrett A. Morgan was born in Paris, Kentucky, on March 4, 1877, and in 1907, he opened a sewing machine repair shop. Garrett Morgan learned to repair sewing machines and to repair clothes when he was just a child because he had to drop out of school to work and to help support his family. Morgan became a very successful businessman. He was also one of the first African Americans to buy a car, and the rest is history. People everywhere on Earth benefit from Garrett Morgan's invention of the traffic signal. He also invented the gas masks that have become standard equipment for the military and fire departments for nearly 100 years.

2. Benjamin Banneker was born in Ellicott's Mills, Maryland, on November 9, 1731. He was a self-educated mathematician, scientist, clock maker, writer, astronomer, inventor, and antislavery activist. Banneker made astronomical calculations and astounded even the experts. He could predict solar eclipses and the tides with pinpoint accuracy. His discoveries, findings, calculations, and even medical advice were published in his *Farmer's Almanacs*. Benjamin Banneker was the first African American to gain recognition in science.

3. Elijah McCoy, "The Real McCoy," was born in 1844 in Colchester, Ontario, Canada, after his parents escaped the United States via the Underground Railroad. When Elijah was little, he and his parents moved back to the United States. Elijah was hired as a furnace keeper when he was a young man. He made sure that train engines always had wood in the furnace. He invented a lubricating cup that would keep locomotive engines from overheating, and his device was so successful that people wanted only McCoy lubricators and would ask for "The Real McCoy." Elijah patented many more inventions, including the ironing board and automatic sprinklers.

Exercise 19

Circle the pronouns and underline their antecedents.

1. Although many people believe that the number 13 is lucky, there are those who believe the number 13 to be unlucky.

2. Most hospitals and high rises do not have a 13th floor, and those that do skip the number 13 and use 14 instead.

3. Some street numbers skip the 13th street because people who are superstitious do not want to live on unlucky streets.

4. Airplanes do not have a 13th row because passengers who fear flying and the number 13 refuse to sit in these ill-fated seats.

5. Some lotteries eliminate the number 13 because it is considered unlucky.

6. Apollo 13 was an ill-fated mission to the moon, and many superstitious people warned that its fate was sealed from the moment the mission was named using the number 13.

7. Money comes to those whose right hand itches.

8. You will pay money out if your left hand itches.

9. Hang a horseshoe in your house for good luck, but do not hang it upside down or your luck will run out.

10. Growing any kind of ivy wards off evil, so many people grow it in and around their homes to bring protection.

11. Never give a knife as a gift or the friendship will end, so married couples should never exchange knives with one another.

12. Knives seen crossing on a table mean that a family quarrel will soon occur; as a result, the number of knives on a table and where to place them should be considered when those who are superstitious set the table.

13. A ladybug in the house is good luck, so don't kill it.

14. Catch a falling leaf on the first day of fall to prevent getting colds all winter, but let it escape your grasp and you surely will get sick.

15. Wishes will come true if they are made while you are cooking fresh onions.

16. An onion will break a fever if you place it under the bed.

17. If a person sees an owl, he/she is believed to be clairvoyant.

18. A student who takes a test with the same pencil that he/she used to study will do better on the test because the pencil will remember the answers.

19. Never leave a chair rocking because an unwanted spirit will sit in it.

20. A person has an unfaithful lover if he/she drops a pair of scissors.

Exercise 20

Circle the pronouns and underline their antecedents.

1. The box jellyfish is found in the Pacific Ocean, and it is considered the deadliest of the jellyfish.

2. Victims of the box jellyfish are instantly paralyzed, or they are killed.

3. The venom of this jellyfish is among the most deadly venoms in the world, and most victims do not survive it.

4. The heart and the nervous system of the victim are attacked by this deadly venom that paralyzes them within a few seconds.

5. A person who is unlucky enough to brush against these tentacles can suffer a heart attack from the intensity of the pain.

6. Each jellyfish grows many tentacles, and they each can measure from 10 feet to 100 feet.

7. Each of the tentacles has thousands of stinging cells.

8. Box Jellyfish are also unique because they have eyes, and they can move rather than simply drift.

9. The box jellyfish is shaped like a box, and that is how it gets its name.

10. Jellyfish do not have a brain, and they do not have bones, yet they have survived on Earth for 650 million years.

11. Some jellyfish grow clusters of tentacles that can contain as many as 150 tentacles per cluster, making them even more deadly.

12. There are hundreds of species of jellyfish, and most of them are beautiful to look at and painful to touch.

13. Stings from jellyfish are the most common beach injuries sustained by humans, and rarely are these stings fatal to them.

14. Jellyfish are more prevalent in warmer waters, but they can exist even in the depths of the oceans.

15. Although jellyfish appear in all colors, some are crystal clear, making them difficult to see.

16. Sea lice are larvae of jellyfish that live mostly in the Gulf of Mexico, and they travel in large clouds or swarms that are almost invisible in the water.

17. Victims of sea lice stings experience rashes, blisters, fever, nausea, and vomiting, and they suffer severe headaches.

18. Sea lice can get into swimsuits and remain there ready to sting the swimmer again when the suit is worn again without washing it.

19. Warning flags are flown along gulf beaches to alert swimmers of jellyfish and sea lice infestations because their stings are dangerous to swimmers.

VERB

Verbs demonstrate a state of being or action in a sentence.
Every sentence has a subject (noun or pronoun) and a verb.

Types of Verbs

Linking Verbs

A **linking verb** connects a subject and its noun or adjective complement.
In other words, a linking verb connects a noun with its description.

Helping Verbs

Helping verbs demonstrate or express time and mood.
Because of helping verbs, the reader understands if an event or action has occurred, is occurring, or will occur.

Regular Verbs

Verbs that form their past tense and past participle by adding **ed** are called regular verbs.

Irregular verbs

Verbs that form their past tense and past participle by changing their spelling are called irregular verbs.

Verb Tenses

Present
I **study** every night.

Past
Last week I **studied.**

Future
Next week I **will study.**

Perfect
I **have studied** a total of 15 hours.

Progressive
I **am studying** all day.

Exercise 21

Circle the verb in each sentence.

1. Rats can last longer without water than camels.

2. The first ice cream bar invented was the Eskimo Pie.

3. South Africa is the largest producer of gold.

4. The world's largest bell is in Russia.

5. Gutzon Borglum took 14 years to carve Mount Rushmore.

6. Leonardo da Vinci was ambidextrous, and he could draw with one hand while writing with the other.

7. In the country of New Guinea, 117 languages are spoken.

8. People never lose their interest in bicycles.

9. The world's most popular flavor of ice cream is vanilla.

10. The shortest sentence in the English language is "I am."

11. Mosquitoes are attracted to people wearing blue before all other colors.

12. The Pacific Ocean is the home of 25,000 islands.

13. The moon is 1 million times drier than the Gobi Desert.

14. A blue whale's tongue weighs more than an elephant.

15. Tiger sharks compete with one another in the womb to determine which one will be born.

16. Sharks can live up to 100 years.

17. More than 7 billion people live on Earth.

18. Humans can survive a month without eating, a week without water, and a week without sleep.

19. Alexander Graham Bell invented the telephone; ironically, his wife and mother were deaf.

20. An elephant's teeth can weigh as much as 9 pounds.

Exercise 22

Circle the correct verb.

1. The cockroach are/is the fastest critter on six legs.

2. Flamingos turn/turns pink from eating shrimp.

3. Bone <u>are/is</u> five times stronger than steel.

4. Nearly one-half of McDonald's profits <u>are/is</u> from Happy Meals.

5. Guests <u>have/has</u> to scuba dive in order to get to the underwater Jules Undersea Lodge in Key Largo.

6. The Earth <u>has/have</u> a volcanic mountain chain that runs 30,000 miles beneath the sea.

7. A sheep and a goat can mate and <u>produce/produces</u> a baby geep.

8. The human hair <u>grow/grows</u> about five inches every year.

9. Mummies <u>were/was</u> once used in Egypt as fuel for trains.

10. A camel's hump <u>is/are</u> not used to store water but to store fat.

11. Camels can drink as much as 20 gallons of water at a time, and the water <u>is/are</u> stored in the bloodstream.

12. The average person <u>shift/shifts</u> 25 times during sleep.

13. Cooking <u>destroy/destroys</u> 90% of the vitamin C that vegetables contain.

14. More artists <u>live/lives</u> in California than in any other state.

15. Polar bears <u>eat/eats</u> as much as 100 pounds of fat during one feeding.

16. The first university <u>were/was</u> built in India in 700 B.C.

17. Humans <u>loses/lose</u> their taste buds as they age.

18. Although fake Christmas trees <u>are/is</u> gaining popularity, approximately 35 million real Christmas trees is/are sold every year.

19. More muscles <u>are/is</u> needed to frown than to smile.

20. A cat's mood <u>is/are</u> demonstrated by the position of its tail.

Exercise 23

Circle the verb in each sentence.

Plant Facts

1. Orchids are grown from seeds so tiny that the seeds are almost invisible.

2. A redwood lodge in northern California was built from the wood of one giant redwood.

3. The Mexican jumping bean is really a seed that contains the larva of a small gray moth.

4. An ear of corn has 800 kernels.

5. Each coffee tree yields only one pound of ground coffee annually.

6. Bamboo can grow as much as three feet in one day.

7. Only oak trees 50 years and older yield acorns.

8. Oak tree roots find their way to water, and that is why it is dangerous to stand under an oak tree during an electrical storm.

9. Corn is gown on every continent except Antarctica.

10. The bottle brush tree that is planted by the front door of a business or home will capture evil spirits before they can enter the dwelling.

11. The candlesticks of the sun plant grow a candle-shaped flower once every seven years.

12. The fragrance of flowers is emitted from the oils they produce.

13. Perfume is made from the oils produced by flowers.

14. Leonardo da Vinci discovered that the rings of a tree trunk revealed its age.

15. The world's largest flower, *Rafflesia arnoldii*, smells like a corpse when it blooms.

16. Dancing grass or the telegraph plant gets its name from the movement of its leaves that occur without a breeze of any kind or strength.

17. The lifespan of the *Welwitschia mirabiils* is from 400 to 1500 years, and it can survive even five years without water.

18. A very shy plant, *Mimosa pudica*, will completely close up when gently touched, but it will reopen shortly after if left alone.

19. The Venus flytrap is a carnivorous plant that feeds on ants and arachnids that are unlucky enough to step upon its leaves and get trapped when the leaves snap closed.

20. The baseball plant curls up into a ball until it rains, and then it opens to catch the water.

Exercise 24

Circle the verbs in each sentence.

1. During the chariot scene in *Ben Hur*, a small red car can be seen in the distance.

2. *Donald Duck* comics were banned in some countries because Donald Duck did not wear pants.

3. At least 100 people every year choke to death from chewing on pencils or pens.

4. The electric chair was invented by a dentist.

5. A pair of rats can produce 1 million offspring in six months.

6. A porcupine can float in the water.

7. Lions can mate 50 times a day.

8. Canada has more lakes than the rest of the world combined.

9. Chicago has the largest Polish population of any other city in the world except for Warsaw.

10. North America has a larger percentage of wilderness than Africa does.

11. A hen lays 19 dozen eggs a year.

12. Cows will produce more milk if they listen to music.

13. Cows cannot walk down stairs.

14. Squirrels should be the symbol for Arbor Day because they plant millions of trees by burying their nuts and forgetting where they buried them.

15. There are more sheep than people in New Zealand.

16. There are more dogs than people in Paris.

Exercise 25

Circle the verb and underline the subject in each sentence.

The Body

1. Hair grows faster on the face than on any other part of the body.

2. The brain is 80% water.

3. The brain does not feel pain.

4. High I.Q.'s yield a higher percentage of dreams.

5. A 10-watt light bulb and the brain operate on the same amount of power.

6. A nerve impulse travels 170 mph to and from the brain.

7. The nail of the middle finger grows faster than the other nails.

8. Fingernails grow faster than toenails.

9. Each human hair has a life span from three to seven years.

10. The small intestine is the largest internal organ.

11. Stomach acids can dissolve razorblades.

12. The lining of the stomach is replaced every four days.

13. The liver is capable of 500 functions.

14. Human teeth begin growing six months before birth.

15. A three-month fetus already has a fingerprint.

16. Overeating diminishes hearing until the food is dissolved.

17. Women have a better sense of smell than men.

18. The ashes of a cremated person average nine pounds.

19. Most people begin snoring by the age of 60.

20. The tongue is the strongest human muscle.

Exercise 26

Circle the verb and underline the subject in each sentence.

1. Celery has negative calories.

2. The glue on Israeli postage is kosher.

3. Fred and Wilma Flintstone were the first couple to appear on television in bed.

4. Bulletproof vests, fire escapes, windshield wipers, and laser printers were all invented by women.

5. Watermelons originated in Africa.

6. The watermelon is actually a vegetable and not a fruit.

7. The largest watermelon, according to the *Guinness Book of World Records*, weighed in at 262 pounds.

8. There are 1200 varieties of watermelons.

9. Some watermelons do not have seeds.

10. The pulp of a watermelon is called meat, and it can be red, yellow, or clear.

Exercise 27

Circle the verb and underline the subject in each sentence.

1. The United States has the highest incarceration rate in the world.

2. More jail cells than condominiums are constructed everyday.

3. Most serial killers are male.

4. Avocadoes have more calories than any other fruit.

5. A lightning bolt travels at 60,000 miles per hour.

6. Seven out of 10 people struck by lightning will survive.

7. Lightning strikes the Empire State building 500 times a year.

8. More people are struck by lightning while on the phone than while outside.

9. Southern California has 10,000 earthquakes a year.

10. At least 10,000 people die every year from earthquakes.

11. Every second, two Barbie dolls are sold.

12. Barbie has more than 80 careers and 40 pets.

13. Pumpkins come in orange, white, green, and blue.

14. Walt Disney never graduated from high school.

15. Walt Disney won 32 Oscars.

16. Walt Disney created Mickey Mouse and was the voice of Mickey Mouse; however, he was afraid of mice.

17. Walt Disney World Resort is the size of San Francisco.

Exercise 28

Circle the correct verb in each sentence.

1. There is/are 38 species of mammals that are/is extinct.

2. Many hundreds of species of mammals is/are considered endangered.

3. Thousands of vertebrate and invertebrate species is/are listed as threatened.

4. Species that is/are considered vulnerable is/are those that is/are at risk because of naturally declining numbers.

5. A high probability of extinction refer/refers to those species that are threatened because of changing conditions in their natural surroundings.

6. Endangered species are those that require legal protection to exist, and their extinction are/is probable.

7. Species that no longer exist is/are categorized as extinct species.

8. The extinction of 70% of all the Earth's species occurred/occurs 65 million years ago.

9. No one <u>know/knows</u> for certain what caused this mass extinction, including the extinction of the dinosaurs at that time.

10. Two theories <u>claims/claim</u> that either the collision of the Earth with an asteroid or volcanic eruptions created drastic changes in the environment and in the atmosphere of the Earth.

11. There are many species of grasshoppers, and each species <u>have/has</u> its own sound.

12. Only grasshoppers of the same species can breed with one another, so the unique sounds of each species <u>are/is</u> used to attract other grasshoppers of the same species.

13. Some frogs can fly and <u>can/could</u> change colors at specific times during the day.

14. A king cobra can kill more than thirty people with a single injection of its venom and <u>are/is</u> the world's most dangerous large snake.

15. Pigs and horses can <u>suffer/suffers</u> from sunburn.

16. Armadillos <u>are/is</u> usually seen only at night because they sleep during the day.

17. Armadillos can also <u>walk/walks</u> under water, and they can <u>hold/holds</u> their breath for six minutes.

18. More often than not, armadillos hit cars rather than the contrary because armadillos <u>jumps/jump</u> straight into the air when they <u>are/is</u> frightened.

19. Other than humans, armadillos <u>is/are</u> the only other animals that can get leprosy.

20. There <u>is/are</u> 50 million armadillos in the United States.

ADJECTIVE

Modifiers: Words That Describe

Adjectives and adverbs are modifiers. When a modifier is misplaced in a sentence, the description is not next to the word or phrase that it is describing, which gives the sentence another meaning from what the writer intended. Oftentimes, the sentence will not make sense if the modifier is misplaced.

Examples

WRONG: The teacher told me what to do with a smile.
RIGHT: The teacher told me with a smile what to do.
WRONG: The man pointed to the dog with the cell phone.
RIGHT: The man with the cell phone pointed to the dog.
WRONG: While dressing, my cell phone rang.
RIGHT: While I was dressing, my cell phone rang.

    Adverbs Describe or Modify Verbs, Adjectives, and other Adverbs.
    They answer questions such as how, when, and where.
    <u>Yesterday</u>, the large dog <u>quickly</u> jumped <u>over</u> the old, dead log.

Adjectives Describe or Modify Nouns.

Adjectives also include a, an, and the.

Adjectives usually appear in front of nouns, and they express which, how many, and what kind of.

As . . . As And So . . . As

Use "as . . . as" to compare. Use "so . . . as" to contrast.

Examples

He is <u>as tall as</u> his father.

He is not <u>so tall as</u> his father.

Either . . . or and neither . . . nor

Use "or" with "either," and use "nor" with "neither." Do not mix and match.

The noun or pronoun closest to the verb will determine whether the verb is plural or singular. The closest antecedent will always determine number.

Examples

WRONG: Either Bob or <u>Mary</u> must raise <u>their</u> hand.

RIGHT: Either Bob or <u>Mary</u> must raise <u>his</u> hand.

WRONG: Neither Bob nor <u>Mary</u> <u>are</u> going to the meeting.

RIGHT: Neither Bob nor <u>Mary</u> <u>is</u> going to the meeting.

Exercise 29

Circle the adjectives in each sentence.

Amazing Facts about the Universe

1. The brightest star in the night sky is the North Star, Sirius.

2. The Earth is in the enormous Milky Way galaxy, which is 1,000,000 light years across.

3. Ice has been discovered on planet Mars.

4. The Andromeda galaxy is the nearest galaxy to the Milky Way galaxy.

5. The hottest planet in our solar system is Venus.

6. The planets Venus, Mercury, Mars, Jupiter, and Saturn are visible without a professional telescope.

7. Thousands of tons of meteoric particles collide with the Earth each year.

8. Only a very small percentage of the universe is visible because most of the universe is composed of dark matter and dark energy.

9. Our sun rotates around the visible center of the Milky Way.

10. The brightest object in the night sky is our moon.

11. Traveling at the speed of light, a small object would take 100,000 years just to cross the Milky Way galaxy.

12. Jupiter is the heaviest planet.

13. The sun does not set in isolated Norway for three months out of every year.

14. The sun is not visible at the North Pole six long months out of every year.

15. The distance to the moon can be measured because of the enormous mirrors that have been left by exploring astronauts.

16. Laser beams are aimed at the moon and bounce off of the large mirrors.

17. There are recorded stars that are larger than our solar system.

18. Our sun has the largest mass in our solar system.

19. The moon is constantly moving away from the Earth, resulting in longer days.

20. The Earth is 1 million times smaller than our sun!

Exercise 30

Circle the adjectives in each sentence.

1. A harsh winter is predicted if a white calf is born at the end of fall.

2. Travelers will have good luck if their travel companion is an old cat.

3. Black cats and black snakes that come toward you are good luck.

4. Someone is walking on your future grave if you feel goose bumps.

5. Standing inside of an unbroken circle will protect you from someone with evil intentions.

6. Pick up a straight pin or a safety pin, and your luck begins; let it lay, and your luck will stay.

7. Never kill a chirping cricket in your house unless you want bad luck.

8. Any kind of wild bird that flies into the house warns of death.

9. Immediately open a door or a window to let the soul from a deceased relative or pet leave.

10. Hold your breath while passing a cemetery or you may breathe in a wandering spirit!

11. Never bury the dead in black clothes because the dead will come back.

12. A howling dog at night senses death before daylight.

13. Never wear new cloths or new shoes to a funeral.

14. Counting the cars in a funeral procession is bad luck.

15. Seeing a funeral procession is good luck unless you count the cars.

16. Never bury a dead relative on a Friday because another death in the family will soon follow.

17. Wild flowers growing on a grave means a good person is buried there; however, weeds growing on a grave means a wicked person is buried there.

18. For good luck while fishing, throw the first fish caught back.

19. You will be taking a pleasant trip if the bottom of your right foot itches.

20. A man will visit if you drop a dinner or salad fork.

ADVERB

Adverbs describe or modify verbs, adjectives, and other adverbs.
   Adverbs express how, when, and where something happens or happened.
   Many modifiers that end in **ly** are adverbs

Exercise 31

Circle the adverbs in each sentence.

1. More money is spent yearly on gardening than on any other hobby.

2. Oddly, dead skin is the cause of most home dust bunnies.

3. The average person laughs 15 times a day.

4. Dogs and cats can accurately hear utra sounds that humans can't.

5. Every year, more people fatally choke on toothpicks than they do on food.

6. People working outside in the summer can profusely sweat as much as four gallons of water daily.

7. A rhinoceros horn is surprisingly made of densely compacted hair.

8. Women automatically blink more often than men.

9. Amazingly, Shakespeare created the word "assassination."

10. More people speak English fluently in China than in the United States!

11. Interestingly, the nose and the ears never stop truly growing.

12. Scissors were skillfully invented by Leonardo da Vinci.

13. Frankly, more people openly fear spiders than they fear death.

14. The eye of an ostrich is usually bigger than its brain.

15. Refrigerate rubber to make it last incredibly longer than it would in the hot sun.

16. Sadly, dragonflies live one day.

17. The dot over an " i " is curiously called a tittle.

18. Astronauts do not eat overly gas-producing foods such as beans before they go traveling into space.

19. Violets are not blue but are clearly violet.

20. Charlie Chaplin entered a Charlie Chaplin look-alike contest and astonishingly lost.

Exercise 32

Underline the adjectives and circle the adverbs in each sentence.

The Weird and Strange

1. Ironically, the king of hearts is the only king without a moustache in a standard deck of playing cards.

2. Amazingly, large casinos in Vegas do not have clocks.

3. The *Mona Lisa* does not have eyebrows because it was quite fashionable during the Renaissance to shave off unsightly eyebrows.

4. A lightening bolt is elementally hotter than the sun's surface.

5. Many left-handed people are accidently killed every year from using products designed for right-handed people.

6. Cat urine eerily glows under a black light.

7. A roach can live up to two weeks with its head cut off and amazingly even lay eggs!

8. People can pawn just about anything in Vegas except human dentures interestingly, which are considered illegal.

9. England is much smaller than the state of Florida.

10. Sneezes surprisingly travel at an incredible speed 100 mph.

11. Three hours of electricity are saved for every glass jar that is recycled.

12. Six thousand lightening strikes occur every minute somewhere on the planet.

13. Ironically, penquins can swim, but they can't fly.

14. Amusingly, elephants can swim, but they can't jump.

15. Tongue prints are as different as fingerprints and incredibly are a very reliable source of identification.

16. The black widow spider kills its partner immediately after mating or during mating if the male spider does not perform.

17. The preying mantis will eat itself if it is kept in a glass jar.

18. Fingernails and hair continually grow after death.

19. Amazingly, fingerprints appear on a developing fetus at 18 weeks.

20. One gallon of oil can permanently contaminate one million gallons of fresh water.

Preposition

Prepositions describe relationships between the words of a sentence.

Usually this description is positional. Prepositions combine with other words to form prepositional phrases that describe when or where something happens.

After / at / above / across
Below / between / beyond / before / beside / behind
In / inside / on / over / under / underneath / with / of

Due to And Because of

"Due to" is a predicate adjective. "Because of" is a prepositional construction.

"Due to" cannot be used to begin a sentence. "Due to" is usually preceded by a helping verb. "Because of" is never preceded by a helping verb.

Examples

WRONG: We were late <u>due to</u> the blowout.
WRONG: His fear of snakes was <u>because of</u> the snake bite he received when he was a child.
RIGHT: His fear of snakes was <u>due to</u> the snake bite he received when he was a child.
WRONG: Due to the wet roads, drive carefully.
RIGHT: Because of the wet roads, drive carefully.

Exercise 33

Circle the prepositional phrase(s) in each sentence.

The Seven Wonders of the Ancient World

1. The three pyramids at Giza in Egypt were completed almost 5000 years ago.

2. The largest of the three pyramids was built by Cheops, and it rises 450 feet into the air and contains 2.3 million blocks that each weigh 2 ½ tons.

3. Nebuchadnezzar built the Hanging Gardens of Babylon, in the ancient city of Mesopotamia, in 600 B.C. to honor his wife, Queen Amuhia.

4. Although it mysteriously disappeared, the Statue of Zeus, built by the Greek sculptor Phidias, at Olympia is considered one of the seven wonders of the ancient world.

5. The statue reached 40 feet high and was made of gold and ivory.

6. The Temple of Artemis at Ephesus existed in 350 B.C., but it was destroyed by the Goths in A.D. 262.

7. The temple was built in 350 B.C. to honor the Greek goddess Artemis.

8. Queen Artemisia had the Mausoleum at Halicarnassus built to hold the remains of her husband, King Mausolus, who died in 353 B.C.

9. An earthquake in 224 B.C. destroyed the Colossus at Rhodes, a bronze statue of Apollo that took the sculptor Chares 12 years to complete.

10. The Pharos of Alexandria was a lighthouse that was built during the third century B.C.

11. The lighthouse was built on the island of Pharos off the coast of Egypt.

12. Unfortunately, the Pharos of Alexandria was destroyed during an earthquake in 224 B.C.

13. This list of the Seven Wonders of the Ancient World was compiled by ancient Greek historians.

14. Most present-day historians agree that this original list is the most widely acceptable as the Seven Wonders of the Ancient World.

15. The Pyramids of Giza are the only surviving wonder of this ancient list of seven.

Exercise 34

Underline the subject and verb and circle the prepositional phrase(s) in each sentence.

1. There are many compiled lists of modern wonders.

2. The following entries represent one acceptable list of popular modern wonders.

3. The Empire State Building was completed in 1931, and it overlooks New York City at 1,250 feet.

4. The world's largest hydroelectric power plant is the Itaipu Dam that was built by Brazil and Paraguay on the Parana River.

5. The Itaipu Dam took 16 years to build and was completed in 1991.

6. The CN Tower, when it was built in 1976, was the world's tallest freestanding structure at 1,814 feet.

7. The Panama Canal took 34 years to build because there were so many obstacles to overcome.

8. The canal spans 50 miles across the Isthmus of Panama and was considered the most expensive project both financially and in human lives lost during construction in American history at the time of its completion.

9. The Channel Tunnel stretches over 31 miles.

10. Twenty-three of those miles are 150 feet below the seabed of the English Channel.

11. High-speed trains encased in tubes carry passengers between the countries.

12. The Netherlands North Sea Protection Works is a series of dams, surge barriers, and floodgates that prevent the country from being flooded during storms.

13. The project was finished in 1986 and is considered by many engineers to be equal in scale to the Great Wall of China.

14. Some scientists believe that the Netherlands North Sea Protection Works will prevent the Netherlands from sharing the same fate as Atlantis, disappearing forever into the ocean.

15. At one time the longest suspension bridge in the world, the Golden Gate Bridge, was completed in 1937.

16. The Golden Gate Bridge, spanning over 12 miles, connects San Francisco and Marin County.

17. More than 80,000 miles of steel were used to construct the bridge.

18. The project took under four years to complete despite the ocean currents, ferocious winds, and thick fog.

19. Many believed that a suspension bridge of this magnitude could not be built considering the natural obstacles.

20. The cables that link the two towers on the bridge are the largest ever made.

Exercise 35

Underline the subject and verb and circle the prepositional phrase(s) in each sentence.

1. The following list of the New Seven Wonders of the World was generated by Internet users.

2. The Great Wall of China was begun in the seventh century, yet it took hundreds of years to complete.

3. The Great Wall of China is the world's longest human-made structure.

4. The wall was built to protect China from the Huns, Mongols, and other invading troops.

5. The Great Wall of China can even be seen from space.

6. The entire city of Petra in Jordan is included in this list.

7. This city was built in 9 B.C. and continued to flourish during the Roman Empire.

8. The Christ Redeemer Statue in Brazil stands 125 feet tall on the Corcovado Mountain.

9. The Christ Redeemer Statue took over five years to build.

10. Incredibly, the statute was built in France, shipped to Brazil, and carried by train up the mountain.

11. The city of Machu Picchu was built 8,000 feet above sea level in the fifteenth century by the Incans.

12. The pyramid at Chichen Itza in Mexico was the center of the Mayan civilization.

13. Visitors can still climb the steps of the pyramid.

14. The Coliseum in Rome, Italy, was built more than 2,000 years ago.

15. The Coliseum is an enormous amphitheater that contained 50,000 seats on graduated levels.

16. The Coliseum is located in the center of Rome, and guests can still visit the remains and stand in awe of its enormity.

17. This immortal amphitheater continues to influence stadium construction throughout the world.

18. Shah Jahan built the Taj Mahal in honor of his dead wife.

19. The Taj Mahal was made of white marble.

20. Although the structure was built in 1630, visitors to India may still tour the Taj Mahal and marvel at its historic significance and unique style of architecture.

Exercise 36

Underline the subject and the verb and circle the prepositional phrase(s) in each sentence.

1. Alcohol can be detected in urine 6 to 12 hours after the last drink.

2. The largest group of pollinators is the bee.

3. The most commonly used word is "the" in the English language.

4. A blue whale eats three tons of food every day.

5. The Presidential Library is the largest library in the United States.

6. Cotton diapers take over six months to break down.

7. The first toothbrushes were produced in the United States in 1885.

8. The Earth is roughly 8,000 miles across, and the deepest hole dug by humans is in Russia and measures only 7.6 miles.

9. The North Pole exists as ice on top of a frozen sea rather than as land.

10. Life began in the seas more than 3 billion years ago.

11. Ice covers one-tenth of the Earth's surface.

12. The largest snowflake on record was 15 inches wide!

13. The common housefly transmits more diseases than any other insect known to humankind.

14. The *Rafflesia arnoldii* is the largest flower on Earth, growing as big as three feet across and weighing as much as 15 pounds.

15. Food is grown on only 11% of the Earth's surface.

16. One-third of the Earth's surface is desert.

17. The mountains in Scotland are estimated to be 400 million years old.

18. Winds in Antarctica can reach 150 miles an hour.

19. The Sahara Desert in North Africa is as large as the United States.

20. A Russian dog sent into space in 1957 was the first astronaut.

Exercise 37

Circle the prepositional phrase and underline the noun in each prepositional phrase.

1. Earth is called the Blue Planet because from space the oceans and the atmosphere make the planet appear blue.

2. The oceans comprise 99% of the Earth's living space.

3. Indonesia, Japan, and the United States have the largest number of active volcanoes.

4. Chinese Mandarin is the most spoken language in the world, and English is second.

5. Winslow, Arizona, is home to the world's largest meteorite crater.

6. The Red Sea is the saltiest sea in the world.

7. The largest city by population is Shanghai, China, with more than 13 million people.

8. Lake Mead is the largest human-made lake in the United States.

9. The Earth is home to 1,200,000 species of animals and 300,000 species of plants.

10. Most of the world's volcanic eruptions occur under the sea.

11. Snails have thousands of teeth.

12. The hair of a cat will stand up all over its body when it is frightened, but the hair will stand up only in a narrow band on its back when the cat is threatened.

13. Armadillos always give birth to four babies.

14. A housecat can sprint at 31 miles per hour.

15. Neil Armstrong's left foot was the first foot to step on the moon.

16. A group of jellyfish is called a smuck.

17. The emperor penguin can grow to a height of four feet.

18. The Saguaros cacti can grow to the height of a six-story building.

19. An octopus has three hearts although they don't all pump blood through them.

20. Butterflies taste with their feet, and that is why they stand on their food.

Exercise 38

Circle the prepositional phrase and underline the noun in <u>each prepositional phrase.</u>

Lucky Rituals

1. Many gamblers wash their hands before placing bets in a casino.

2. Stall 3 in a restroom is considered a luck changer if things are going wrong.

3. Making a wish while tossing a coin in any fountain or while seeing the first star of the evening will make the wish come true.

4. Throwing spilled salt over the right shoulder will fend off bad luck.

5. Decorating the house using the principles of Feng Shui will bring luck into the home and to all who live there.

6. Dragons placed in precarious positions in the home bring good fortune.

7. The three-legged toad sitting next to a stack of money will certainly bring wealth to its owner.

8. Decorate with bats to bring happiness into the home.

9. Fish in the home whether live or decorative objects are considered very lucky.

10. An elephant with its trunk up will bring kindness and strength into the home.

11. Tie three Chinese coins, the ones with holes in the center, together with red ribbon to bring instant money luck.

12. Sweeping the floor on New Year's Day will sweep away the luck, so don't sweep or clean on the first day of the year.

13. Clothes worn inside out will bring good luck to the wearer.

14. To see a black snake in front of you is good luck.

15. A Southern charm is to carry an alligator's tooth to bring new money into the home.

16. Hands that are washed with chamomile soap will draw money into them.

17. Hang a horseshoe over the door to protect the house and to bring good luck.

18. Carry nutmeg or pyrite to draw money.

19. A silver dime in the purse or wallet will bring luck and protection.

20. Cinnamon carried in the purse or wallet will bring safety and luck.

SUBJECT AND VERB AGREEMENT

Subjects and their verbs must agree in number. A **singular subject** must have a **singular verb**. A **plural subject** must have a **plural verb.** Plural nouns generally end in s while plural verbs do not: several *trees grow*. Singular nouns generally do not end in -s while singular verbs do: a *tree grows*.

Remember to cross any prepositional phrases *before* identifying the subject and verb.

Exercise 1

Circle the subject and correct verb in each sentence.

1. Dreams **has/have** many interpretations.

2. Dreaming of a murder **warn/warns** the reader that a life-changing event may occur.

3. Witnessing or committing a murder in a dream **are/is** a warning that the dreamer needs to control his or her anger.

4. Rough water in a dream **mean/means** that the dreamer may be facing an obstacle.

5. Smooth water in a dream **are/is** a sign of peaceful times to come.

6. Dreaming of surgical operations **are/is** a sign that a personal relationship will be repaired.

7. Rabbits in a dream **indicates/indicate** a birth announcement.

8. Good luck **is/are** sure to follow a dream of a rainbow.

9. Betrayal **follows/follow** a dream of a rat.

10. Snakes that surface in a dream **is/are** good luck unless the dreamer is bitten.

11. Dreams usually **represent/represents** issues the dreamer is facing in real life.

12. Dreaming of suffocation **are/is** a sign of stress in the dreamer's life.

13. A dreamer who **are/is** robbed should stop wasting money.

14. Storms that appear in dreams **symbolize/symbolizes** that confusion and disorder will occur in the dreamer's life.

15. Dreaming of being restrained **means/mean** that the dreamer believes that someone or something is a barrier in his or her life.

Exercise 2

Circle the subject and correct verb. Cross out any prepositional phrases.

1. Mammals **is/are** carnivores because they eat meat, but reptiles, amphibians, and insects **is/are** also carnivores.

2. Some carnivores like humans also **eat/eats** vegetation.

3. Omnivores **is/are** carnivores that eat vegetation as well as meat.

4. Omnivorous animals **eats/eat** just about anything.

5. The largest of all cats **is/are** the tiger.

6. Tigers **hunts/hunt** their prey alone, and they do not live in prides like lions do.

7. Tigers **is/are** night hunters.

8. Many people **believes/believe** that the tiger lives in Africa.

9. The Bengal tiger **lives/live** in India and Asia.

10. The largest of the tigers **are/is** the Siberian tiger.

11. Both the Bengal tiger and the Siberian tiger **is/are** facing extinction.

12. After tigers mate, they **go/goes** their separate ways.

13. The survival of the cubs **is/are** the responsibility of the mother.

14. Many people die every year in the rice fields of India because of tiger attacks.

15. The tigers **attacks/attack** the workers from the rear.

16. To reduce the chance of being attacked from behind, the workers **wears/wear** face masks on the back of their heads.

17. Leopards **live/lives** in Africa and **attacks/attack** humans as well.

18. Leopards **is/are** bold enough to enter large cities that border their territory.

19. Their coats **are/is** tan and have black spots

20. Some people **believe/believes** that leopards are spirits that have taken animal form.

Exercise 3

Circle the subject and the correct verb.

1. Leopards that have black coats **is/are** called black panthers.

2. Humans **kills/kill** the leopard for its beautiful coat, and that is the reason the leopard is on the endangered list.

3. The jaguar **is/are** also on the endangered list because it is killed for its beautiful coat.

4. The jaguar **is/are** found in Central and South America.

5. Jaguars **hunts/hunt** near fresh water, feeding mostly on turtles and fish.

6. People walking near the water **knows/know** to look up into the trees because jaguars like to sleep on hanging branches.

7. Jaguars **attacks/attack** their prey by piercing their heads with their fangs.

8. Both jaguars and leopards **is/are** often overlooked because they blend in among the surrounding foliage.

9. Keeping jaguars and leopards as pets **is/are** illegal in the United States.

10. Some cultures **honors/honor** the jaguar as a god, and the people **makes/make** icons of the jaguar.

Exercise 4

Circle the verb and the correct subject.

1. Many **animal/animals** will signal a warning before they attack, but the African bull elephants will immediately attack when their young are threatened.

2. Bull **elephant/elephants** use their tusks as their weapon of choice when they are competing for a mate.

3. Elephant **tusk/tusks** can grow up to 10 feet long and can weigh up to 150 pounds each, so elephants use these tusks to puncture their adversaries.

4. Elephants travel in herds, and their **baby/babies** are called calves.

5. **Elephants/Elephant** send out a low frequency sound to summon the herd to come and encircle endangered calves, resulting in an army of threatening tusks that only poachers with guns can overcome.

6. **Rhino/rhinos** will also charge any intruder that threatens their calves or comes into their territory.

7. Rhinos can weigh up to three tons and, in spite of their weight, can charge at 30 miles per hour.

8. Like humans, **rhino/rhinos** make trails that they use like roads throughout their territory.

9. An angry **rhinos/rhino** will charge any intruder that ventures onto its trail.

10. Rhinos are well aware of the power that they have because of their size and strength, and **it/they** know that few are brave enough to challenge them.

Exercise 5

Circle the subject and correct verb in each sentence.

1. Real buffalo **live/lives** only in Africa, India, and Asia.

2. The buffalo in America **is/are** really bison.

3. Bison **are/is** related to the buffalo and even look like buffalo.

4. Bison and buffalo **protects/protect** their young by surrounding them like the elephants does/do.

5. Baby lions **are/is** called cubs.

6. Lions **live/lives** in dens rather than in a herd.

7. Dens **are/is** smaller than herds and consist/consists of several families of males, females, and cubs.

8. Unlike the tiger that preys alone, lions **works/work** as a team to kill their prey.

9. The female lion **is/are** called a lioness, and she **have/has** the responsibility of finding the prey.

10. Female lions will **work/works** together to surround and confuse the prey.

11. Female lions, like the jaguar, **attacks/attack** the head of the prey, but instead of biting the head, they **bite/bites** the neck until the prey is dead.

12. After the prey is dead, the female lions **step/steps** aside to let the males and the cubs eat first.

Exercise 6

Circle the subject and the correct verb in each sentence.

1. Jellyfish **defend/defends** themselves by using their tentacles.

2. The tentacles **is/are** filled with paralyzing poisons that are released when the tentacles come into contact with a predator.

3. The size of a jellyfish **range/ranges** from barely an inch to 10 feet without including the tentacles.

4. The tentacles **adds/add** another 100 feet to the size of the jellyfish.

5. Jellyfish **is/are** not limited to particular climates or to particular marine depths but can be found throughout the world on the surface of seas or on the bottom of oceans.

Exercise 7

Circle the subject and correct verb in each sentence.

1. Coral reefs **has/have** been on earth for millions of years.

2. The Great Barrier Reef **is/are** the largest living thing on earth.

3. Thousands of individual reefs **makes/make** up the Great Barrier Reef.

4. There **is/are** also hundreds of islands among this enormous reef.

5. The Great Barrier Reef **are/is** parallel to the coast of Australia.

6. Coral reefs **grow/grows** in shallow water.

7. Thousands of marine species **flourishes/flourish** on coral reefs.

8. Venomous sea snakes, jellyfish, and octopus **makes/make** the coral reefs their home.

9. The Great Barrier Reef **is/are** one of the seven wonders of the world.

10. The Great Barrier Reef **are/is** over 100,000 square miles long.

VERBS

Every sentence contains a subject and a verb. A **verb** is the part of speech that shows action in the sentence like *jump, talk, study, run,* or appeals to the senses like smell, touch, sight, sound, or demonstrates a state of being like *seems, is, are*, and *appears*.

Exercise 1

Circle the verb and underline the subject in each of the following sentences.

1. Scientists believe that the Earth was formed from an explosion of expanding heated gas and dust billions of years ago.

2. The oceans were formed from rainstorms that lasted thousands of years, and the land was molded from violent volcanic eruptions.

3. Oxygen was created as a product of these violent changes, and life was formed.

4. Prehistoric life refers to creatures that lived before humans.

5. Bacteria that were single celled and microscopic were the first life forms to appear in the oceans.

6. Chlorophyll developed inside the bacteria, allowing it to thrive and grow because the bacteria could get its sustenance from the sun.

7. As chlorophyll developed, it released oxygen into the air.

8. As single-celled organisms grouped together, new life forms were created.

9. Among the first creatures to develop nearly 2,500 million years ago was the jellyfish.

10. Sponges and corals appeared much later, approximately 600 million years ago.

11. The first fish appeared almost 500 million years ago.

12. These fish lived on the bottom of the seas and oceans.

13. The first fish were covered in thick plates like armor instead of thin scales like they have today.

14. Prehistoric fish began to evolve about 350 million years ago.

15. Scientists refer to this period of change as the Devonian Period or the Age of Fish.

16. Fish were the most important creatures on Earth during this time because some fish developed legs and became the first amphibians to walk the Earth.

17. The Devonian Period was characterized by warm climates that fostered the evolution of lungs in the first amphibians and the appearance of the first plants.

18. The transformation of fins to limbs and the development of lungs occurred over millions of years.

19. Darwin's Theory of Evolution is the belief that all life has descended from the first single-celled bacteria and evolved naturally through adaptation.

Exercise 2

Circle all of the verbs in the following sentences.

1. Shooting stars, also called falling stars, are trails of light that can be seen in the night sky.

2. The trails of light appear as meteors that are vaporized while entering the Earth's atmosphere.

3. Meteoroids are made up of dust and rock that burn up as they enter the Earth's atmosphere.

4. The fleeting trail of light is called a meteor.

5. Meteors can be seen throughout most nights.

6. Meteors that enter the atmosphere at the same time produce a brilliant strand of lights called a meteor shower.

7. Most people do not realize that hundreds of tons of rock and dust enter the Earth's atmosphere every day.

8. Meteoroids that hit the surface of the Earth are called meteorites.

9. Meteorites that hit the surface of the Earth are not usually balls of fire because they have already been cooled by the atmosphere by the time they slam into the surface.

10. Spectacular meteor light shows are common sights in August.

Exercise 3

Circle all of the verbs in the following sentences.

1. Bats are the only mammals that can fly, and they mostly fly at night.

2. Bats have been around for nearly 50 million years.

3. There are nearly 1,000 living bat species.

4. Bats are nocturnal animals, or they are crepuscular.

5. Nocturnal means active at night, and crepuscular means active during the twilight of dawn and dusk.

6. Echolocation is a sophisticated form of sonar that bats use for navigating and finding prey.

7. Bats are more appreciated and understood by people today for their important role in the ecological balance of nature.

8. Bats are natural enemies of night-flying insects and can consume as many as 10,000 mosquitoes a night.

9. Bats are also important pollinators of plants.

10. Bats can pollinate many hundreds of species of plants, including topical fruits like bananas and mangos.

11. Bat excrement acts as a fertilizer, helping plants to grow by supplying them with rich nutrients.

12. Without the bat, many plant species would disappear along with the animals that depend on these food sources to survive.

13. Bats are very versatile and adaptable; they are found in all regions of the earth.

14. Because bats are mainly insectivorous (insect eaters), they are abundant in tropical regions where insect populations are heavy year-round.

15. The number of insects that a bat colony can consume in one night is staggering.

16. As many as 300 tons of insects may be eaten in one night by a colony of bats, so imagine the devastating effect the unchecked population growth of mosquitoes would have on the world without the bat.

17. Hanging upside down by their hind feet is the way that bats really do sleep.

18. Several thousand bats can make up a bat colony.

19. The size of bats commonly varies from one inch to 16 inches.

20. The wing span of some discovered bats was measured beyond six feet!

Verbs are identified by their function in the sentence.

Action verbs *show movement.*
The lizard *leaped* to catch the nearby moth.
Linking verbs connect nouns to adjectives, pronouns, or other nouns and illustrate a state of condition or being.
The man *appears* tall.
The man *is* tired.

Helping verbs identify the time of the action.
The student *had* studied for the test.   *Had* indicates the action has occurred.
The student *is* studying for the test.   Is indicates the action is occurring.
The student *will* study for the test.   *Will* indicates the action will occur.

The following are common helping verbs:

am	has	does
is	had	done
are	could	will
was	should	would
were	do	
have	did	

Exercise 4

Circle the helping verb and underline the action verb in the following sentences.

1. Most animals have lived peaceably among themselves.

2. Animals will attack if they feel threatened or sense that their young are threatened.

3. Animals will also attack when they are hunting for food.

4. When an animal feels threatened, it will attack or give a warning signal.

5. Male polar bears will fight each other for courtship rights to a female polar bear.

6. Strong and healthy males will most likely win in courtship battles to obtain a mate.

7. Many animals will fight to protect the territory where they live.

8. They will risk their lives to defend their territory from other animals.

9. Some animals will mark their territory with their scent or use sound as a warning to intruders to stay away.

10. The male crocodile will protect its young by carrying the babies in its mouth.

11. Even birds like the giant cassowary, which stands more than five feet tall, will fight to defend its territory.

12. Large birds like the cassowary, geese, and ostrich have been known to attack and even kill humans who threaten their chicks.

13. These enormous birds use their talons to slash and tear open their enemies.

14. Geese will also attack humans and can easily break a man's leg or arm with their powerful wings.

15. Geese are sometimes used as watchdogs, warning their owners of intruders by loud honking noises.

16. Like the ostrich and the emu, carrowaries cannot fly, but they can run quickly on land and can easily overcome an adversary.

17. Ostriches stand up to eight feet tall, and they can weigh as much as 300 pounds.

18. They can use their legs to defend themselves by kicking their adversaries.

19. Eagles look threatening, but they do not attack humans.

20. Like the eagle, the hawk also looks threatening, but it doesn't attack humans either.

PRINCIPAL PARTS OF VERBS

There are four principal parts of verbs: past, present, past participle, and present participle. These parts of verbs express time and help to form past, present, and future verb tenses.

Think of the word tense as meaning time. Past tense would be past time. Present tense is present time, and future tense is future time.

Present	Past	Past Participle always has a helping verb	Present Participle always has a helping verb the main verb ends in -**ing**
walk	*walked*	*had walked*	*is walking*

Present Tense Verbs (Present Time Verbs)

Present tense verbs show that action **is** taking place now or that the action **is** routine.

I *am driving* to school	Action in progress is called **present progressive**.
You *are driving* to school.	Action in progress is called **present progressive**.
He *is driving* to school.	Action in progress is called **present progressive**.
They *are driving* to school.	Action in progress is called **present progressive**.

I *drive* to school.	I *have* my book.	The **present** action is routine.
You *drive* to school.	You *have* your book.	The **present** action is routine.
He *drives* to school.	He *has* his book.	The **present** action is routine.
They *drive* to school.	They have their books.	The **present** action is routine.

I *have driven* to school.	Action that is recent is called **present perfect.**
You *have driven* to school.	Action that is recent is called **present perfect.**
He *has driven* to school.	Action that is recent is called **present perfect.**
They *have driven* to school.	Action that is recent is called **present perfect.**

Notice that the **present perfect** is formed with **have** or **has** and the past participle.

Past Tense Verbs (Past Time Verbs)

Past tense verbs show that action occurred in the past or that the action **was** routine in the past.

I *was driving* to school.	Action that was in progress is called **past progressive.**
You *were driving* to school.	Action that was in progress is called **past progressive.**
He *was driving* to school.	Action that was in progress is called **past progressive.**
They *were driving* to school.	Action that was in progress is called **past progressive.**

I *drove* to school.	The action was completed.
You *drove* to school.	The action was completed.
He *drove* to school.	The action was completed.
They *drove* to school.	The action was completed.

I *had driven* to school.	Action that occurred before a certain time is called **past perfect.**
You *had driven* to school.	Action that occurred before a certain time is called **past perfect.**
He *had driven* to school.	Action that occurred before a certain time is called **past perfect.**
They *had driven* to school.	Action that occurred before a certain time is called **past perfect.**

Notice that the **past perfect** is formed with **had** and the past participle.

Future Tense Verbs (Future Time Verbs)

Future tense verbs show that action **will** occur in the future.

I *will be* driving to school.	Future action that will continue is called **future progressive.**
You *will be* driving to school.	Future action that will continue is called **future progressive.**
He *will be* driving to school.	Future action that will continue is called **future progressive.**
They *will be* driving to school.	Future action that will continue is called **future progressive.**

I *will drive* to school.	The action will be completed.
You *will drive* to school.	The action will be completed.
He will drive to school.	The action will be completed.
They *will drive* to school.	The action will be completed.

I *will have driven* to school.	Action that will occur before a certain time is called **future perfect.**
You *will have driven* to school.	Action that will occur before a certain time is called **future perfect.**
He *will have driven* to school.	Action that will occur before a certain time is called **future perfect.**
They *will have driven* to school.	Action that will occur before a certain time is called **future perfect.**

Notice that the **future perfect** is formed with **will have** and the past participle.

Exercise 5

Underline the present tense verb in the following sentences.

1. Vampire bats do not suck blood from their victims.

2. They lick, rather than suck, a tiny amount of blood from a puncture wound that they make from their razor-sharp teeth.

3. The bats land on large animals like horses and cows and make a tiny puncture on the hide with their teeth.

4. The animal usually is unaware that it has been bitten and is not harmed from the tiny puncture mark.

5. The blood loss from the animal is minimal, even though the bat may be too full to fly away.

6. The vampire bat weights less than one once, so even a drop of blood is substantial to the tiny bat.

7. Bats can search for food at speeds of 60 mph.

8. Vampire bats have heat sensors on their noses that are sensitive to warm blood spots on the victim's body.

9. Vampire bats take 30 minutes to lick the droplets of blood; as a result, humans are rarely the victims.

10. Baby vampire bats drink milk instead of blood.

Exercise 6

Underline the present perfect verb in the following sentences.

1. I have studied three days for the test.

2. John has studied only two days for the test.

3. Latonya has seen the movie.

4. Steven has worked at Walmart for five years.

5. Sandra has read the novel three times this year.

Exercise 7

Underline the present progressive verb in the following sentences.

1. I am studying for the test.

2. Jan and Tony are driving to school.

3. Tom is walking two miles every day.

4. Amanda has been walking every day.

5. The students have been studying in groups.

Exercise 8

Underline the past tense verb in the following sentences.

1. Yesterday, I had my car.

2. This morning, I rode the bus to school.

3. The students had to turn in their assignments.

4. I walked home from the mall.

5. I saw the movie last night.

Exercise 9

Underline the past perfect verb in the following sentences.

1. I had worked at the park.

2. Trisha had studied for the test.

3. Jim and Tom had taken the test.

4. Steven had seen the movie.

5. Randall had seen the movie, too.

Exercise 10

Underline the past progressive verb in the following sentences.

1. The doctor was rescheduling her patients.

2. The streetlights were blinking on and off.

3. The stars were twinkling like fireflies.

4. The grieving dog was howling all night.

5. The neighbor was ringing the doorbell.

Exercise 11

Underline the future tense verb in the following sentences.

1. The bus driver will collect the money.

2. The train will stop at noon.

3. The store will close next week.

4. My mother will drive us to the mall.

5. The students will pass the state exam.

Exercise 12

Underline the future perfect verb in the following sentences.

1. I will be happy when I graduate.

2. Harold will be here tonight.

3. Grandmother will leave me her favorite ring.

4. Janet will make the reservations tonight.

5. Troy and Thomas will run for student government.

Exercise 13

Underline the future progressive verb in the following sentences.

1. Harold will be arriving tonight.

2. Troy and Thomas will be running for student government.

3. I will be auditioning for the play.

4. Tyler will be applying for the job.

5. I will be driving the car to school.

REGULAR AND IRREGULAR VERBS

Regular verbs do not change their spelling to form past and past participle. The tenses are formed by adding **–d** or **–ed** to the present tense verb.

Present	Past	Past Participle	Present Participle
talk	talked	**had** talked	**have/has** talked
jump	jumped	**had** jumped	**have/has** jumped

Irregular verbs change their spelling to from past and past participle.

Present	Past	Past Participle	Present Participle
write	wrote	**had** written	**have/has** written
go	went	**had** gone	**have/has** gone

Some common irregular verbs:

Present	Past	Past participle
rise	rose	**had** risen
fall	fell	**had** fallen
bring	brought	**had** brought
eat	ate	**had** eaten
tell	told	**had** told
drink	drank	**had** drunk
swim	swam	**had** swum
come	came	**had** come
take	took	**had** taken
hide	hid	**had** hidden
bite	bit	**had** bitten
begin	began	**had** begun
do	did	**had** done
freeze	froze	**had** frozen
lie	lay	**had** lain
lay	laid	**had** laid
sit	sat	**had** sat
set	set	**had** set

A note about **to lie, to lay, to sit, to set:**

Verb	Definition	Simple Present	Simple Past	Past Participle
Lay	*to put or set something down*	*lay*	*laid*	*laid*
Lie	*to rest or recline*	*lie*	*lay*	*lain*
Set	to put or lay Something down	set	set	set
Sit	to rest or be seated	sat	sat	sat

Infinitives [TO + VERB] are not verbs. Infinitives function as nouns, adjectives, and adverbs.

To win the race was my ultimate goal.
To win is a <u>noun</u> because it is the subject of the sentence.

I brought a paper *to read* while I wait.
To read is an <u>adjective</u> because it modifies the paper.

I practiced running everyday in order *to win* the race.
To win is an adverb because it explains why I practiced running.

Exercise 14

Underline the infinitive in each of the following sentences.

1. To fly, a bat propels itself off the ground by its legs.

2. A jaguar will blend in with leaves to hide from other predators.

3. Female alligators will attack predators to protect their babies.

4. To escape hungry birds, chameleons can blend into their surroundings.

5. Radio frequencies can be adjusted to eliminate static.

6. Mother cats will carry their babies by the nape of the neck to transport them to a safer area.

SUBJECT AND VERB AGREEMENT

A verb must agree with its subject in number and person. Singular subjects take singular verbs, and plural subjects take plural verbs. Singular means one, and plural means more than one.

Amanda works at Walmart.
Amanda is a **singular** noun. She is **one** person. **Works** is a **singular** verb even though it ends in **s**.

People drive too fast on the interstate.
People is a **plural** noun. People means more than one person. **Drive** is a **plural** verb although it does not end in **s**.

A *knife is* on the table.
Knife is singular. The verb **is** is singular.

A *knife and fork are* on the table.
The **knife** and the **fork** are two things on the table. The subject **knife and fork** is plural. **Are** is a plural verb.

While many plural nouns end in -**s,** plural verbs do not.
Cypress *trees grow* very tall.

While many singular nouns do not end in -**s,** singular verbs do.
A cypress *tree grows* very tall.

Exercise 15

Circle the verb in the following sentences and underline the subject.

1. Authors use a number of techniques to bring a story to life.

2. Setting is one way that an author makes a story seem real to the reader.

3. The location of the story contributes to the story's development.

4. Time, weather, and mood also help to create the story's setting.

5. The events that take place in the story are known as the plot.

6. How the events of a story unfold help to develop the storyline.

7. The plot is created through a conflict that the main character or characters encounter.

8. The major events of the plot impact the main character in significant ways.

9. The main character in a story does not have to be human.

10. Main characters can be animals or things.

Exercise 16

Circle the correct verb in the following sentences.

1. Some lizards *do/does* not have legs and *resembles/resemble* snakes.

2. Glass lizards *grow/grows* as large as four feet, and because they do not have legs, they *are/is* often mistaken for snakes.

3. These lizards *have /has* dark brown stripes and *live/lives* in logs and trees.

4. Unlike snakes, though, they *have/has* eyelids and external ear openings.

5. The pink worm lizard *is/are* also a native of Florida.

6. The worm lizard *grows/grow* to approximately 16 inches.

7. It *resembles/resembles* an earthworm and *has/have* neither eyes nor legs.

8. The smallest North American lizard *is/are* the gecko.

9. Geckos are crepuscular like bats and, as a result, *are/is* usually only seen at sunrise or sunset.

10. They *have/has* very distinct toes and large eyes and *is/are* very distinguishable from other lizards.

11. It almost *appears/appear* that they have suckers on the bottom of their feet because of their ability to cling to walls and ceilings.

12. The fine bristles on the bottom of their toes *act/acts* like hooks and not like suckers.

13. Nearly all lizards can *regenerate/regenerates* their tails if they *are/is* broken off and they *lay/lie* eggs.

14. Geckos are seen throughout Florida and *are/is* relatively harmless.

15. Lizards *are/is* vital to the subtropical environmental ecological balance because they *thrive/thrives* on insects and *help/helps* to keep the insect population in check.

   Active voice is created when the subject of the sentence completes the action.
   Tom drives his car to school.
   Tom (the subject of the sentence) is doing the driving.

Passive voice is created when the subject of the sentence receives the action.
The car was driven by Tom.
The car is not doing the driving.

Exercise 17

Identify the following sentences as either active voice or passive voice.
  Write **A** or **P** in the blank.

1. _____ The Magna Carta is considered the most famous British document even though it was signed in 1215.

2. _____ King John was forced to sign the Magna Carta that guaranteed the rights of the individual, including a trial by jury.

3. _____ The Magna Carta also assured a system of checks and balances of power, so that even kings and queens were subject to the laws of the land.

4. _____ This document laid the foundation for constitutional government.

5. _____ Like the Magna Carta, the Declaration of Independence declared the rights of the people.

6. _____ The Declaration of Independence cites the fundamental principles of a democratic government.

7. _____ The Declaration of Independence states that "All men are created equal."

8. _____ Thomas Jefferson wrote the Declaration of Independence, and he presented it to Congress on July 2, 1776.

9. _____ On July 4, 1776, the Declaration of Independence was adopted.

10. _____ John Hancock, who was the president of the Second Continental Congress, was the first person to sign the declaration, so when people say "put your John Hancock here," it means to sign a document.

CHAPTER 4

PRONOUNS

Pronouns can replace nouns. They can act as subjects in a sentence, take the place of objects, and demonstrate possession. **Pronouns** can also label the noun it is replacing as male, female, or genderless. Father, brother, husband, uncle, and Mr. Jones, for instance, can be replaced with *he* or *him.* Mother, sister, wife, aunt, and Mrs. Jones can be replaced with *she* or *her.* Car, table, tree, and river can be replaced with *it.* A group of males, a group of females, and a group of things are referred to as *they* or *them.* To show ownership, **possessive pronouns** are used. The students studied at *her house, his house, their house, my house, your house, our house.*

TYPES OF PRONOUNS

Personal Pronouns

Pronouns that refer to people, places, or things are called personal pronouns. Personal pronouns can be singular or plural. Pronouns that take the place of subjects are called subjective pronouns. Pronouns that take the place of objects are called objective pronouns, and pronouns that show possession are called possessive pronouns. Choosing the correct pronoun case can usually be done by sound.

Subjective Case Pronouns

Tom and I/me walked to school. Choosing I or me can be done by reading the sentence using I without saying the name Tom, and then reading the sentence using me without saying the name Tom.

> *I walked to school.*
> *Me walked to school.*

I is a subjective pronoun and can take the place of a subject in a sentence. Since subjective pronouns act as subjects in a sentence, they need verbs. The pronoun me does not sound right when it is used with a verb. In the sentence, *I walked to school*, I is the subject and walked is the verb; therefore, **Tom and I walked to school** demonstrates the correct pronoun case.

Subjective   Pronouns

Singular		Plural
he	_____	they
she	_____	they
I	_____	we
you	_____	you
it	_____	they

Exercise 1

Choose the correct pronoun in each of the following sentences.

1. The Nobel Prize has been awarded every year since **its/it's** creation in 1901.

2. Alfred Nobel left provisions in **his/their** will to fund the prize to worthy recipients who/whom made contributions in the fields of science, medicine, literature, and world peace.

3. Alfred Nobel wanted those **who/whom** benefited humankind to be recognized.

4. **He/him** also wanted to encourage the greatest minds on earth to use there/their knowledge for the betterment of humankind.

5. **Them/those who/whom** are awarded the Nobel Prize receive a gold medal and hundreds of thousands of dollars.

Exercise 2

Choose the correct pronoun in each of the following sentences.

Women inventors did not publically appear until the end of the 1800's. Women were not allowed to

own property, so she/they could not own a patent. They/she could not even sign legal agreements, so

there/their husbands or fathers or brothers had to sign for them. As a result, no one really knows how

many women inventors there were throughout history. Although some women were able to patent their/there inventions during the 1800's, many more were denied legal patents. Some of the inventions

by women include the syringe, bulletproof vests, life raft, electric hot water heater, windshield wipers,

and the muffler.

Objective Case Pronouns

Tom walked to school with Jane and I/me. Choosing I or me can be done by reading the sentence using I without saying the name Jane, and then, reading the sentence with me without saying the name Jane.

Tom walked to school with I.

Tom walked to school with me.

Me is an objective pronoun and can take the place of the noun in the prepositional phrase. Objective pronouns are used without verbs. Tom walked to school with Jane and me demonstrates the correct pronoun use.

Objective   *Pronouns*

Singular		Plural
him	_____	them
her	_____	them
me	_____	us
it	_____	them
you	_____	you

Exercise 3

Choose the correct pronoun in the following sentences.

1. John Banks said that the chair of the committee and **he/him** would announce the winner.

2. Candice and **she/her** will deliver the material tonight.

3. The student turned in **his/her** or their essay on time.

4. Each student contributed **their/his** or her opinion during the meeting.

5. Every swimmer must have on **their/his** or her life jacket.

6. Tammy or the twins are bringing **her/their** sodas to the party.

7. The twins or Tammy is bringing **their/her** sodas to the party.

8. The man **who/whom** left his jacket is at the door.

9. Mr. Jones, **who/whom** is at the door, left his jacket.

10. Everybody will stay after class to finish **their/his** or her notebook.

Possessive Pronouns

Possessive pronouns are used to show ownership.
   The house belongs to Tom or ***Tom's house*** can be written using a possessive pronoun as ***his house***.

Possessive   Pronouns

Singular	Plural
his	whose
hers	their
her	theirs
its	your
whose	yours
your	our
yours	ours
my	
mine	

Exercise 4

Circle the possessive pronoun in each of the following sets.

1. Alligators are abundant in Florida and can make nearly any body of fresh water **there/their** home.

2. Alligators mate in the spring and emit a deep bellowing sound to summon **their/there/they're** potential mates.

3. Several months after mating, the female gator builds **her/hers** nest.

4. She/her uses dirt, leaves, and sticks to construct **her/their** nest.

5. **Her/she** nest is called a mound, and it can reach a height of two or three feet.

6. **Her/she** lays up to fifty eggs, and **she/her** buries **them/they** in the center of the mound.

7. The mother gator protects her/their young 24 hours a day and will attack anyone **whose/who's/who** approaches **her/hers** nest.

8. A group of baby alligators is called a pod, and the baby gators are protected by **their/they're** mother for one to two years.

9. Although alligators can be seen in the wild from Texas to North Carolina, **their/there** main habitat is Florida.

10. Alligators are not found anywhere else on earth other than the United States except in China, but **their/there** sightings in China are rare.

Interrogative Pronouns

Interrogative pronouns are used to ask questions.

who	*Who* is coming to dinner?
whom	To *whom* did you give the dinner invitation?
whose	At *whose* house are we having dinner?
which	*Which* night is the dinner?
what	*What* dish am I supposed to cook for dinner?

Reflexive Pronouns and Intensive Pronouns

myself	I passed the driving test *myself*.
himself	He sings to *himself* in the shower.
herself	She walked down the alley by *herself*.
yourself	You should give *yourself* some time off.
itself	The car started up by *itself*.
ourselves	We drove the boat *ourselves*.
yourselves	Save money by doing the work *yourselves*.
themselves	The students need to review for the test *themselves*.

THERE IS *NO* SUCH PRONOUN AS *THEIRSELVES.*

To remember reflexive pronouns, think of looking at *yourself* in the mirror.
Tom looked at *himself* in the mirror.
Jane looked at *herself* in the mirror.
To remember intensive pronouns, think of starting a project by yourself and how excited you will be when you complete it. I painted the house *myself*, and it looks great!

Exercise 5

Fill in the blank with the correct reflexive or intensive pronoun.

1. Stewart_____ passed the driving test.
2. Mary was shocked that she painted the house_____.
3. You need to say to _____, "I can do it."
4. The students planned the project_____ and presented the idea to the teacher.
5. We completed the requirements _____ and received our certificates.

Demonstrative Pronouns

Demonstrative pronouns express a specific relationship with an object without naming it.

this	*This* is the right one.
that	*That* is the wrong one.
these	*These* should be included on the test.
those	*Those* have been eliminated.

Demonstrative pronouns should be followed by a noun in order to make the reference clear.

This address is the right one.
That address is the wrong one.
These pronouns should be included on the test.
Those trees have been eliminated.

Exercise 6

Add a noun to each sentence to make the reference clear.

1. That_____ is the nicest design.
2. Those_____ were on the summer reading list.
3. This_____ is my favorite.
4. These_____ are on sale.
5. This_____ is too wrinkled to wear.

PRONOUN AGREEMENT

Pronouns must agree with their antecedents in number. The noun that the pronoun refers to is called the antecedent. If the noun is singular, the pronoun must be singular. If the noun is plural, the pronoun must be plural.

The *boys* picked up *their* uniforms from the coach.
Mr. Jones left *his* wallet on the table.
Mary studied for *her* test last night.

Exercise 7

Circle the pronoun and its antecedent in each sentence.

1. Pit-vipers like water moccasins are common in Florida, and they can be found living near any fresh water habitat.

2. Water moccasins are very aggressive and will attack swimmers who have made vibrations or ripples in the water, and they have even been known to strike cows that are standing in shallow water.

3. Moccasins can strike their victims under water without warning and can strike from tree limbs.

4. They are also called cottonmouths because the inside of their mouth is white.

5. Rat snakes are also native to Florida, but they are not venomous like water moccasins.

6. They eat mostly rats and help to rid the environment of these disease- carrying rodents.

7. The Eastern diamondback rattlesnake, however, is probably the most threatening pit-viper in the South, and it is the most dreaded.

8. The diamondback strikes to kill its victims.

9. The diamondback has a six-foot strike distance, and it will strike anyone or any animal that enters its strike zone.

10. There have been reports of diamondback strikes even after the snake has been killed because its nervous system still remains active for a period of time, and many myths surrounding the diamondback developed as a result.

11. The diamondback can strike, recoil, and strike again in less than a second and before the victim realizes he or she has been bitten.

12. Like the diamondback, pigmy rattlesnakes are also found in the palmetto flatwoods of the South, and they are just as aggressive as the diamondback and the water moccasin.

13. However, the pigmy rattlesnake rarely grows larger than 20 inches, so its size does not make the snake look dangerous.

14. Nevertheless, the strike of a pigmy can be as lethal, and it will strike repeatedly when it feels threatened.

15. Many firefighters have been bitten by these deadly snakes as they battle brushfires in snake infested palmetto flatlands.

Exercise 8

Match the correct pronoun with its antecedent in each sentence.

1. The skink is a beautiful, shiny lizard that is indigenous to Florida and is sometimes mistaken for a snake because **it/they** has a long snakelike tail.

2. Skinks can grow as large as 15 inches, and **they/it** appear in all colors.

3. Bright blue skinks are easily identifiable as non-threatening lizards, but **their/it's** shiny black counterparts are often mistaken for snakes.

4. Skinks are only poisonous if **they/it** are eaten.

5. Skinks do not strike, but they will bite if **they/it** are picked up.

6. However, the bite from a blue or a black skink is not considered dangerous because **it's/its** teeth cannot penetrate human skin.

7. The orange skink, however, does inflict a painful bite and can hang onto a predator like a cat that attacks **it/them**.

8. Geckos are abundant in Florida, but **they/them** are harmless.

9. Geckos do not look like other lizards because **they/it** have large eyes and distinct toes that look like suckers.

10. Geckos can be seen after dark clinging to walls and ceilings, eating gnats and moths that **they/them** catch flying near **them/it**.

Indefinite	*Pronouns*
someone	somebody
anyone	everybody
everyone	no one
each	anybody
every	none
neither	anything
either	nobody

Indefinite pronouns do not refer to anyone or anything specific. They are matched with singular antecedents and they take singular verbs.

Right	Every student turned in his or her essay.
Wrong	Every student turned in their essay.

Right	Someone left his or her books on the bench.
Wrong	Someone left their books on the bench.

When using either/or and neither/nor, the noun that follows or and nor determines what the verb is and what the referring pronoun is.

Right	Either Aunt Mary or the ***twins are*** driving me to school.
Wrong	Either Aunt Mary or the ***twins is*** driving me to school.

If ***Aunt Mary*** follows ***or,*** the singular verb is used.

Right	Either the twins or ***Aunt Mary is*** driving me to school.
Wrong	Either the twins or ***Aunt Mary are*** driving me to school.

Exercise 9

Choose the correct pronoun and verb.

1. The mysterious creature Bigfoot is named because footprints measuring up to 19 inches long, purportedly belonging to it/the creature, **have/has** been found.

2. There **have/has** been many sightings of Bigfoot in the Pacific Northwest; however, scientific proof of **its/it's** existence **has/have** not been established.

3. The compilation of reported Bigfoot sightings has determined that thousands of **these/them lives/live** in the mountains of the Pacific Northwest.

4. The footprints **have/has** been used to estimate the height and weight of the creature/it.

5. Bigfoot creatures **is/are** estimated to reach heights of nine feet and to weigh as much as 1000 pounds as determined by the size of **there/their** footprints.

ADJECTIVES AND ADVERBS

Adjectives and **adverbs** are words that describe. Adjectives and adverbs are called modifiers because they change or modify the information in a sentence. **Adjectives** describe nouns and make those nouns come to life. *The dog jumped over the log* is a flat sentence. The dog is not a specific dog, so a story about this dog cannot develop. The sentence: *The large, black and white spotted dog quickly jumped over the old, rotten log* uses adjectives and adverbs to bring this dog to life as a specific dog.

Adjectives make it possible to differentiate one noun from another noun. **Adverbs** describe adjectives, verbs, and other adverbs. Saying that the *dog quickly jumped* tells the reader that the dog might be young and agile. Adverbs help to establish the tone of the sentence as well. If the writer had used *cautiously jumped*, *awkwardly jumped*, or *slowly jumped* instead, the reader would have a different perception of the condition of the dog and a sense of what the situation surrounding the dog might be. If the dog cautiously jumps, then the dog might be fearful of what is on the other side of the log. If the dog awkwardly jumps, then perhaps the dog is young or is disabled to some extent. **Quickly, cautiously, awkwardly,** and **slowly** are adverbs, and they are describing how the dog jumped.

Exercise 1

Circle all adjectives and/or adverbs in each of the following sentences.

1. The planet Earth is made up of many layers of rock.

2. The inner core of the Earth is an amazing 750 miles thick.

3. This inner core is solid primarily iron and nickel; however, the core that surrounds this solid rock is liquid rock.

4. Molten rock referred to as mantle rock completely covers the layer of liquid rock.

5. The Earth's mantle is 1,800 miles thick.

6. Above the mantle layer is the 500-mile-thick lithosphere.

7. The lithosphere is extremely hard, outer-level crust where humans live.

8. Even with modern equipment, it is impossible to dig a hole through the Earth.

9. Humans have drilled into only a fraction of the earth's thick mantle.

10. Drilling through the Earth's inner core will probably never be accomplished by humans.

Exercise 2

Circle the adjectives and/or adverbs in each of the following sentences.

1. Earthquakes and volcanic eruptions are caused when molten rocks abruptly lift while cooled rocks simultaneously sink.

2. The cooler rocks are quickly heated by the energy from the core of the Earth and begin to instantly rise again.

3. Convection currents are caused by the constant heating, sinking, and rising of the rocks.

4. This intense movement caused by convection currents created the plates that hold the oceans and the continents.

5. Convection currents purportedly cause earthquakes to occur somewhere in the world every day.

COMPARATIVE AND SUPERLATIVE ADJECTIVES

Comparative adjectives are used to compare or distinguish two nouns.

John is *taller* than Ron.

The letters -**er** are added to adjectives that compare.
Think of adding two letters to compare two things.

If the adjective sounds funny when -**er** is added to it, use the word **more** in front of the adjective instead.

Wrong   Sue is *intelligenter* than her sister. More should be used in front of intelligent instead of adding an -**er** to the word.

Right   Sue is *more intelligent* than her sister.

Superlative adjectives are used to compare or distinguish between three or more nouns.

John is the *tallest* student in the class.

The letters -**est** are added to adjectives that compare a noun with two or more other nouns. Think of adding three letters to compare three things.

If the adjective sounds funny when -**est** is added to it, use the more **most** in front of the adjective instead.

Wrong   Sue is the *intelligentest* student in the class.

Right   Sue is the *most intelligent* student in the class.

John is *tall*.   *tall* is an adjective

John is *taller* than Mike.   *taller* is a comparative adjective

John is the *tallest* member of his family.   *tallest* is a superlative adjective

 **Exercise 3**

Check whether the adjective is comparative or superlative.

	Comparative	Superlative
1. wider	_____	_____
2. longest	_____	_____
3. more beautiful	_____	_____
4. smallest	_____	_____
5. most brilliant	_____	_____
6. brighter	_____	_____
7. happiest	_____	_____
8. sweeter	_____	_____
9. more intelligent	_____	_____
10. happier	_____	_____

TYPES OF ADJECTIVES

Descriptive Adjectives

Descriptive adjectives modify nouns or pronouns by answering **which one, how many,** and **what kind of.** Descriptive adjectives create imagery by forming word pictures.

The *large, black and white spotted* dog quickly jumped over the *rotten* log.

Three fluffy, yellow kittens played with the *large* ball of *red* yarn.

The Articles a, an, and the

Articles are also adjectives and are used to introduce and limit nouns.

A, an, and **the** are never used in a sentence without referring to a noun.

The <u>student</u> will be listening to *a* <u>story</u> during class before writing *an* analytical <u>essay</u>.

Personal or Possessive Adjectives

These adjectives are like the possessive pronouns *her, his, their, our, your, my,* and *its.* These pronouns are considered adjectives when they modify nouns.

>   *His* book was left on the desk.

Demonstrative Adjectives

These adjectives are like the demonstrative pronouns *these, those, this,* and *that.*
  These pronouns are considered adjectives when they modify nouns.

That <u>test</u> will be easy.	*That* is an adjective modifying the noun *test.*
These <u>notes</u> are typed.	*These* is an adjective modifying the noun *notes.*
That will be easy.	*That* is a pronoun, taking the place of the noun *test.*
These are typed.	*These* is a pronoun, taking the place of the noun *notes.*

Exercise 4

Circle the descriptive adjective in the following sentences.

1. Devastating floods are common in China.

2. In 1887, the flooding of the Majestic Yellow River killed more than 900,000 people in China.

3. Tropical storms have also resulted in devastating floods.

4. Cyclones are tropical storms that are deadlier than hurricanes.

5. Cyclones that emerge from the Indian Ocean are so deadly that human fatalities have been recorded in the hundreds of thousands.

6. A devastating cyclone that struck Bangladesh in 1970 killed over 500,000 people.

7. Florida is also the site of some of the world's most deadly hurricanes.

8. The enormous damages from hurricanes Andrew and Charley amounted to tens of billions of dollars.

9. The damages from Hurricane Katrina have been estimated to exceed $100 billion dollars, making it the largest natural disaster in the history of the United States.

10. Hurricane Katrina struck southeast Louisiana on August 29, 2005, and resulted in nearly 2,000 deaths.

11. Naming hurricanes in order to more easily record and track them began in 1951.

12. The military alphabet was used to name these destructive storms until 1953.

13. Women's names were exclusively used until 1979 when men's names were added to the infamous list.

14. Naming hurricanes makes it easier for trained meteorologists to follow the potentially dangerous track of the storms.

15. The names of devastating storms are retired and are no longer used.

16. Hurricanes are named each season in alphabetical order.

17. The Sumatra earthquake, measuring a magnitude of 9.3, struck off the coast of the Indonesian Island of Sumatra on December 26, 2004, and the destructive tsunami that was created resulted in the deaths of nearly 300,000 people.

18. Tsunamis are tidal waves that are caused by underwater earthquakes.

19. Tidal waves develop in the Pacific Ocean, and they do not occur as often as Atlantic Ocean hurricanes.

20. Tidal waves reach heights of 100 or more feet, and they travel at amazing speeds of nearly 500 miles per hour.

COORDINATION

Sentences are connected in order to create a unified and coherent flow of information by eliminating short choppy sentences. There are three ways to connect sentences.

1. Coordinating Conjunctions

    for, and, nor, but, or, yet, so

    They can easily be remembered by thinking of the acronym **FANBOYS**.

Examples

Pat hated work, **but** he liked school.
Pat bought the book, **yet** he did not intend to read it.
Pat studied for his test, **for** he wanted to pass the course.
Pat wanted to buy a new car, **so** he saved his money for a down payment.

Note: A comma always comes in front of a coordinating conjunction and never after it.

2. A second way to coordinate sentences is to use a conjunctive adverb.

Commonly used conjunctive adverbs accordingly, furthermore, moreover, also, hence, as a result, however, nevertheless, thus, indeed, therefore,otherwise, consequently, instead, undoubtedly, finally, likewise, thereafter, further, meanwhile, similarly

Examples

Pat hated work; however, he liked school.
Pat wanted to buy a new car; therefore, he saved his money.
Pat registered for a math class; furthermore, he registered for a history class.

Note: A semicolon always comes in front of a conjunctive adverb and a comma after it. A third way to coordinate sentences is to use a semicolon.

Examples

Pat hated work; he liked school.
Pat wanted to buy a new car; he saved his money.
Pat registered for a math class; he registered for a history class.
Note: Coordination can only be used to connect sentences. There must be a subject and a verb on each side of the connector.
Note: Sentences are also called independent clauses. A clause is a group of words. Independent clauses are groups of words that contain a subject and a verb and express a complete thought.

Coordination Patterns

I ; I	[Independent clause] ; [Independent clause]
I , for I	[Independent clause], for [Independent clause]
I , and I	[Independent clause], and [Independent clause]
I , nor I	[Independent clause], nor [Independent clause]
I , but I	[Independent clause], but [Independent clause]
I , or I	[Independent clause], or [Independent clause]
I , yet I	[Independent clause], yet [Independent clause]
I , so I	[Independent clause], so [Independent clause]
I ; however, I	[Independent clause]; however, [Independent clause]

Exercise 1

Underline the connecting word(s) in each set of sentences.

Rain Forest Facts

1. Rain forests used to cover 14% of the Earth's surface, but that percentage has been reduced to less than 6% now.

2. Environmentalists predict that the rainforests will disappear because of deforestation by 2050; however, total destruction could occur sooner.

3. Environmentalists estimate that deforestation because of mining and logging is destroying nearly 100 acres of rainforests per hour; as a result, nearly 50,000 species of plants and animals are disappearing forever.

4. Indigenous tribes of the rainforest are disappearing as well, and their language and their knowledge of plants and animals will disappear, too.

5. The Amazon Rain Forest contains more than a billion acres, and it covers the areas of five South American countries.

6. Rain forests recycle carbon dioxide into oxygen, and because the Amazon Rain Forest is so large, it is responsible for 20% of the world's oxygen.

7. One-half of the world's 10 million species of plants and animals live in the rain forests, and, collectively, the rain forests are the source of one-half of the world's fresh water.

8. Nearly 100% of the world's natural foods originally came from the rain forests; in addition, much of the world's natural pharmaceuticals come from the rain forest, including powerful anticancer drugs.

9. Scientists have examined only a small percentage of the plants that flourish in the rain forest, and they believe that the cures to cancer and other deadly diseases can be found in the rain forests.

10. The resources of the rain forest are perpetual and renewable; however, mining for minerals has left the rain forest stripped of life and forever barren because nothing will grow on the land again.

11. The rain forest took 200 million years to develop, yet humans will destroy the rain forest within the next 30 years, burning 100 million acres a year.

The Titanic

1. J.P. Morgan owned the company that built the Titanic, and the company insisted that the ship was unsinkable.

2. The building of the Titanic took approximately 3000 men and more than $7 million, but the cost did not include enough life rafts to save the passenger.

3. New ships are traditionally christened to keep them safe at sea; however, the Titanic was not christened, so many people believe that is the reason it sank.

4. The christening of ships is usually done in public ceremonies, and even royalty have taken part in the elaborate rituals.

5. The Titanic collided with an iceberg during its maiden voyage on Sunday night, April 14, 1912, and the unchristened Titanic began to sink.

6. Only 705 people survived out of the 2,208 total passengers and crew aboard the ship, for the ship did not carry enough lifeboats for everyone on board.

Exercise 2

Correct the following run-on sentences using any method of coordination.

1. Ants have six legs, each leg has three joints.

   _____

2. Most ants can lift 20 times their body weight some ants can lift 100 times their body weight.

   _____

3. The life of an ant is roughly two months they have to get a lot accomplished in a short period of time.

   _____

4. The antennae are used for smell and touch ants do not have tongues.

   _____

5. The strong jaws of the ants are not used for chewing, they are used for squeezing the liquid from their food.

   _____

6. Ants do not have two eyes, they have compound eyes that are made up of many eyes.

   _____

7. Each ant has two stomachs they do not function the same way.

   _____

8. One stomach is used to hold food for other ants the other stomach is used to hold food for itself.

   _____

9. The exoskeleton of the ant is not like human skin, it is like a protective hard shell.

   _____

10. There are thousands of species of ants they live on every continent on Earth.

    _____

11. Ants live in colonies that range from thousands to millions of ants, each ant has a position in the colony.

    _____

12. Each colony has one or two queen ants their job is to lay eggs.

_____

13. Worker ants care for the eggs, they defend the nest from intruders.

_____

14. Worker ants also look for food they are responsible for keeping the nest clean.

_____

15. In order to defend themselves and the nest, some ants sting, some ants spray acid.

_____

16. To increase the number of worker ants in a weak colony, eggs and larva are stolen from a strong colony, they are taken to the weak colony.

_____

17. Some ants are nomadic they are constantly on the move, taking their eggs and larva with them.

_____

18. Some species of ants fly, they are often mistaken for termites.

_____

19. A keen observer can tell the difference between a termite and a winged ant the common observer usually cannot tell the difference.

_____

20. Termites have a head and a body and straight antennae winged ants have three body parts and bent antennae.

_____

Exercise 3

Use a semicolon to connect the following run-on sentences.
   Circle the semicolon for easy visibility.

1. The first glue was made from fish some people think the first glue was made from horses.

2. The windshield wiper was not invented by a man it was invented by a woman, Mary Anderson, in 1903.

3. Alexander Graham Bell invented the telephone many people do not know that his mother and wife were deaf and could not help him with the sound.

4. In 1821 when Louis Braille was 12 years old, he invented Braille it is a coded writing system for the blind.

5. He published his first Braille book in 1829 some people burned the book because it was thought to be the secret language of the devil.

6. Earle Dickson invented the band-aid in 1921 he saw that his wife needed to cover the cuts that she got from preparing daily meals.

7. The Yo-Yo is not a recent invention it was used as a weapon in the Philippines for more than 400 years.

8. The name Yo-Yo means "come back" in the native language of the Philippines the name has remained an appropriate one.

9. Bette Nesmith used her kitchen blender to mix up a liquid that would cover up typing mistakes there was yet not a product that easily corrected typing errors.

10. Her liquid mixture became Liquid Paper the world was changed forever.

Exercise 4

Add a second sentence using a coordinating conjunction.

1. During your lifetime, you'll eat about 60,000 pounds of food.

   _____

2. Thomas Edison, light bulb inventor, was afraid of the dark

   _____

3. It's against the law to slam your car door in Switzerland

   _____

4. In Bangladesh, students as young as 15 can be jailed for cheating on their finals

   _____

5. The most common name in the world is Mohammed

   _____

6. Babe Ruth wore a cabbage leaf under his cap to keep him cool. He changed it every 2 innings

   _____

7. In Tokyo, people can buy toupees for their dogs

_____

8. If you know a (male) millionaire who happens to be married, the most likely profession of his wife is a teacher

_____

9. A flamingo can eat only when its head is upside down

_____

10. Sixty-one thousand people are airborne over the United States at any given time

_____

Exercise 5

Add a second sentence using a conjunctive adverb.

1. Soldiers from every country salute with their right hand

_____

2. *60 Minutes* on CBS is the only TV show that does not have a theme song or music

_____

3. Cats can hear ultrasound

_____

4. The Olympic flag's colors are always red, black, blue, green, and yellow rings on a field of white because at least one of those colors appears on the flag of every nation on the planet

_____

5. Every day more money is printed for Monopoly than for the U.S. Treasury

_____

6. One-third of the land in the United States is owned by the government

_____

7. There are no venomous snakes in Maine

_____

8. Chimps are the only animals that can recognize themselves in a mirror

_____

9. Hawaii is moving toward Japan four inches every year

_____

10. February 1865 is the only month in recorded history not to have a full moon

_____

Exercise 6

Underline the place in each sentence where a semicolon should be inserted.

1. Every point of light in the sky is a star except the moon, the planets, and satellites the sun is a star, too.

2. Stars are grouped according to their size some are dwarfs while others are giants or supergiants.

3. Stars are large gaseous masses of hydrogen and helium the sun is approximately 5 billion years old, and it is considered a dwarf star.

4. Red dwarfs are the most common stars they are smaller than our sun and are not clearly visible, except for those red dwarfs that are close to the Earth.

5. White dwarfs are smaller than the Earth they are invisible to us because their nuclear power has burned out.

6. Following the red dwarfs in number are the red giants these stars are larger and brighter than our sun.

7. The supergiants are the largest and the rarest of the stars the supergiant, Betelgeuse, which is located in Orion, is estimated to be 600 million miles across.

8. The life expectancy of stars varies their size and mass determines their life span.

9. Ten billion years is considered infancy to many red dwarfs these red dwarfs will continue to fuse hydrogen into helium for another 60 billion years.

10. Some stars become unable to resist the continuous force of gravity on their core, the core collapses, and the star explodes.

11. The exploding star is called a supernova stars that continue to collapse without exploding may eventually disappear, leaving only their gravity to suck in everything that comes near.

12. One theory about collapsed supernovas is that they create black holes scientists are coming closer to proving the theory true.

13. A nebula is a cloud of cosmic gas and dust a nebula usually appears as a colorful mist.

14. The misty areas around stars are nebulas many times they are visible to the naked eye.

Exercise 7

Underline the place in each sentence where a coordinating conjunction should be inserted and write the coordinating conjunction that would best connect the sentence in the blank in front of the sentence.

1. _____ The Earth is part of the system of stars known as the Milky Way the Milky Way or Galaxy is comprised of about 200 billion suns.

2. _____ All of the stars that are seen from Earth are part of the Milky Way, this galaxy is the only one that we can without a telescope.

3. _____ The Milky Way is so large that it would take our sun 240 million years to make a complete orbit the Milky Way is located in a cluster of 30 galaxies.

4. _____ Galaxies are also grouped into clusters and superclusters scientists believe that there are billions of galaxies.

5. _____ This cluster of galaxies is a part of a larger group of clusters called a supercluster gravitational forces hold the clusters together.

6. _____ Scientists believe that areas without gravity exists between the superclusters that remain separated from one another as a result.

7. _____ Telescopes are needed to view galaxies beyond ours much can be seen with the naked eye.

8. _____ The surface of the moon can be seen without a telescope the holes that appear on the moon's surface are the scars left by objects that have collided with the moon.

9. _____ The moon has mountains, valleys, and crater holes it is made up of crushed rock and ice.

10. _____ Recent discoveries include finding water on the moon methane and carbon dioxide are also present.

Exercise 8

Underline the place in each sentence where a conjunctive adverb should be inserted and write the conjunctive adverb that would best connect the sentence in the blank in front of the sentence.

The moose lives in Northern North America; however, it lives mainly in the forests rather than in the mountains.

1. _____ The moose is a member of the deer family it is larger than the deer.

2. _____ Shoving and bunting other moose is what a moose uses its antlers the antlers are strong because they are made of bone.

3. _____ Moose do not fight one another to the death the weaker of the two in battle simple walks away.

4. _____ Moose antlers drop off in the winter they start to grow again in the spring.

5. _____ Every year the antlers grow larger than the antlers from the previous year they grow stronger.

6. _____ Female moose do not grow antlers they do not have the same defense that males have.

7. _____ Male moose are called bulls they can weigh as much as 1,400 pounds.

8. _____ A bull moose can exceed a height of seven feet his antlers can spread seven feet.

9. _____ The largest antlers in the world belong to the bull moose they are not effective weapons.

10. _____ More effective in battle are the hooves both male and female moose use their sharp hooves to defend themselves.

Exercise 9

Add a period to separate the following sentences. Remember to capitalize the first word of the second sentence.

1. Ray Bradbury published *Farenheit* 451 in 1953 the novel reflected the events concerning the expansion of communism.

2. Bradbury predicted the influence that television would have on the American public he believed this negative influence would be determined by the increase in social crimes.

3. *Farenheit 451* was set in a futuristic society this society banned all books and burned them.

4. People who had books hidden were arrested their houses were burned down along with the books.

5. Bradbury warned society against willfully giving up its freedoms he showed people what life would be like without the knowledge gained from religion, science, and philosophy.

   Run-on sentences are independent clauses that have not been properly connected. A **fused run-on** occurs when two sentences are connected without punctuation. A **comma splice run-on** occurs when two sentences are connected with nothing but a comma.
   Baby alligators live in a <u>pod their</u> likelihood of survival is increased because they band together for two years.
   No punctuation connects these two sentences, so it is a fused run-on.
   The sound that an alligator makes is called a <u>bellow, alligators</u> will bellow nonstop to attract other alligators during mating season.
   Only a comma is used to connect these two sentences, so it is a comma splice run-on.

Exercise 10

Identify each sentence as either a fused run-on or a comma splice run-on. Indicate in the blank with an **F** or **CS**.

1. _____ The United States Constitution was the creation by fifty-five delegates who met on May 25, 1787 at the Constitutional Convention held at Independence Hall in Philadelphia as a result the United States Constitution was adopted in 1788.

2. _____ James Madison is considered the "Father of the Constitution," he created a system to check and limit the powers of Congress, the Supreme Court, and the president.

3. _____ The first ten amendments of the United States Constitution guarantee individual liberties they are called the *Bill of Rights*.

4. _____ The First Amendment guarantees freedom of religion, freedom of speech, and the freedom of the press it also guarantees the right to petition and the right to assemble.

5. _____ The Constitution that was adopted in 1788 did not have the *Bill of Rights* they were added later.

CHAPTER 7

SUBORDINATION

Commas are not placed in sentences according to one's breathing pattern. Commas are placed in a sentence according to the kind of phrase and where it is attached to the sentence. There are definite patterns for learning the punctuation of phrases.

Subordination Patterns
P, I [Phrase] <u>comma</u> [Independent clause]
From the age of the dinosaurs, alligators have existed.

I P [Independent clause] <u>no comma</u> [Phrase]
Do not use a comma before a dependent clause and a prepositional phrase that end a sentence.
The American alligator can be found <u>from as far west as Texas to as far north as North Carolina and as far south as Florida.</u>

I, P [Independent clause] <u>comma</u> [Phrase]
Use a comma before phrases beginning with a, an, ing word, and which.
Alligators also inhabit China, <u>which is the only other place on the earth where alligators exist.</u>

½ I, P, ½ I   The phrase is in the middle of the sentence with commas around the phrase.
Florida, <u>comprising the most concentrated alligator population on earth,</u> is also home to a small population of crocodiles.

½ I P ½ I   The phrase is in the middle of the sentence with no commas around the phrase.
Female alligators <u>that are protecting their young</u> are the most aggressive alligators.

Use commas around phrases beginning with **which** but not around phrases beginning with **that**. A phrase beginning with **which** is considered nonrestrictive information (information that is not required). A phrase beginning with **that** is considered restrictive information (information that is required). Information set within commas can be removed. Think of the commas as handles on a basket.

The basket can be removed.

Examples

P,I   <u>Beside the chimney,</u> a slight crack had appeared.

IP   A slight crack had appeared <u>beside the chimney.</u>

I,P   I plan to visit Alaska, <u>a place I have wanted to see all my life.</u>

IPI   The lady <u>who has three cats</u> lives next door.

   Note: No commas are used when the relative pronoun refers to a nonspecific noun.

No commas are used when the interrupting phrase begins with the relative pronoun "that."

I,P,I   Mrs. Jones, <u>who has three cats</u>, lives next door.

   Note: Commas are used when the relative pronoun refers to a specific noun.

Commas are used when the interrupting phrase begins with the relative pronoun "which."

List of Subordinators

A subordinator is a word that is so powerful that it can reduce a sentence to a phrase. "The child screamed" is a sentence. "Because the child screamed" is a subordinate clause. It is not a sentence although it does contain a noun and a verb.

when, while, since, before, after, until, wherever
because, since, as,
if, unless,
although, even though, despite, in spite of
while, where, whereas

Exercise 1

Circle the subordinator in each sentence.

1. While okra is usually boiled or fried, it can be dehydrated and eaten as a snack.

2. Vegetables and fruit retain their nutrients even though they have been dehydrated.

3. Flowers can be dehydrated and used in potpourri because their fragrant oils remain active.

4. Because cloves can be boiled, they can be used to make a delightful household fragrance.

5. Vinegar can be sprayed throughout the house to eliminate unwanted odors because the vinegar smell will evaporate.

6. Whenever odors build up in the refrigerator, place a box of opened baking soda in the refrigerator door to neutralize the odors.

7. Salt can be sprinkled over the carpet so that odors are trapped and then picked up whenever the floor is vacuumed.

8. All door knobs and handles in a house should be disinfected after a family member has been ill.

9. Disinfectant wipes should also be used to clean the computer keyboards after someone has sneezed on the keys.

10. People who take elevators should wipe the floor selection buttons because so many people have touched the buttons while making prior selections.

Identifying fragments

Fragments are parts or pieces of sentences, so they do not express a complete thought. Fragments are incomplete sentences because they are missing either subjects or verbs. A group of words without a subject or a verb does not express a complete thought.

Example

"After school today" does not have a subject nor a verb. The reader is left wondering what will happen after school today.

Some fragments occur in groups of words called dependent clauses. Dependent clauses are often difficult to recognize as fragments because they contain a noun and verb. However, dependent clauses cannot stand by themselves because they do not express a complete thought.

Example

Because the dog barked all night. The reader is left wondering what happened as a result of the dog barking all night.

The group of words has a noun, "dog" and a verb, "barked," but it does not express a complete thought. Because is a subordinator. Subordinators are words that reduce sentences to incomplete thoughts. "The dog barked." is a complete thought, but after "because" is added to the words, the complete thought is lost, and the reader needs more information to make the meaning clear.

Exercise 2

Indicate whether each clause is a sentence or a fragment by labeling with an "S" or an "F."

1._____ Because turnip greens are bitter.

2._____ Calcium is responsible for the bitter taste of turnip greens.

3._____ Because turnip greens are a cruciferous vegetable.

4._____ Cruciferous vegetables because turnip greens are considered among them.

5._____ Cruciferous vegetables produce flowers in the shape of a cross.

6._____ Should be eaten to maximize the benefits.

7._____ Turnips have been eaten since prehistoric times.

8._____ Between a cabbage and a turnip to produce a rutabaga.

9._____ Crossing a turnip and a cabbage produces a rutabaga.

10._____ Rutabagas are grown in the fall.

PARENTHETICALS: ELEMENTS THE WRITER USES TO INTERRUPT THE SENTENCE

They indicate slight emotion and are offset with commas.

Examples

She won't, to be honest with you, make it to work on time.
This hat, I believe, is yours.
He did, however, voice his opinion.

Exercise 3

Insert commas where needed. Circle the commas for easy visibility.

Powerful World Brands

1. Google is the world's most powerful brand.

2. It was incorporated on September 7 1998 in a garage in Menlo Park California but Google did not go public until August 19 2004.

3. In terms of market capitalization General Electric is the world's second largest company.

4. With a brand value of nearly $55 billion Microsoft is the third largest brand and world's largest software company.

5. Invented as a medicine in 1885 by Dr. John Pemberton in Covington Georgia Coca-Cola is the world's fourth largest brand.

6. With 300 million customers China Mobile is the world's largest mobile phone operator and the fifth largest brand on Earth.

7. Primarily because of its cowboy image Marlboro is the sixth largest worldwide brand.

8. The world's largest retailer of groceries and toys Walmart is the seventh largest brand.

9. The world's largest financial services organization is Citigroup and it is the world's eighth largest brand.

10. IBM is the world's largest information technology employer and the ninth leading brand name.

11. The Toyota Motor Corporation is the largest auto company with revenues exceeding 200 billion so it is the tenth largest brand.

 **Exercise 4**

Connect the following sentences using coordination or subordination.

Vacation Wonders

1. Nearly 5 million people visit the Grand Canyon every year and camp in the Grand Canyon National Park. The Grand Canyon is located in Arizona and is a gorge that has been created by the Colorado River, erosion, and wind.

    _____

    _____

2. The South Island of New Zealand has 10 national parks. These parks feature glaciers, fjords, lakes, forests, and beaches.

    _____

    _____

3. Cape Town, South Africa, is rich with beautiful scenery, beaches, boating, and multicultural events. The best time to visit is in the summer.

    _____

    _____

4. Las Vegas is the entertainment capital of the world. This largest city in Nevada offers visitors a fantasy vacation, glamorous casinos, and first-rate shows and entertainers.

    _____

    _____

5. New York is the place to visit for fine art, fashion, Broadway shows, and fine dining. Central Park in the summer cannot be missed.

    _____

    _____

6. For mountain climbing and hiking, travelers should vacation in the Canadian Rockies. There are two national parks to visit that offer skiing and snowshoeing in the winter.

    _____

    _____

7. Machu Picchu allows the traveler to experience a sense of euphoria. This mystical, isolated vacation destination is located in Peru and is considered to be the home of the gods.

    _____

    _____

8. Venice, Italy, is a great tourist destination. Venice is built on 317 small islands that are connected by 400 bridges. Tourists can take romantic gondola boat rides through the 150 canals that encircle the city.

_____

_____

9. Victoria Falls is the most beautiful waterfall in Africa. Activities include elephant safaris, water rafting, and cultural shopping. Zambia is on one side of the falls and Zimbabwe is on the other side.

_____

_____

10. Hong Kong is the place to visit anytime in the fall. Hong Kong is an oriental treasure. The city is filled with mysticism, culture, beautiful scenery, and luxurious shopping and dining.

_____

_____

11. For cultural traditions, historical landmarks, and Victorian seaports, Port Townsend, Washington, is the perfect vacation spot. Lively music, art, and breathtaking scenery are a few of the many amenities that this magical city offers.

_____

_____

12. For historic house museums, beautiful beaches, Hemingway memorabilia, luscious bars, and street entertainment, Key West, Florida, is the place to visit. Key West is a year-round destination. The sultry breezes and constant average temperature of 84 degrees make it appealing anytime of the year.

_____

_____

13. The Vegas of the Middle East is Dubai. Come to Dubai to enjoy the life of the rich and famous. Dubai is an oasis in the middle of the desert.

_____

_____

14. Hauntingly beautiful Fiji in the Pacific Ocean is a must travel destination. Relax on the scenic beaches, sleep all day in a hammock, walk quiet and solitary paths, or enjoy the excitement in an all-inclusive resort. Fiji offers the traveler many choices.

_____

_____

15. Costa Rica is the perfect Caribbean vacation destination. Exotic animals, rain forests, beautiful beaches, and sultry breezes await the traveler.

_____

_____

Exercise 5

Underline the subordinator in each sentence.

Weird Stuff

1. Since Seinfeld loved the Superman image, a Superman appears somewhere in every episode of *Seinfeld*.

2. Although undetectable to the touch, most lipstick contains fish scales.

3. Do not try to suppress a sneeze because you can rupture a blood vessel.

4. It is physically impossible for pigs to look up into the sky whenever they are standing.

5. More than 50 % of the people in the world have never made or received a telephone call because they live in areas or countries that do not have this luxury.

6. Even though many of them do not speak English, 90 % of New York City cabbies are recently arrived immigrants.

7. Although living past 100 is becoming more common, only one person in 2 billion will live to be 116 or older.

8. In ancient Egypt, priests plucked every hair from their bodies, including their eyebrows and eyelashes whenever they performed sacred rituals.

9. Even though people are encouraged to eat healthy, Americans on average eat 18 acres of pizza every day.

10. Honey is the only food that does not spoil even if it is left on the shelf for years and years.

Exercise 6

Add a second sentence using a subordinator.

1. Antarctica is the only continent without reptiles or snakes

_____

2. In the Caribbean there are oysters that can climb trees

_____

3. The youngest pope was 11 years old

_____

4. Iceland consumes more Coca-Cola per capita than any other nation

_____

5. Armadillos can be housebroken

_____

6. Peanuts are one of the ingredients in dynamite

_____

7. Ancient Egyptians slept on pillows made of stone

_____

8. The average person has more than 1,460 dreams a year

_____

9. One in every four Americans has appeared on television

_____

10. It's against the law to have a pet dog in Iceland

_____

Exercise 7

Add commas when needed to the following sentences. Circle the commas in order to make them clearly visible. Some sentences are correct.

1. Prehistory refers to the time in Earth's history before language was written.

2. This period in history is called the Prehistoric Era and it extended from the beginning of time to approximately 1,200 years B.C.E.

3. Prehistory is divided into the Stone Age, the Bronze Age, and the Iron Age.

4. During the Stone Age hominids started using stone tools.

5. Hominids are ancestors of modern day *Homo sapiens*.

6. Since the discovery of the remains of the Neanderthal man in Germany in 1856 scientists have placed hominids in the Stone Age.

7. After the discovery of these hominid remains the term Neanderthal man has been used to represent all prehistoric hominids.

8. During the Paleolithic Period which is the first part of the Stone Age Neanderthal man existed by hunting and gathering.

9. Neanderthal man existed over four million years ago.

10. When the earth underwent global change and began to warm the Paleolithic Age ended.

11. In the Neolithic Period that followed the Paleolithic Period Neanderthal man advanced from hunting and gathering.

12. Farming and cultivating characterized the activities of the Neanderthal man during this period.

13. When man began to progress and to make tools and weapons from metal the Bronze Age began.

14. The Bronze Age lasted until approximately 2500 B.C. when iron was discovered.

15. The term Iron Age is used to refer to the next period in human development.

16. The use of iron significantly changed the development of civilization because iron tools made farming easier.

17. The strength of iron tools made clearing the land and cutting down trees possible.

18. Iron tools which are very durable lasted longer.

19. Most elements have a name and a year associated with their discovery.

20. Gold, silver, and iron have existed since prehistoric times and neither dates nor names are associated with their discovery.

Exercise 8

Add commas to the following sentences. Circle the commas in order to make them clearly visible. Some sentences are correct.

1. The Prehistoric Age ended with the use of iron.

2. The ancient Greek and Roman civilizations existed during the Classical Age that lasted from the end of the Iron Age to about 500 C.E.

3. During the Classical Age humankind developed quickly.

4. The ancient Greeks and Romans made lasting contributions in literature, art, science, philosophy, and medicine.

5. The philosophers Socrates, Plato, and Aristotle and the poet Homer and the dramatist Sophocles are proof that humankind influenced the modern world.

6. The Hippocratic Oath taken by every physician is evidence of the influence that Hippocrates has had on medicine.

7. Following the Classical Age was the Medieval Period.

8. The Medieval Period beginning in 500 C.E. is also referred to as the Middle Ages and as the Dark Ages.

9. The Medieval Period lasted until the end of the 1400s when the Roman Empire collapsed.

10. The Medieval Period was given the name Dark Ages because it was a period overshadowed by the bubonic plague which wiped out one-third of the population of Europe and barbarism.

11. Millions of innocent people who were accused of witchcraft were also executed.

12. The Middle Ages was also the period of the Crusades.

13. The Crusades were Christian military exploits that attempted using religious wars, battles, and campaigns to recover Palestine (The Holy Land) from the Muslims and restore it to the Christians.

14. The Crusades were unsuccessful in securing Israel from the Muslims but the resulting expansionism because of the Crusades strengthened and unified Europe moving it into a period of the celebration of the human spirit.

15. This age of revival of human creativity from 1450 C.E. to 1600 is called the Renaissance which means "rebirth" and the Dark Ages of human history came to an end.

16. Ancient Greek and Roman philosophies resurfaced during the Renaissance.

17. During this age of rediscovery humankind studied the cultures and the beliefs of the ancient Greeks and Romans.

18. Out of the Renaissance emerged Michelangelo, Shakespeare, Leonardo da Vinci, and Machiavelli.

19. Some of the world's greatest minds came out of this period.

20. Because of the great minds that surfaced during the Renaissance humankind moved into the period called The Enlightenment.

Exercise 9

Underline the phrases in the following sentences.

1. The Enlightenment, lasting through the 1700s, is also called The Age of Reason.

2. This period became known as the Age of Reason because the philosophers of this era emphasized the use of reason to make decisions, solve problems, and discover the truth.

3. Contributions in science, education, law, and politics were made during the Age of Reason.

4. Superstition, ignorance, and social and political injustice were examined, discredited, and criticized by the great scholars.

5. The mysteries of the universe were mathematically examined and defined.

6. The essence of humankind and the laws of nature became the focus of this period.

7. The Romantic Movement strengthened the interest in humankind.

8. The Romantic Movement allowed humans the time to think about their interrelationships and personal growth.

9. Humankind's need to look inward and to understand the nature of humankind's relationships was not a primary concern for very long.

10. The Industrial Revolution, which began in Great Britain in the 1700s, spread to the United States.

CAPITALIZATION

CAPITALIZATION

Capitalize the first word of a sentence, the pronoun **I**, proper nouns, and the first word of a direct quotation.

Months of the year:

January	July
February	August
March	September
April	October
May	November
June	December

Days of the week:

Monday

Tuesday

Wednesday

Thursday

Friday

Saturday

Sunday

Streets, cities, states, counties, countries, continents:

Tampa

Florida

Hillsborough County

United States

North America

Dale Mabry Highway

Seventh Avenue

All words that represent cultures and languages are **always capitalized** regardless how the word is used.

Spanish bean soup

English muffin

German shepherd

Greek salad

American dream

Cultures, languages:

English	European
French	American
Spanish	African
Greek	Cuban
Italian	Mexican
Indian	Asian

Bodies of water:

Atlantic Ocean

Pacific Ocean

Indian Ocean

Gulf of Mexico

Hillsborough River

Tampa Bay

Lettuce Lake

Parks, attractions:

Lowry Park

Yellowstone National Park

Disney World

Busch Gardens

Sea World

Strawberry Festival
Museum of Science and Industry

Schools:
Hillsborough Community College
Hillsborough High School
University of South Florida
Edison Elementary School

Titles:
Mrs. Jones
Mr. Jones
Dr. Jones
Uncle Jones
Aunt Jones
Governor Jones
President Jones
Minister Jones

President, when referring to the President of the United States, is always capitalized with or without a name. Titles used in the place of names are always capitalized. Sit *Father* next to *Grandpa* at the dinner table. An easy way to determine if the title replaces a name is to substitute a name for the title.

Sit *Tom* next to *Jim* at the dinner table.

Titles of publications, movies, telecasts, media:
Frankenstein
10 Connects
Family Matters
The Oprah Magazine
"The Story of an Hour"

Italicize the titles of whole productions like movies, magazines, newspapers, television shows, and CDs. Use quotation marks around parts of the whole like short stories, poems, chapters, scenes, articles, and songs.

Historical periods, wars:
World War I
Renaissance
Civil War
Great Depression
Victorian Era

Religions and religious sects:
Christian
Catholicism
Baptist
Catholic
Voodoo

Holidays:
Christmas
Halloween
Kwanzaa
Thanksgiving
Columbus Day
Mother's Day
Martin Luther King, Jr. Day

The words *north, south, east,* and *west* are capitalized when they represent regions and are not capitalized when they represent compass directions.

Birds fly *south* in the winter.	**South** is used as a direction.
Birds fly to the *South* in the winter.	**South** is used as a region.

Do not capitalize the seasons (*summer, winter, spring, fall*) unless the term is part of a title.

Do not capitalize subjects unless the subject title represents a culture, language, or religion: *English, math, biology, chemistry, Spanish, history.*

Capitalize the title of course names: *Introduction to Math 101, Organic Chemistry 435, English Composition 101.*

Exercise 1

Circle each letter that needs to be capitalized.

The Presidents

1. the eight presidents who never attended college are washington, jackson, van buren, taylor, fillmore, lincoln, a. johnson, and cleveland.

2. the following presidents attended harvard: j. adams, j. q. adams, t. roosevelt, f. roosevelt, rutherford b. hayes, j. f. kennedy, and george w. bush.

3. eighteen presidents who never served in congress are washington, j. adams, jefferson, taylor, grant, arthur, cleveland, t. roosevelt, taft, wilson, coolidge, hoover, f. roosevelt, eisenhower, carter, reagan, clinton, and g. w. bush.

4. the most common religious affiliation among presidents has been episcopalian, followed by presbyterian.

5. the ancestry of all 44 presidents is limited to the following heritages, or some combination thereof: dutch, english, irish, scottish, welsh, swiss, german , and african.

6. the oldest president inaugurated was Reagan.

7. the tallest president was lincoln at 6'4".

8. the fourteen presidents who served as vice presidents are j. adams, jefferson, van buren, tyler, fillmore, a. johnson, arthur, t. roosevelt, coolidge, truman, nixon, l. johnson, ford, and george h. w. bush.

9. for two years the nation was led by a president and a vice president who were not elected by the people. after vice president spiro t. agnew resigned in 1973, president nixon appointed gerald ford as vice

president. nixon resigned the following year, which left ford as president, and ford's appointed as vice president, nelson rockefeller, second in line.

10. the term "first lady" was used first in 1849 when president zachary taylor called dolley madison "first lady" at her state funeral. it gained popularity in 1877 when used in reference to lucy ware webb hayes. most first ladies, including jackie kennedy, are said to have hated the label.

11. james buchanan was the only president never to marry.

12. presidents lincoln, garfield, mckinley, and kennedy were assassinated in office.

13. assassination attempts were made on the lives of jackson, t. roosevelt, f. roosevelt, truman, nixon, ford, carter, reagan, george h. w. bush, clinton, and g. w. bush.

14. eight presidents died in office: harrison, taylor, lincoln, garfield, mckinley, harding, f. roosevelt, and kennedy.

15. presidents adams, jefferson, and monroe all died on the 4th of july.

16. kennedy and taft are the only presidents buried in arlington national cemetery.

17. lincoln, jefferson, f. roosevelt, washington, kennedy, and eisenhower are portrayed on u.s. coins.

18. adams and jefferson were the only presidents to sign the declaration of independence, and they both died on its 50th anniversary, july 4, 1826.

19. barack obama worked his way through college, aided also by student loans and scholarships.

20. obama was elected president of the united states on november 4, 2008.

Exercise 2

Underline the letters that should be capitalized.

1. All major league baseball umpires must wear black underwear while on the job in case their pants split.

2. San francisco cable cars are the only national monuments that move.

3. Abraham lincoln's dog, fido, was assassinated too.

4. The california department of motor vehicles has issued six driver's licenses to six different people named jesus christ.

5. There are more than 87,000 americans on waiting lists for organ transplants.

6. The average child recognizes more than 200 company logos by the time he/she enters first grade.

7. Amusement park attendance goes up after a fatal accident because many people want to ride the same ride that killed someone.

8. For every ton of fish that is caught in all the oceans on our planet, there are three tons of garbage dumped into the oceans.

9. Japanese and chinese people die on the fourth of the month more often than any other dates because of the superstition associated with the number four as unlucky.

10. There are an average of 18,000,000 items for sale at any time on ebay.

11. Albert einstein never knew how to drive a car.

12. The cruise liner queen elizabeth 2 moves only six inches for each gallon of diesel fuel that it burns.

13. Most elvis impersonators are of asian descent.

14. There are only three types of snakes on the island of tasmania, and all three are deadly poisonous.

15. The united states has 5% of the world's population, but 25% of the world's prison population.

16. One out of five people in the world lives on less than $1 per day.

17. Thirty-five billion e-mails are sent each day throughout the world.

18. There are 150,000,000 cell phones in use in the united states, more than one per every two human beings in the country.

19. For every person on earth, there are an estimated 200 million insects.

20. If you disassembled the great pyramid of cheops, you would get enough stones to encircle the earth with a brick wall twenty inches high.

Exercise 3

Circle the word that should be capitalized in the following sentences.

1. Uncle jim looked for the baptist church that was located on main street.

2. The atlantic ocean borders east florida.

3. Hillsborough community college is on 15th street.

4. The hillsborough river runs through tampa.

5. I love to visit the museum in ybor city.

6. Shakespeare performed his plays at the globe theater in London.

7. The class will take a trip to a national park this summer.

8. The manatees are protected in florida.

9. I have a german shepherd.

10. Tom and my grandmother will be here saturday.

11. Janet called the priest to bless her new home.

12. The mayor will speak at graduation.

13. He did not have breakfast because he is out of cheerios.

14. To get to my house, turn left at the light and head west.

15. My family spent the weekend at the gulf.

16. Henry and i ran to walmart to get the supplies.

17. We went to visit the university.

18. The game was held at the stadium.

19. Harriet will take biology, math, and english in the fall.

20. I studied the dark ages in history class.

Exercise 4

Circle the words that should be capitalized in the following sentences.

1. My favorite grocery store is publix.

2. Sarah and aunt jane will lead the discussion.

3. On monday, the instructor will give the class a test on the brain.

4. I will take my bible and my spanish book with me this weekend.

5. The students will watch the movie freedom writers.

6. Are you going to subway for lunch?

7. In january, my classes begin.

8. I can't wait until summer gets here.

9. Halloween and valentine's day are my favorite holidays.

10. The field trip to alaska and canada will be fun.

11. He was raised catholic but his father is jewish.

12. Steven and uncle leonard will be going to europe this winter.

13. The funland is a drive-in theater in tampa.

14. My brother leroy will be playing in the finals.

15. Joan gave me a saint christopher medal for my birthday.

16. The university of south florida is located on fletcher ave.

17. Walking along gandy bridge is dangerous.

18. The textbook has a chapter on astronomy.

19. I enjoy studying the sun, the moon, and the stars.

20. We live next to the zoo.

OTHER MECHANICS AND USAGE

PARALLELISM

Parallelism means using the same structure to demonstrate two or more ideas.

Examples of Parallel Constructions

Students must bring *pencils, paper, notes, and pens* to the workshop.

To find the treasure, each team must *follow* directions, *ask* questions, *and think* logically.

Some television cartoons encourage children *to act* aggressively, *to imitate* poor role models, and *to develop* poor study skills.

My daily exercise routine includes *stretching, walking, and jogging.*

Examples of Nonparallel Constructions

Students must bring *pencils that are sharpened, lined paper, class notes, and pens with either blue or black ink* to the workshop.

To find the treasure, each team must *follow* directions, *be sure to ask* questions, and *think* logically as a group.

Some television cartoons encourage children *to act* aggressively, *poor role models*, and *developing* poor study skills is another negative effect from television cartoons.

My daily exercise routine includes *stretching, walking, and I sometimes like to jog.*

Exercise 1

Underline the parallel structures in each of the sentences below.

1. The meanings of common dream symbols and images can be found in dream interpretation books.

2. A dream of falling into a bottomless pit may either mean that the dreamer's current concern is irresolvable or mean that the concern is unimportant.

3. Angels who appear in dreams may mean the dreamer will receive an important message or warning.

4. Dreaming of animals may be significant because animals can represent the dreamer and can offer guidance through instinctive problem-solving techniques.

5. The dreamer should research the animal that appears in the dream and should study the animal's behavior.

6. Balloons attached to strings may either represent a forthcoming celebration or represent an emotional release.

7. Dreaming of a monster under the bed may mean that a secret will be revealed while dreaming of a monster in the closet may mean that a secret will be kept.

8. Giving birth or hearing about a birth in a dream can foreshadow a new experience.

9. A person who feels stripped of energy, dignity, identity, or importance may dream of bones.

10. Dreaming of bridges may mean that a divided or disconnected situation will be resolved.

11. To dream of a burial or a funeral may symbolize the end of an unwanted situation or habit.

12. Dreaming of riding public transportation may mean the need to accept a general consensus and the need to conform.

13. If the dreamer sees shoes, the message can represent the need to flee or to escape a current situation.

14. The dreamer feels in control if he or she dreams of driving a car, but the dreamer needs to slow down if he or she dreams of speeding.

15. The dreamer needs to let go of the past if he or she is in a cemetery or in front of a gravestone.

16. Being chased in a dream may indicate that the dreamer is running away from responsibility, but pursuing in a dream may indicate that the dreamer is running toward responsibility.

17. Buying new clothes means accepting new ideas.

18. Giving away clothes may foreshadow that the dreamer will give advice or will give help to someone in need.

19. Detours in a dream show the dreamer that alternative viewpoints should be considered or that new directions should be taken.

20. Alligators that appear in dreams may be a warning to avoid gossip that can be destructive.

Exercise 2

Correct the nonparallel sentences.

1. Dreaming of darkness in a dream signifies fear, secrets, or it could mean confusion and chaos in the dreamer's life.

   _____

   _____

2. If the dreamer sees his or her own death, the dreamer can expect a change or eliminating a habit could be the meaning.

   _____

   _____

3. Driving through a detour, or if the driver runs over a detour means that the driver is ignoring the signs to take another approach concerning a current situation.

   _____

   _____

4. To dream of drowning or a dream of sinking is a sign that the dreamer is overwhelmed.

   _____

   _____

5. Open windows in a dream symbolize the need to escape, but seeing closed windows means the dreamer feels like barriers are affecting a current situation.

   _____

   _____

6. Volcanic eruptions in a dream are a warning that the dreamer is about to have problems to deal with.

   _____

   _____

7. Tornadoes in a dream are a warning that the dreamer will be emotionally shattered or warn the dreamer that he or she will be moving to a new location.

_____

_____

8. The dreamer who falls or trips should think before making a decision and asking for assistance will also be helpful.

_____

_____

9. Confronting monsters and to confront aliens is a positive sign that the dreamer will successfully face an adversary or problem.

_____

_____

10. The dreamer who is fighting is being warned that to deal with the adversary or situation having confidence is needed.

_____

_____

Exercise 3

Identify whether the following sentences are parallel or nonparallel by writing a **P** or an **NP** in the blank next to each sentence.

1. _____ To see an approaching fog or being surrounded by a fog warns the dreamer that it is unwise to face a situation without plan of action.

2. _____ Some cultures believe that to dream of frogs signals an epiphany is about to occur within the dreamer.

3. _____ If the dreamer feels compelled to control and to manipulate, gang involvement may be the subject of the dream.

4. _____ To see a group from a distance may mean that the dreamer feels impacted by the opinion of a particular group also including family members.

5. _____ Dreaming of cutting hair may show the dreamer that wisdom must be used to make a critical decision.

6. _____ Falling into a hole means the dreamer will be caught off guard.

7. _____ Negative dreams about the home signal that feeling safe is a problem the dreamer is facing.

8. _____ Beware the kiss of death in a dream because it means the dreamer will be betrayed.

9. _____ Ladders in a dream warn that hard work is required to accomplish a goal.

10. _____ To dream of finding money represents good luck, but a lost opportunity is the meaning when dreaming of lost money.

DANGLING AND MISPLACED MODIFIERS

Modifiers add description and clarification to other words or groups of words. When the word is missing that the modifier is describing, the problem is called a dangling modifier. When the modifier is separated from the word it is describing, the problem is called a misplaced modifier. Dangling modifiers and misplaced modifiers can distort the intended meaning of the sentence.

Dangling Modifiers

When the alarm clock sounded, the coffee was made.
Corrected: I made coffee when the alarm clock sounded.

Wanting to have some fun, the fair was a planned activity.
Corrected: I attended the fair because I wanted to have some fun.

Missing the school bus, the class was attended late.
Corrected: I attended class late because I missed the school bus.

Having finished the housework, the car was washed.
Corrected: After I finished the housework, I washed the car.

To pass the exam, class notes have to be studied.
Corrected: In order to pass the exam, I have to study my class notes.

Misplaced Modifiers

The dog was taken to the park on the leash.
Corrected: On the leash, the dog was taken to the park.

The mail was delivered to the correct address that was lost.
Corrected: The mail that was lost was taken to the correct address.

Cracked, the lady returned the vase to the store.
Corrected: The lady returned the cracked vase to the store.

The students turned in late essays who missed class.
Corrected: The students who missed class turned in late essays.

With three legs, the man discarded the chair.
Corrected: The man discarded the chair with three legs.

Exercise 4

Draw an arrow from the incorrectly placed modifier to where it should be placed in the sentence.

1. Sunning next to the screen, the man saw the snake.

2. The house burned down in the news.

3. Broken beyond repair, the man replaced his watch.

4. The students studied for the test in groups.

5. The dog bothered the neighbors who barked all night.

6. Some species of birds are recorded by scientists migrating 10,000 miles.

7. Broken windows and dented doors were repaired by the carpenter in the house.

8. Up the tree, the dog chased the squirrel.

9. The meteor was recorded by the observer shooting across the sky.

10. Diving for fish, the lady watched the pelican.

Exercise 5

Rewrite the following sentences, correcting the misplaced modifier.

1. While dressing, the phone rang.

_____

_____

2. The alarm sounded while studying.

_____

_____

3. After taking the picture, the negative was developed.

_____

_____

4. Class was attended late taking the bus.

_____

_____

5. The car stalled taking the driving test.

_____

_____

NUMBERS
Figures or Words

Use words for numbers below 10 and figures for numbers above nine.

> When a number begins a sentence, use words.
> The first *12* callers will receive free park passes.
> The first *five* callers will receive free park passes.
> *Twelve* callers will receive free park passes.

Dates

Use figures after the month and words before the month.

> April 10
> 10th of April   (is also acceptable)
> tenth of April

Addresses

Use figures for house numbers and street numbers. Ordinals can also be used to avoid confusion. Usually, numbers one through nine are spelled out.

> 22nd Street
> First Street
> 1st Street (the ordinal use is also acceptable)
> Hwy 41
> 4321 Dale Mabry Hwy
> Seventh Avenue

When two numbers, representing two different things, are side by side, use figures for one and words for the other to avoid confusion.

> ***Page 19, two exercises must be completed***
> ***222 Seventh Avenue***

Money

Use figures to express money amounts. Use the $ symbol for dollars and the word **cents** for amounts under a dollar.

> $85   (do not use zeros to represent no change)
> $85.25
> 25 cents   (do not use a decimal .25 cents)

Exercise 6

Identify the correct usage of numbers in the following sentences.

Write **F** above numbers that should be figures, **W** above numbers that should be words, and **C** above correctly used numbers.

1. 22 people witnessed the strange object in the sky.

2. Students who scored ninety or higher on the midterm could exempt the final exam.

3. The board was two feet long and 14 feet wide.

4. I paid for one dozen bagels, but I only had 7 in the bag.

5. John will be twenty-one next month.

PUNCTUATION

Colons [:]

Use a colon to introduce a list, directions, definitions, explanations, direct quotations, after a salutation, and to indicate time.

> *Four members were inducted into the club: Jane, Tamika, Jose, and Robert.*

> *Follow these directions to the park: Head east on Hillsborough Avenue, turn left on 56th Street, turn right on Fletcher Avenue, turn left at the Lettuce Lake Park entrance.*

> *Here is what I am going to do: study, study, study.*

> *The applicant must have the qualifications to run the office: filing, typing, computer experience, personal communication skills.*

> *Robert Jones: "The widest part of the river is its weakest point."*

> *Dear Mr. Jones:*

> *5:18 p.m.*

Dashes [—]

Dashes are used to indicate an extenuation of thought, a parenthetical statement or phrase, and to represent a range of numbers or dates.
> *Last night—or did I already tell you—Jack called.*
> *2003–2008*

Parentheses [( )]

Use parentheses to set off interruptions, biographical dates, and in-text citations.
> *Yesterday (I had a premonition before it happened) I had a flat tire.*
> *(1933–2001)*
> *(Jones, 1997, p. 32)*

Hyphens [-]

Hyphens are half the length of dashes and are used to divide words at the end of a line and to connect two or more words to make a new word, when adding some prefixes to nouns, and between double-digit numbers written as words.

> *con-*
> *vention*

self-explanatory directions

ex-husband

twenty-two

Quotation Marks [" "]

Use quotation marks to set off directly quoted material and titles of short stories, songs, poems, articles, play acts and scenes, and chapters of books.

> *Governor Jones said, "I am not going to run for re-election."*
> *"I am not going," Governor Jones said, "to run for re-election."*
> *I just read Edgar Allan Poe's short story "The Masque of the Red Death."*

Exercise 7

Correct the rest of the sentences using the lines under each sentence.

1. Alice Walker's Every Day Use is my favorite short story.

   _____

   _____

2. Jeff Rand 1967-2005 left his fortune to his cat.

   _____

   _____

3. Campers will need to pack the following items blanket, pillow, plate, fork, cup, and bottled water.

   _____

   _____

4. Tonight's lecture will be called self improvement of the masses.

   _____

   _____

5. Last night I received a call from Henry much to my surprise.

   _____

   _____

APOSTROPHES

There are three uses of apostrophes.

1. Apostrophes are used to show that letters or numbers have been eliminated or omitted.

   Apostrophes are placed in contractions to show where letters have been omitted.

Examples

cannot   can't

- The apostrophe is placed to show where the "n" and the "o" have been omitted.

Common Contractions

It is = it's
Should not = shouldn't
Would not = wouldn't
Did not = didn't
They are = they're
Could have = could've
We will = we'll
She will = she'll
He will = he'll

Apostrophes are used to form possessives.

- Add an apostrophe and "s" to the singular form of a noun to show ownership. ('s)

  The student's book was left on the desk. (The book was left by one student.)

- Add an "s" and apostrophe to the plural form of a noun to show ownership. (s')

  The teacher returned the students' papers. (All of the students received their papers.)

- Add an apostrophe and "s" to plural nouns that do not end in "s."

  The children's toys were left outside. (The toys belonging to the children were left outside.)

- Add an apostrophe and "s" at the end of a singular compound noun. ('s)

  My sister-in-law's car is in the shop for repairs.

- Add an apostrophe and "s" after the second name if both people own the same item.

  Tom and Jane's house. (Tom and Jane own the house together.)

  Tom's and Jane's houses. (Tom and Jane each own a house.)

Apostrophes are used to illustrate plural letters (or numbers).

I have three I's in my name.

My telephone number has four 0's.

Exercise 8

Use apostrophes to make contractions of the following words.

1._____ we will

2._____ did not

3._____ I am

4._____ was not

5._____ were not

6._____ will not

7._____ we were

8._____ they will

9._____ we are

10._____ is not

11._____ you are

12._____ who is

13._____ you have

14._____ I would

15._____ that is

16._____ where is

17._____ have not

18._____ do not

19._____ does not

20._____ has not

Exercise 9

Add an apostrophe to show possession, and rewrite the word in the blank.

1. _____ The childs toy in on the floor.

2. _____ The mothers luncheon will honor all grandmothers, too.

3. _____ Sandys shoes are on the steps.

4. _____ The womens department is on the second floor.

5. _____ Todays menu is posted.

6. _____ Saturdays class is cancelled.

7. _____ The citys mayor will be interviewed.

8. _____ The cities mayors will be interviewed

9. _____ The childrens summer reading list is published.

10. _____ The mans hat is on the table.

CHAPTER 10

WRITING PATTERNS

A paragraph is a developed thought. We automatically develop our thoughts when we talk to others. We add details and examples to help the listener create a visual of what we are talking about and what we are explaining because we want the listener to share our experiences. We want the same interaction from our readers. We want our readers to share our experiences, too, so we add description and examples to our writings. Paragraphs are used to help the writer deliver a thought to the reader. Like essays, paragraphs structure and organize our thoughts.

   A basic paragraph has 8 to 12 sentences.

   • The first sentence is the topic, or the main idea, of the paragraph.

   Note: Single paragraph writing is often required for posting discussion board responses in online classes.

Example

Tampa is an interesting city to visit.

   • The body of the paragraph tells why Tampa is an interesting city to visit.

The body of the paragraph is composed of descriptions and explanations.

Generally, three reasons or details are included in the body of the paragraph to support the main idea. Sometimes these three reasons or details are called prongs.

> **First,** Tampa is the home of the NFL Tampa Bay Buccaneers and the Raymond James Stadium where the Buccaneers play their home games. Buccaneer souvenirs can be bought throughout the city. **Second,** Tampa has a beautiful performing arts center that features a variety of plays, musicals, and concerts that appeal to all ages. The Performing Arts Center is located in downtown Tampa, overlooking the beautiful Hillsborough River that runs throughout the city. **Third,** Tampa has the perfect weather year round with an average temperature of 83°. Outdoor activities such as hiking, camping, picnicking, swimming, boating, and cycling are always an option. It is easy to be a spectator or a participant in outdoor sports any time of the year. In addition, outdoor concerts are always available to those who want to enjoy cultural events under the stars.

- Notice that transitions are used to connect the sentences. The transitions, "first," "second," and "third" are used to establish coherence within the paragraph.
- The final sentence is the conclusion of the paragraph and restates the main idea.

Tampa has the amenities to satisfy the new and the experienced traveler and offers the perfect vacation experience.

The developed paragraph allows the writer to create an image in the mind of the reader.

Example

Tampa, Florida is an interesting city to visit. First, Tampa is the home of the NFL Tampa Bay Buccaneers and the Raymond James Stadium where the Buccaneers play their home games. Buccaneer souvenirs can be bought throughout the city. Second, Tampa has a beautiful performing arts center that features a variety of plays, musicals, and concerts that appeal to all ages. The Performing Arts Center is located in downtown Tampa, overlooking the beautiful Hillsborough River that runs throughout the city. Third, Tampa has the perfect weather year round with an average temperature of 83°F. Outdoor activities such as hiking, camping, picnicking, swimming, boating, and cycling are always an option. It is easy to be a spectator or a participant in outdoor sports any time of the year. In addition, outdoor concerts are always available to those who want to enjoy cultural events under the stars. Tampa has the amenities to satisfy the new and the experienced traveler and offers the perfect vacation experience.

TYPES AND PURPOSES OF PARAGRAPHS AND ESSAYS

Paragraph and essay writing can be constructed according to the intended purpose.

Narrative

The narrative approach is intended to inform or to tell a story. Most students begin the writing process by telling stories about themselves.

The following transitions are often used to relate the events in the story:

for instance, for example, although, because, however, in addition, since, nevertheless, then, yet, but, while

Descriptive

The descriptive approach is intended to create a picture in words that appeals to the reader's senses. By describing specific details using the senses of sight, sound, smell, touch, and taste, the writer allows the reader to share in the experience.

The following transitions are often used to connect the specific details:

for example, furthermore, for instance, in contrast, as a result, because

Process

The process approach is intended to show the reader how to do something or to explain how something is done.
The following words are often used to connect the steps in the process:

first, second, third, finally, during, afterwards, before, last, then

Illustration

The illustration approach is like a narrative essay with many examples and is comprised of mostly examples. It is the type of essay that most students use for essay exams because the student is demonstrating his or her knowledge of the exam subject.
The same transitions are used to connect examples:

for instance, for example, although, because, however, in addition, since, nevertheless, then, yet, but, while

Compare and Contrast

The compare and contrast approach is used to show similarities and differences in related topics, ideas, people, or things.
The following words are often used to show similarities and differences:

like, but, similar to, unlike, similarly, likewise, while, compared to, in contrast, contrasted with, on the contrary, also, however, although, yet, even though, conversely, regardless

Persuasive

The persuasive approach is intended to convince the reader to accept a particular point of view or to undertake a certain action.
The following words are often used to convince or persuade:

although, indeed, in fact, of course, accordingly, consequently, hence, so, therefore, thus, as a result

Definition

The definition approach is intended to define by using examples and illustrations to clearly explain, classify, characterize, and label what a term means.
The following words can be used as definition essay transitions:

indeed, in fact, surely, furthermore, moreover, in addition, for example

Cause-and-Effect

The cause-and-effect approach is intended to show the causes and the consequences of events.
The following transitions can be used to demonstrate cause and effect:

due to, because, but, therefore, as a result, consequently, so, since

Classification

The classification approach sorts and organizes things, people, and ideas into categories.
The following transitions are used to classify:

first, second, third, finally, the first group, the second group, another, similarly

A list of writing topics

a learning experience
a bad decision
a good decision
someone you trust
someone you do not trust
your favorite hobbyyour favorite sport
why are sports important
your favorite holiday
your favorite day of the week
your favorite relative
effective study skills
the ideal job
the perfect pet
your favorite piece of furniture
why you love your car
your favorite vacation
recommend a good movie
warn against a bad movie
the difference between two people in your life
similarities of two foods that you like

Exercise 1

Write a three-prong statement for each of the following.

1. Why you would recommend a movie

_____

_____

2. Why you think sports are important

_____

_____

3. A decision that you are glad that you made

_____

_____

4. What you like about your favorite holiday

_____

_____

5. What is the ideal job

_____

_____

Exercise 2

Choose one of your topics above and develop an eight to twelve sentence paragraph, using your own paper.

What type of format are you going to use? _____

Exercise 3

Write a good topic for each of the following types of writing approaches.

1. Narrative

_____

2. Descriptive

_____

3. Process

_____

4. Illustration

_____

5. Compare/contrast

_____

THE THESIS, TOPIC SENTENCES, AND BASIC STRUCTURE

Writing paragraphs and writing essays require the same organizational skills. Paragraphs and essays have a specific purpose:

Both contain a thesis statement, supporting details, and a conclusion. Paragraphs usually represent the planned addition of more ideas to an essay; however, paragraphs can exist alone and can be self contained, having an introduction, body, and conclusion.

Whether writing a paragraph or writing an essay, **the topic has to be narrowed** so that it can be discussed in the given space. The easiest way to narrow a topic is to divide the topic into three sections or characteristics.

<u>Topics</u>

Pets
Educational programs
Fashion
Music

<u>Narrowed</u>
<u>Topics</u>

Dogs as companions
<u>Thesis statement with three ideas</u>
Dogs make wonderful companions for the elderly, for children, and for the handicapped.

The benefits of *Sesame Street*
<u>Thesis statement with three ideas</u>
Sesame Street encourages children to develop reading skills, to imitate good role models, and to learn problem-solving skills.

Hats, jewelry, and dresses
<u>Thesis statement with three ideas</u>
The Elizabethan Era fashion was characterized by flamboyant hats, heavy jewelry, and colorful dresses.

Jazz beginnings
<u>Thesis statement with three ideas</u>
The history of jazz includes social constraints, political issues, and personal relationships.

The paragraph	The five-paragraph essay	
Thesis or topic sentence	**Topic sentence**	
Supporting details	**Thesis statement**	paragraph 1
Conclusion	Background information	introduction
	Topic sentence	
	Point 1	paragraph 2
	Supporting details	body
	Topic sentence	
	Point 2	paragraph 3
	Supporting details	body
	Topic sentence	
	Point 3	paragraph 4
	Supporting details	body
	Conclusion	
	Restate points 1-3	paragraph 5
	Conclusion	

Exercise 4

Write a thesis statement for each of the following narrowed topics.

1. A person who influenced your life

2. Your favorite vacation

3. Your favorite movie

4. The qualities of a best friend

5. The perfect job

Exercise 5

Revise the following vague thesis statements.

1. That was the worst movie I have ever seen.

2. I will never forget my first car.

3. He/she did not have the qualities I was looking for in a spouse.

4. My senior trip to Disney World was a blast.

5. Thanksgiving is my favorite holiday.

Generating ideas for your essay paragraphs come from the three elements or characteristics listed in the thesis statement.

> *I love to take cruise vacations because of all the amenities.*
> *I love to take cruise vacations because of the food, the entertainment, and the port of call shopping.*

Ideas for each of the three parts can be created by brainstorming.

<u>Under buffets</u>
Dessert bars
24-hour ice cream fountain
Salad bars
Early breakfast
Late breakfast
All-day lunch available
All-you-can-eat servings
Casual dinner or formal dinner
24-hour pizza
Ice sculptures

<u>Under entertainment</u>
Movies
Bingo
Dances
Children's activities
Comedy shows
Deck games
Lounges
Casino
Pool party

<u>Under port of call tours</u>
Shopping
Bicycle tours
City tours
History
Culture
Beach
Snorkling
Museums
Straw market

These ideas will become supporting details and examples in the paragraphs headed by each of the parts.

Outlines help to organize the ideas into paragraphs.

Title _____

I.   Introduction
    A. _____ Attention grabber
    B. _____ Three-prong thesis statement
    C. _____ Background information
II. Body
    A. _____ Topic sentence
        1. _____ Support
        2. _____ Support
        3. _____ Support
    B. _____ Topic sentence
        1. _____ Support
        2. _____ Support
        3. _____ Support
    C. _____ Topic sentence
        1. _____ Support
        2. _____ Support
        3. _____ Support
III. Conclusion
    A. _____ Restate thesis
    B. _____ Summary

A list of essay topic ideas for practice:

Favorite vacation	Unhealthy lifestyle
Favorite movie	Important dates
Worst movie	Important decision
Worst vacation	College life
Family celebrations	High school life
Family customs	Entertainment
Perfect spouse	Hobbies
Perfect wedding	Children
Healthy lifestyle	Laws

Regardless of the purpose, most essays have a number of common writing steps.

1. Once you have been given the purpose of the assignment such as to describe, or define, or argue a topic, decide what subject you are going to develop.

   - Make sure that your topic is not too broad.
   "Communication has changed over the years" is too broad and cannot fully be discussed in a short essay or research paper. A more narrowed topic is "The way people send mail has changed since the creation of e-mail."

   Adapting the argumentative/persuasive topic:

   - Do not use opinion statements like "I think" or "I believe" because opinion statements are not arguable. Everyone has a right to have an opinion. Use third person.

     Argument: Television cartoons encourage children to act aggressively.

     Opinion: I think television cartoons encourage children to act aggressively.

   - Choose a topic that your audience would see as a concern.

   - Choose a topic that you find emotionally interesting.

2. Create an outline as a guide to structure the layout of your ideas.

   - A standard five-paragraph format essay has been provided for you in this chapter.

3. Write a topic sentence and a thesis statement to begin your essay.

   - The topic sentence is your umbrella statement that your topic discussion will fall under.   "The way people send mail has changed since the creation of e-mail."

   - Follow your topic sentence with a thesis statement that breaks down the topic into three sections. These three sections will be the three body paragraphs of the essay.

     E-mail has replaced traditional stamped mail because sending e-mail is faster, cheaper, and easier.

4. Gather information like facts, statistics, and background information about your topic.

5. Fill in the format of the outline, including your supporting details.

   - You can use bullets of information or complete sentences in your outline.

6. Write your introduction, beginning with the topic sentence and followed by the thesis statement. Lengthen and strengthen your introduction by adding background information about your topic.

   - The introduction should be your strongest paragraph because it is the foundation of the essay.

   - Do not use announcement statements like "In this essay I am going to discuss."

     Do not use comments like "I think" or "I believe."

   - Unless you are writing a personal narrative, do not use first person "I."

     Do not use second person "You."

     Use third person "he, she, they, we, people."

   - Do not ask the reader questions.

7. Write the conclusion, beginning with the topic sentence. Restate the main points of the essay.

   • Do not add any ideas that were not discussed in the essay.

   • Leave the reader with something to think about. Do not add questions to your conclusion.

8. Write the body of the essay, using the outline as a guide.

9. Review and revise your essay, correcting any errors prior to final submission.

APA Citations

In-text citations are used to reference the material of others within the written text of your document. Use the author's last name and the year of publication as the source.

Note: Use the MLA link below for MLA citation examples.

Short Quotations

"Effective writing stimulates reflection and promotes change" (Ronson, 2010, p. v).

According to Ronson (2010),

"Effective writing stimulates reflection and promotes change" (p. v). The full citation must appear on the reference page at the end of the document.

Long Quotations

Long quotations of four or more lines are typed in a block format. Quotation marks are not used because the format itself indicates that the material is quoted. According to Dr. Ronson (2010),

> Anyone can learn to write. There are writing rules and grammar mechanics that guide and direct the learning process. Effective writing is a powerful instrument to have at your command. Effective writing can improve your confidence and, ultimately, your quality of life. (p. v)

Paraphrasing

Restating someone's ideas without using the author's exact words is called paraphrasing and is cited by using the author's last name and year of publication.

Effective writing is a skill that anyone can learn (Ronson, 2010).

Cite summaries the same way, using the author's last name and year of publication.

The Mechanics of Citations

Capitalize titles of sources.

Capitalize proper nouns.

Italicize titles of books, movies, journals, newspapers, and magazines that are typed.

Underline these titles if they are handwritten.

Use quotation marks around titles that represent parts, pieces, or sections of whole works such as chapters, short stories, acts, scenes, and articles.

Only capitalize the first word of the title in a citation on the reference page.

Avoiding Plagiarism

Plagiarism is the act of using another's works, material, or property without giving credit to the author or to the owner or source of the material. Plagiarism is illegal. College students who are found guilty of plagiarism can be dismissed from school. It is easy to avoid plagiarism by using in-text citations and references. Properly citing borrowed work only takes a few seconds.

The following sites demonstrates how to use citations properly.

http://www.umuc.edu/library/libhow/apa_examples.cfm

http://owl.english.purdue.edu/owl/resource/560/01/

The following sites will help you format your citations:

www.easybib.com/

http://www.calvin.edu/library/knightcite/

www.citationmachine.net/

www.noodletools.com/

Read more about plagiarism from the following sites:

http://www.plagiarism.org/

http://owl.english.purdue.edu/owl/resource/589/01/

http://www.writing.northwestern.edu/avoiding_plagiarism.html

http://www.indiana.edu/~wts/pamphlets/plagiarism.shtml

The following site demonstrates how to use MLA and APA citations properly.

http://owl.english.purdue.edu/owl/resource/747/01/

Keeping a Portfolio

A portfolio is a compilation of a student's work that helps to reflect academic growth in a specific area.

A good way to measure whether you have progressed during a school term or if you have improved your skills in a certain subject is by keeping a portfolio. For instance, if you keep all of your returned writing assignments in a specific folder, you can look at your essays at the end of the term for areas of progress or improvement since the first assignment at the beginning of the term. You can keep a portfolio for your assignments in any of your classes. Artists and photographers keep portfolios of their work, so they can easily see areas that need improvement and areas that show improvement in the development of their artistic skills. You can use your portfolio to set goals, and you can record your accomplishments as you recognize success. You will be surprised at how much your writing will improve with practice. Your portfolio will also be a mirror of your attitudes, thoughts, and dreams.

STORIES
TO
INSPIRE

Annika

An old man sat quietly on the bench at the end of the pier and looked out into the ocean. It was a moonless night and the black horizon appeared ominous and unreachable. He seemed to be preoccupied with his thoughts and hardly gave any notice to the man and his son who fished near him. A large, bronze statue of a lady clutching a lantern separated them. A small obscure inscription under the lantern she held read "Until you return".

The young man read the inscription and questioned his father about its meaning. "Dad," this must be Annika, the lady the pier is named after. Do you know who she is?"

The father and son were visitors of this small town. "I don't know, Son," he answered, "she must be part of the town's local history."

They fished in silence for a while until the old man spoke. "Looks like a storm is approaching," he said. The storm was still out in the distance, but they could see the flashes of lightning across the sky, and they could feel the wind picking up and could see the water splashing against the pilings of the pier. "We've got about an hour before she hits," he added.

"You have probably watched a lot of storms come in from here," the father said to the old man.

"Not on this pier" he remarked, "because it's new, but I sat for hours on the dock that used to be here and watched Annika hold the light. She rarely spoke nor took her eyes off of the water, but I think that she was glad that I was here waiting with her."

"She's the lady in the statue," the son said. "And Annika is the name of the pier," he added.

"Annika never saw the pier; it was built after she disappeared," the old man pronounced. "The pier replaced the dock that stood here until the hurricane dragged it into the sea. Some people think that the sea came for Annika, too. I wasn't here that night, but I kind of think that it might be true." The old man looked out into the sea as if he were searching for her, still.

"Why did she come to the dock every night?" questioned the father.

The old man settled back upon the bench and motioned to the father and his son to set their fishing gear down. They obeyed and sat down on the adjacent bench; then the old man began.

During the 1920's this town was a small fishing village. We probably had 100 families living here and they were fed and cared for from the sea's bounty. Annika's father and her two brothers were fishermen, so it was natural that she marry a fisherman, too. Jacob was his name. She and Jacob grew up together. Their families were neighbors. Annika and Jacob played in the same yard and many times were cared for in the same house. The women helped out each other when the men were out to sea. Annika's mother and Jacob's mother were very close friends and combined their strength when the men were gone.

Annika and Jacob got married in 1926. Annika was just 16 and Jacob was 17. By today's standards, Jacob would still be a boy, but back then he was considered a man and he had to do a man's job. He had been going out on the fishing vessel since he was fourteen. He was used to hard work. Besides, people back then didn't think about alternatives. Sometimes the men would be gone a month or more at a time. They would come home with raw and swollen hands and many times with broken spirits. The sea takes it toll after a while. But like a woman, it sure takes a hold of a man's soul and he always goes back no matter what kind of beaten he has endured. Above all else, though, the sea demands respect and commitment. A slothful hand will eventually pay the price of a watery grave. The sea doesn't forgive, they say; and it never forgets.

Shortly after Jacob and Annika were married, Jacob, along with Annika's father and brothers, set out for an early fall harvest. The winter fronts begin in October and they bring with them some terrible storms. The men were hoping for one more good haul before the storms began.

Annika promised that she would stand on the dock and hold a lantern every night and wait for Jacob's return. She said that he would be able to see the light two days away and that would give him the strength and the will to make it home. Many times the men didn't make it home. Either a storm overcame their vessel or illness or infection from injuries sustained by the nature of the job would overcome them. Either way, the sea determined that too. The sea always kept what she wanted one way or another.

Before he left, Jacob had surprised Annika with a beautiful flowered dress that he had ordered from a catalog especially for her. That was the only way to buy new clothes because we didn't have department stores like we have now. It was the most beautiful dress that she had ever seen. It was white with pink and yellow flowers all over it. It had lace around the bottom and blew about her ankles as she walked. With her long golden hair, she looked like an angel standing on the end of the dock holding a staff of light to help the lost find their way home.

She was wearing this dress when Jacob left. She stood on the end of the dock even after the boat long disappeared from sight. He asked her to wear it again when she came to meet him at the dock upon their return. It was customary for the first person who saw a returning vessel to ring the village bell, alerting everyone to the men's safe return. At the sound of the bell, everyone gathered at the dock to either assist the men with their haul or to greet them home. Jacob knew that Annika would have time to slip into her dress when she heard the bells announcing the return of his vessel.

The men expected to be gone three weeks, but Annika waited every night on the dock as she had promised Jacob, holding the lantern to guide them home when the men were ready. They never returned. Annika's mother was grief stricken at the loss of her husband and her two sons, and she died within the year. Annika grieved in a different way. For sixty years, she waited for Jacob's return. She stood on the dock every night, wearing her flowered dress and holding the lantern. Her dress became faded and raged, but I don't think that she saw it that way. She never remarried and she never developed close relationships with anyone. Perhaps she thought it too painful.

The people of the village thought that she had gone mad, losing her father, her two brothers, and her husband, and many offered to get her medical help. After awhile, she became like a permanent fixture on the dock, and people paid little attention to her. The old man stopped for a moment and looked at the statue as if he were remembering.

"What happened to her?' the young man asked. "You said she disappeared."

"Like I said," he continued, "I wasn't here the last night Annika was seen on the dock. I wish I had been here, but there's nothing that I can do about that now." The old man glanced over at the young man's father. A sadness came over the old man's face that the father wanted to ask him about, but the old man quickly turned his head toward the statue and finished his story as if he were telling it to Annika herself.

Nearly 25 years ago, the sea port opened about two miles from here, and the old dock was no longer used by the fishermen. Annika still came out every night, though, and held up her lantern. The new port and dock had plenty of modern lights that were used to guide the boats in, but I guess Annika had been shining her light so long that it was the only thing that she knew to do, and it was her way of showing Jacob that she had never forgotten him.

The morning after the last night that Annika was seen, her lantern was found still burning and at the end of the dock. No trace of her was ever found. Some believe that she fell into the sea. Some believe that she jumped. I believe that she saw Jacob coming and ran to meet him.

The old man, the father, and his son were quiet for a while. Then the old man added. "That was about eight years ago. Since then, the old dock broke loose during a hurricane and this pier was built in its place. It felt funny coming out here and not seeing Annika and her light." The old man looked up into the face of the statue. "Until you return," he whispered.

The old man, the father, and his son stood on the pier for a long time and looked out upon the sea—even after it started to rain.

Annika

SOMETHING TO THINK ABOUT

Have you ever lost someone that you love? What happened? What helped you to recover from your grief?

Why do you think Annika returned to the pier every night for 60 years? Why couldn't she continue with her life after the disappearance of her husband?

Have you ever had an unforgettable experience with the sea? What happened and how did you change because of your experience?

What do you think happened to Annika?

When the Silence Broke

Michael appeared to be like any other college student. He came to class the first day donning his book bag on his back, plenty of pens and pencils and, of course, his brand new unopened textbook. Michael sat in the first seat adjacent the chalk board. He never took his eyes off of me as I discussed the course requirements and distributed the syllabus. He continued to come to class everyday. He was always on time and always had his book open when class started. He copied everything I wrote on the board. He never asked questions like the other students, and he never laughed at my jokes like the other students. Occasionally, though, he would smile when I looked at him, yet he never said a word.

For some reason, students rarely think of grammar as an interesting subject, so I reminded them regularly what page in the workbook I was covering. I began to notice that Michael was never on the right page. Oftentimes, I looked him straight in the face and told him what page the rest of the class was on and asked him to join us. Occasionally, he would smile at me, yet he never said a word. I didn't know then that he couldn't. Michael was mute and deaf. He could not talk to me nor could he hear me. Under that blonde hair and behind those blue eyes, Michael lived in a silent world.

"Why didn't you tell me?" I asked him. I could not understand signing, so he wrote his explanation. He said that there was a shortage of tutors and note takers for disabled students, and that he was on a waiting list for assistance. He said that he did not want to disrupt the class nor impose upon me to alter my methods to accommodate him. Many times my back is to the students and I am talking to them as I am writing on the board. He told me that he could lip read and he was able to understand my explanations when I was close to him and in front of him. He missed everything when my back was turned. "I would never have turned my back if I had known," I said. "And you missed all of my great jokes," I added, just hoping to see him smile.

For the next two weeks, I made a point of lecturing in front of Michael. I wrote all explanations on the board, including workbook page numbers, so he could follow along more easily. I had a thousand questions to ask him, and I wanted to get to know him and to help him, but I limited my conversations with him because he labored so hard to write everything down that he wanted to say. I realized that most of us take our verbal skills for granted. It only takes a few moments without much of a concerted effort to verbalize an emotion or make a comment. If the only means of communication we had was through our writing skills, there would be little said and a great deal missed. Michael and I had both suffered the loss.

Michael continued in class nearly half way through the term without the assistance of an interpreter. His grades reflected his need for additional help, yet his attitude never changed. He tried to comprehend and he tried to get the notes down and he tried to make sense out of a quiet world. He sat silent in his seat day after day. Even when he removed his books from his back pack, or when he got his tablet and pencils out of his bag, he was silent. It seemed that he made no sound at all no matter what movement he made.

Sometimes when he smiled at me, his eyes would catch mine and then would pierce my soul. I felt exposed, emotionally. I believe he was trying to tell me that it was okay, that he had learned to cope long before he entered my class, and that he accepted his limitations. But it was I who felt limited and handicapped. It was my job as an English professor to teach students how to effectively communicate, to show them the importance of effective communication. Michael helped me to learn that effective communication is far more than mechanics and punctuation. It involves emotions, consideration, interest, and a willingness to share and to give and to accept. I wanted to communicate with him. I wanted to break the silence. I just didn't know how.

Finally, Michael was assigned someone who could. One morning when I walked into the classroom, Michael was waving his arms, and smiling, and signing as fast as his fingers and hands would move. He hadn't noticed that I was standing inside the doorway of the classroom. I stood watching him for a few minutes. I felt like I had witnessed a flower bloom. Michael had never met his interpreter before that morning when she walked into class looking for him. He talked and laughed with her as if they had been friends for years. The only magic that she used was a common language. She talked with him through signing. At last he had someone to be his voice. She became the paper to his pencil.

When Michael noticed that I was standing nearby, he reached out and took my hand, drawing me closer to him and the interpreter. His excitement filled the room and every student who walked in was drawn to his desk. Michael was talking to me so fast that the interpreter laughed and asked him to slow down because she couldn't keep up. He wanted to tell me everything about his life, his family, his dreams, and his silence. He thanked me for trying to help him. And then he thanked me for taking the time to listen.

I stepped back as his classmates gathered around him. He spoke to everyone of them, and the room was filled with the fragrance of spring. After class was dismissed, I sat for a long time in the stillness, thinking about the silence. What a tragedy it would have been if the silence had never been broken. So much would have been lost.

When the Silence Broke

SOMETHING TO THINK ABOUT

Have you ever had someone in your life whom you felt like you could not communicate with? Why did you feel this way? What happened to the relationship as a result?

Do you think that relationships are damaged because of a lack of communication? What happens when people do not talk to one another?

Can you remember when you had a problem but you were afraid to discuss it? Did you feel alone? Did you have to work the situation out by yourself, or did you finally open up and ask for help? What was the outcome? Were you glad that you asked for help?

Why are some people easier to talk to than others? What kind of listener are you?

The Scent of Death

"Those who have been in my presence never forget it. Those who have seen me never live to tell it."

The two sisters had not left his side since he was admitted to the hospital. He had a private room, so they were allowed to stay with him and sleep on the sofa or in the chair that was next to his bed. No one expected him to live more than a couple of hours, but he remained lingering between life and death for nearly two weeks.

"Whom do you think will come and get Dad when he dies?" the older sister asked of the younger. The younger sister knew that she meant who in spirit form would come and assist their father in his heavenward journey.

"Maybe Uncle Brent will come for him, or maybe Grandmother will come for him," the younger sister answered. Uncle Brent was Dad's brother who had died ten years earlier, and Grandmother was Dad's mother who passed away many years ago when the sisters were children.

During the two weeks that the girls remained with their father, they talked about many things, but death was always the prevailing topic. Although their father was comatose, they held his hands and spoke to him of death and dying. "Do not be afraid to die, Dad; someone will come for you and show you the way toward the light. You will not have to make the journey alone," they assured him. Both sisters believed in an afterlife and knew that their father believed as well. The doctor had said that their father could not hear them, and did not know that they were even in the same room, but the girls knew differently. He had always disliked being alone, and they felt that he feared making the journey alone from life, and that is why his heart continued to beat even though his lungs were mechanically manipulated to breath. They knew that he would go when someone came to show him the way.

"Do you think that we will know when someone comes to get him? Do you think that we will see a light or see the curtains blow or see the wings of an angel?" asked the older sister.

"I don't know," the younger sister answered, "but I don't want Dad to leave without saying goodbye."

"I think that he will let us know," lamented the older sister.

And so he did.

Although they had never experienced the moment of death prior to the death of their father, they knew when it was time.

"Do you smell it?" the younger sister inquired.

"It has filled the whole room," the older sister said. "It wasn't here a moment ago."

"It's an odd sickening-sweet smell. I feel like I can hardly breath," the younger sister cried. "Have you ever heard the expression 'the sweet smell of death'?" she sobbed. "I always thought that was an expression, but I guess this is what death smells like."

The smell of death permeated everything in the room, and within a few moments, it was over. No curtains blew and no shadows crossed the floor.

"I'm sorry girls," said the attending nurse who came running at the older sister's call for help. Although the nurse was nearby, Death had already taken him by the time she entered the room. And with him left the smell of death.

"Did you smell it?" the younger sister asked the nurse. Although the smell was no longer in the room, the nurse knew what the younger sister was talking about. "I have many times in the past," she said. "It only lingers for a few seconds, and then it is gone. It is a smell that you will never forget. I'm truly sorry about your father," she said.

That night the sisters went home, believing that they had left death behind. However, the younger sister's dog recognized the ethereal scent that had attached itself to their clothing. After sniffing their clothing, the younger sister's beloved pet cowered in the far corner of the yard and howled the remainder of the night.

"Even the animals will know my scent and will acknowledge my presence."

Not long after the death of their father, the older sister's turn to meet Death came. The two sisters talked of death again many times.

"I'm afraid to die," she told the younger one; "do you think Dad will come to get me?"

"I'm sure he will," she answered, truly believing that he would not allow his eldest daughter to make the journey alone.

The two sisters now lived far apart, one in Florida and one in California. The younger sister had a ten month old baby at home and would not see her sister again. "When Dad comes to get you," she cried, "say goodbye before you leave."

"I'll be the one wearing vanilla," the older sister said. It was the last time they talked of death, and it was the last time the younger one saw her sister alive.

"I didn't mean to wake you," she said to her husband, "but I can't sleep. I'm going downstairs to get some water." She looked at the clock as she got out of bed. "2am," she thought. "Tomorrow I am going to be exhausted." When she started down the stairs, she nearly tripped and she let out a soft scream.

"Are you all right?' her husband asked. "Yes," she answered. "I tripped on your house shoes," she said. "I don't have any house shoes," he laughed.

When she looked down, the shoes were gone. "I must be seeing things," she said, and she continued down the stairs and walked into the dining room. On top of the table was a pair of glasses that she recognized from her childhood. Now she knew the owner of the shoes.

"Hello, Dad," she said. "I've missed you." A shadow crossed the kitchen wall, and the scent of vanilla filled the room. "Thank you, Sis, for coming to say goodbye." "I love you both," she whispered as the tears streamed down her face.

Moments later the phone rang. "Your sister has passed away," her mother said. Her mother had been staying with her sister the last few months, taking care of her and her family.

"I know, Mom," she said. "Sis woke me up to say goodbye."

The Scent of Death

SOMETHING TO THINK ABOUT

Have you ever been in the presence of someone who was dying? Or have you ever had a near death experience? What do you remember that may have affected your understanding of death and dying? Do you believe that people do have guides to assist them with dying? Do you recall ever having an experience with Death? How did you know that Death was nearby?

Have you ever had an experience with a ghost or a spirit? What happened? Were you afraid?

What are your viewpoints concerning an afterlife? Do you believe that death offers another life? What do you base your beliefs on?

Do you believe that people can sense the presence of death? Do you believe that animals can sense death? What do you base your beliefs on?

What do you believe it is that people and animals recognize about death's presence? Have you ever had an experience to base your beliefs on?

A Child's Strength

To the adult, it is a faded memory. To the child that is locked deep inside of the adult, the memory is vivid and the pain is real. The vividness of the experience and the pain the child felt have been lost through distance and time: distance because it is the safest place for the adult and time because it has been thirty years in memory.

The child walked the two miles to school as she did every morning. She never missed a day of school. It was the only place that she felt safe.

Recess was the first activity of each morning. She was not athletic, and she did not like playing sports or getting dirty, but today she would bounce the basketball on the court and even aim occasionally at the basketball hoop. She appeared to be a happy child. She was good natured, friendly, and popular. These characteristics came easily to her. She was comfortable with her classmates. It wasn't other children she feared.

While she and some of the girls in her class were playing and talking, the teacher announced that recess was over. When she looked up, in response to the teacher's voice, a hard dribbled basketball sprang from the court and hit her tiny seven year old hand, bending her pinky finger back until it snapped, clearly breaking the tiny bone.

Already standing alone, she watched as the ball continued its course down the court. She heard the teacher call for her to return the ball and join the other children in line for the ritualistic single-file procession back into the classroom. She didn't notice the pain at first, but soon the finger turned black and her whole hand swelled noticeably larger than its mate. She felt ill from the pain; however, she kept her hand hidden from the teacher. Her teacher would have been kind to her, and she would have been gentle with the broken finger. The child wanted her teacher to know that she was hurt and in pain. But she did not want her teacher to send her home, so she endured the pain. Soon the blackness of the bruising spread past her wrist. The child hid her suffering for nearly four hours before the teacher discovered the child's pain and called her aunt and uncle. They could not come to get the child, so she was told that she would have to walk home. She didn't expect anyone to come. The child learned early in life that no one would ever come, except teachers. Her teachers had always been nice, and they had been there at school everyday. She always felt comforted in knowing that her teacher would always be in her classroom everyday, unless she was really sick, but still she knew that if her teacher stayed home because she was sick, that she would be back as soon as she recovered. The child knew that her teacher would think that it was the right thing to do to send the child home, and that is why the child did not tell the teacher about her broken finger. She never told her about home either.

Home was with her aunt and uncle who acted as guardians in the absence of her parents who worked long hours. It was there that she was neglected and abused and, for fear of losing her life, was silenced never to reveal the treatment she received at their hands, especially her uncle's. This seven year old child found the strength to endure both physical and emotional pain. That was what she knew to do. No one had ever told her that she had an alternative. That knowledge would come much later, too late for the child.

The little girl held her swollen finger close to her chest, and she silently cried as she made her walk home last a long time.

A Child's Strength

SOMETHING TO THINK ABOUT

Can you remember a time when a teacher befriended you? How did the teacher help you?
Should the little girl have told the teacher that her aunt and uncle were abusing her? What could the teacher have done to help?
Have you ever had to endure pain because you were afraid to face the consequences?
Did you ever have to face an unpleasant situation alone? Where did your strength come from? What was the situation?

The Snake

The father carried his three year old son upon his shoulders. Except for the sound of the father's footsteps, the path along the riverbank was peaceful and still and quiet. The man walked ahead of his wife. "The air is crisp and comfortable," said the husband, "so we should keep an eye out for snakes." It was not uncommon to see a cottonmouth hanging from a tree limb near the river or to see one snoozing in a sunny clearing.

The father and his son continued down the path, forgetting all about the snakes. But the mother did not forget about them. With every step, she searched the ground and the trees until her hike became a quest. She soon became fearful for the safety of her husband and child, and she advised them to slow down and not to venture off of the path as they had been doing.

As she expected, she saw the snake. It was moving slowly toward the path, and it would cross directly in front of her husband and child. She had lived in Florida all of her life, and she had seen many kinds of snakes. She knew that this snake was not a venomous one. But because she had been looking for a poisonous snake, that is what she saw in this one.

She stood frozen on the path for what seemed an eternity until she screamed and broke into tears. Perspiration instantly trickled down her face. A collision of her husband and child with the snake was certain, and gripped with fear, she stood and watched. Her husband stopped and searched in the direction of her eyes. They all watched as the seven foot long, 12 inch diameter snake crossed directly in front of them on the path.

The sunlight danced off the ebony* skin of this magnificent, beautiful, and harmless snake. The Indians believe that it is good fortune to have a snake cross your path. This experience should have been a celebration of good fortune, but the excitement was lost because of the mother's fear.

Don't allow unfounded fear to manifest* danger where there is none. Fear is a gripping emotion that transforms the magnificent, the beautiful, and the harmless into a deadly evil monster.

*EBONY: black
*MANIFEST: show, display

The Snake

SOMETHING TO THINK ABOUT

Have you ever been so consumed with finding something ugly or negative about a situation that you missed the joy that the experience could have brought you?

Have you ever misjudged a person?

What changed your impression of that person?

Have you ever been misjudged because someone failed to see the good in you?

How did you feel?

Did you do anything to change that negative perception of you?

The Hug

Jack and Michelle had planned a long awaited weekend escape to the mountains. They were leaving on the ten hour drive to the cabin following Michelle's evening college class that she was teaching. With a full time job and several adjunct college classes, personal time is limited, restricted, and controlled.

It was nearly 10:00 p.m. when Michelle dismissed her class. She quickly gathered her materials and attempted a fast exit. However, the student was faster in her movement to obstruct the teacher than Michelle was in fleeing. "I need to talk to you," the student said. Michelle still had an hour drive home from the campus. She felt frustrated and put upon when the student stopped her. She looked at her watch to signal to the student that she wanted to make the conversation short.

"I wanted to tell you," the student said, "how much I have enjoyed your class. You are a wonderful teacher, she added. And I just wanted to thank you." They talked for what seemed a few minutes; then the student hugged the teacher and left. Michelle felt as if a heavy load had been lifted from her shoulders.

She felt alive and energetic as she got into her car to head for home. When Michelle looked at the clock in the car, she was surprised that 14 minutes had passed. She felt like she had been detained only seconds.

While she was on the interstate heading home, she thought it strange that she was all alone without another car in sight. The interstate looked ominous* and foreboding*. Then literally out of no where, it seemed, an old car appeared directly beside her. A thick white cloud of exhaust fumes engulfed her car as the clunker sped ahead of her. She had to slow down to almost a stop because the cloud was so thick that she could not see the road in front of her. When the cloud disappeared, Michelle could not believe what she had come upon. Within a short distance from her car, there was a ten car accident that completely blocked all lanes of the interstate. Fire and ambulance rescue had not arrived yet, but she could hear them quickly approaching from behind her. As she looked around in disbelief, she noticed that the old clunker that had critically obstructed her view was no where in sight!

There was no way around the accident because even the emergency lanes were blocked, and the accident occurred on a raised section of the interstate where railings flanked the sides from a fifty foot drop to the street below. By habit, she glanced at the clock in her car. Another 14 minutes had passed! The student's kind words that kept Michelle on campus possibly played a part in sparing Michelle from the accident. But who or what was in the old clunker and what happened to it? How could that car have made a cloud of smoke so thick that it completely obstructed her view and then disappeared? What intervened that night to protect Michelle may never be revealed to her. All she knows is that a chain of events to protect her from harm began with a kind word.

Take every opportunity to stop and say a kind word to someone because it may be more valuable than you think. And never take for granted when kindness is shown to you because it could just be a blessing in disguise.

*OMINOUS: menacing, unfavorable
*FOREBODING: forewarning, threatening

The Hug

SOMETHING TO THINK ABOUT

Were you ever frustrated about a delay that later turned out to be in your best interests?

What caused the delay?

What was the outcome?

Some people believe that a closed window means an open door. Did you ever have a window closed and later discovered that a door opened in its place, offering you a better opportunity?

What happened and how long did you have to wait?

Have you ever changed someone's attitude or the course of his or her day or the direction of his or her life by your kind words or encouragement?

What did you say that made an impact on someone's life?

Has someone's kind words ever influenced your mood or a decision you had to make?

What were the circumstances?

The Eggs and the Snake

My husband, George, asked me to check the chickens' nest boxes for eggs several times during the day because the hens were pecking holes into their eggs as soon as the eggs were laid. Hens will peck their eggs if they sense that they are in danger. My two grandchildren, who love to gather the eggs, were with me all day Sunday, so I let them run out and check the nest boxes for me. They gathered two or three eggs each trip.

The children noticed that the chickens were acting strangely, but the children did not notice anything that could be threatening the chickens. I continued to check the eggs throughout the following week. The hens were still pecking the eggs that weren't quickly gathered, so I continued to watch for any sign of what was making the chickens nervous. Still, I saw no reason for their apprehension*.

When George came home for lunch on Thursday, he checked the boxes because I had been so busy that I had forgotten to check them. I was in the kitchen preparing lunch when I heard his yell. Coming out of the chickens' nest box was a rattlesnake at least six feet long! We could see that it had already eaten the eggs that had been laid since morning.

Had the chickens sensed the coming of the snake, or had the snake been hiding in the nest box all week? We could not see into the nest boxes. In order to retrieve the eggs, we had to reach into the dark boxes and feel for the eggs. George, my grandchildren, and I had been protected from putting our hands on the snake hidden in the box. We didn't know the snake was there, but the chickens did. The snake was there whether or not we sensed it or saw it. Just because something is hidden from sight doesn't mean that it is not there. I have since learned to always be on guard for hidden snakes. I am thankful that my family and I were protected from the venom* lurking in the dark. I wonder how many times have I, my husband, my children been protected without our knowledge by an unseen hand.

*APPREHENSION: concern, anxiety, fear

The Eggs and the Snake

SOMETHING TO THINK ABOUT

Can you remember a time when you would have been in danger had you not been stopped or prevented from acting?
Did something unexplainable protect you?
Did you have an intuitive feeling about impending danger or harm to you or to someone you know? What did you do?
Have you ever taken a different route because you felt like something bad would happen if you didn't?

The Lizard and the Moth

Late one evening a large lizard rested on the outside screen of the kitchen window. It remained immobilized* as it waited in the dim light. Within minutes, a moth appeared at the window. It fluttered about periodically, scraping the screen as it attempted to reach the light coming from the kitchen on the inside of the window.

The lizard darted at the moth several times and missed catching it, but the moth continued to flutter at the window, ignoring the attacks on its life by the lizard. The moth, it seemed, was undisturbed by the presence of the lizard. Finally, the lizard was successful in capturing the moth. As the lizard left the screen, the moth could be seen in the lizard's mouth. The moth was still fluttering, but there was every indication that it would not be for long.

Many times we are warned of impending danger. Either we instinctively know when to avoid impending danger, or we are given signs from the physical environment to avoid dangerous situations and encounters. The moth knew that it was in danger. It even had a portion of its wing bitten off, but the moth ignored the warnings and, of course, suffered the consequences of its ignorance. The moth allowed itself to be victimized.

Many people suffer mental and physical harm because they allow themselves to be victimized. The moth could have flown away and easily escaped its certain doom, but it chose not to escape; thus, it became the lizard's dinner.

*IMMOBILIZED: fixed, unmoving

The Lizard and the Moth

SOMETHING TO THINK ABOUT

Are you or have you ever been victimized by someone else?
What are or were the circumstances surrounding you?
Why do or did you allow someone to dominate you?
How did that make you feel?
What changed the situation?
Did you change as a result?
Have you ever caused someone emotional or physical pain?
What were the reasons behind your actions?
How did that make you feel to hurt someone?
What actions did you take to change the situation?

The Christmas Tree

Every Christmas the search begins for the perfect Christmas tree. The driving force of the search continues until the ultimate aesthetic* selection is made. It is as if the life of the tree embodies* the meaning of Christmas, and not until the perfect tree is in the perfect position and perfectly decorated that the spirit of Christmas is released.

The search began this year at the largest Christmas tree lot in town, where right there in all their glory were 50 rows of gorgeous trees. Somewhere among those trees was the perfect tree. As anticipated, one tree stood out from the rest, literally. Alone, isolated, and segregated from all the other trees, stood the most pathetic looking tree on the lot. In fact, it was so ugly that it seemed ill-fated to remain unselected and on the lot until it became dry and brittle and finally discarded, never having experienced the ornamentation of the Christmas tree attire*.

There was something different about this tree though. It seemed to have feelings, and a sense of gripping sadness emanated from its branches. The thought of the tree haunted the shopper for two days after she and her family left the lot. "It's ridiculous to feel sorry for a tree," her husband said. "If you bring that tree home, you'll be disappointed with it the whole season," he added. There was something different about this tree, she felt, and she knew they had to go back and get it. "I think the tree is beautiful," she said to her family. "You will see it that way too," she promised them.

The lot attendant laughed at the idea that someone was interested in this tree, and he offered to sell it at 50% off of the standard lot price for a tree of its size. A nearby shopper looked at the attendant in disbelief that he should ask so much to get it out of sight. And so the family took this sad little tree home. They adorned it with lights, ornaments, and love, and tenderly topped it with the Christmas angel before they retired for the evening.

As the family slept, the tree transformed. By morning, the branches of the tree had expanded beyond the width of the French doors that served as its backdrop. No other tree could have been this beautiful. Everyone who came to visit during that Christmas season commented on the beauty of the tree and went to the same lot in search of another one like it. But, of course, no others like it could be found.

When the pictures of this beautiful tree were developed, a distinct white light could be seen enveloping the tree. The family has this picture on display in their home. There are those who questioned the origination of the white light, but this family knows the truth behind its radiance. The tree had spread its branches to thank the family for seeing its hidden beauty and magically transformed, it seemed, as a reflection of their love. There are those who believe that trees have souls. Maybe the camera caught a glimpse of this one.

People are like Christmas trees. They come in all sizes and textures and fullness. Some are ignored and left unadorned. Some are cherished and, as a result, transform to reflect the love from those around them. And like the Christmas tree, their time on Earth is short. Maybe the light surrounding the tree was a reminder that we need to give our attention, our time, our encouragement, and our support to those we love so they can spread their branches and radiate and experience all the fullness of life.

*AESTHETIC: artistic, tasteful
*EMBODIES: consist of, contains
*ATTIRE: apparel, dress, garments

The Christmas Tree

SOMETHING TO THINK ABOUT

Do you believe that a camera can pick up a supernatural image?

Have you ever taken a picture of something unexplainable?

What do you think it was?

Have you ever had a supernatural experience?

What happened?

Do you believe that people cannot reach their full potential without the love and support of those around them?

Why is it so important?

The Card

A plethora* of fireworks blazed the full cover of the birthday card that Robin had given to her husband. The picture was one dimensional, but it was pretty. While looking at the card, her husband noticed the instructions on the back explaining how to see the 5-D image on the front cover.

Robin and her husband followed the instructions, and after approximately fifteen minutes of concerted* focusing on the cover, a fifth dimensional image appeared in place of the fireworks. The fireworks on the front of the cover did not obscure the 5-D image. The image could not be seen until the eyes made the adjustment in their focus. When the 5-D image appeared, the fireworks disappeared automatically and were replaced by an entirely different image.

Both images were simultaneously* present, but only one could be seen at a time. The 5-D image could only be seen after the viewer was aware that it existed and adapted the eyes so that the conscious brain could accept the image.

How many times do we look around us and not even see what is really there, or we misinterpret what we see, or we believe that there is only one interpretation of a given situation. There may easily be another way of looking at a situation. Believe that there is another solution and another option and another alternative, all of which are just as real and just as valid, and you will find tolerance, acceptance, and understanding.

*PLETHORA: abundance, shower, deluge
*CONCERTED: joint, cooperative, united
*SIMULTANEOUSLY: together

151

The Card

SOMETHING TO THINK ABOUT

Have you ever misinterpreted what you saw or heard?
What happened as a result?
Have you ever been discriminated against or stereotyped?
How did you feel to be excluded because someone thought that you were different?
What was the situation?
Did you do anything to change that person's opinion of you?

The Sandman

He felt uneasy, sitting on the porch in the dark, alone and called for his sister to join him. She was putting her child to bed and told her brother that she would be out momentarily. This was his first visit to his sister and her husband's vacation mountain home. He liked the serenity that the cabin and its mountain view afforded. The surroundings were peaceful and quiet and uninhabited by other people. He watched as the shadows quickly disappeared with the setting of the sun, transforming the trees and thicket of the close banked woods into opaque monoliths. The bantam light from an occasional firefly was the extent of what he could see as he looked out into the darkness. The quarter moon barely reflected any light, and the stars were obscured by the storm clouds, making the night appear unusually solemn. The creek seemed particularly loud, and he was certain that the rumbling water cascading over the rocks muffled any other sounds that may have tried to penetrate the stillness.

He shifted his position in the chair; then he glanced behind him through the window on the porch for sight of his sister. He could hear her talking to her husband and son, and he knew that she would be more than a moment. He felt uncomfortable as he sat there waiting for her to come out. Although he knew the truth about the originator of his fears, he still listened for the voice of the Sandman when he looked out into the night. As if by impulse, his ears were straining now to hear above the sound of the creek that which he prayed he would never hear again.

"Mom, will you leave the lamp on?" he started as he heard his six year old nephew ask of his mother as she tucked him into bed. "And will you leave the window open so I can hear the creek?"

He had been six years old when he learned to sleep with the light on; "that was nearly fifty years ago," he sighed as he thought about that small boy who was taught to be afraid of the dark. "and I still sleep with a light on in my bedroom." "But many people do," he rationalized, talking to himself. "I wish that I could fall asleep with the windows open, listening to the creek, but I haven't slept with a window open since I was a boy," he thought, remembering the night they shut.

When he was a child, he slept in the back bedroom of the house. The old house that he grew up in didn't have air conditioning, so his mother kept the windows of the house open most of the time. His bedroom windows didn't have screens on them, but no one seemed to worry about what might ingress or egress from those windows. He lay there in bed every night bathed by the dim light of the moon as it filtered through the room, and he fell asleep to the sound of the crickets. He never feared what was on the outside of the windows in the dark until he was conditioned to.

He remembered that it was a quiet night, except for the chirping of the crickets. Then they stopped chirping, or seemed to, because the only sound he heard was a deep, whispered, ominous voice that issued from the blackness on the other side of the open window. Every word uttered was clearly audible. "I am the Sandman," the voice said. "And I come in the night and creep up on little boys who are still awake and sprinkle sand in their eyes to make them sleepy."

He was terrified as he listened to the faceless voice. At six years old, all things are possible in the light as well as in the dark. He had never felt fear before, and he lay in bed with his gaze fixed upon the open window. The sweat rolled down into his eyes, stinging them as he attempted to keep them open and focused in the direction of the voice.

"I live out here in the dark, and I am always out here, waiting for you," the voice continued.

He wanted to scream and to run to his mother, but his lungs wouldn't obey the command to scream, and his legs wouldn't move. His mind and body were paralyzed with fear, and he lay there helplessly at the mercy of the voice in the dark.

"I am the Sandman," the voice said again, "and I will always be out in the dark watching you."

He held his breath, as the Sandman spoke, until he was forced to gasp for air. Then the voice was silent. He starred out into the darkness all night, never shutting his eyes for fear that the voice and its body would emerge from the dark and swallow him whole.

His fears subsided only when the morning came and the sun finally crept into his room. He looked out his window, but all he saw were the hedges that bordered the fence in the yard. He closed his window the following night and never slept with it open again. He never slept in the dark again, either. And he never told a soul why.

Suddenly, he was startled by the sound of his sister's voice as she flung open the door leading onto the porch, and he nearly fell out of the chair.

"Okay, I'm ready for a cigarette," she yelled.

"Your mind must have been somewhere out there in the dark," she laughed. "I didn't mean to startle you," she said.

"Did I ever tell you what our cousin, Jeff, did to me when I was six years old?" he asked his sister as he looked out into the night, lighting his cigarette.

The Sandman

SOMETHING TO THINK ABOUT

Have you ever felt afraid of the dark? What was it that you were afraid of?

Has someone or something ever frightened you so badly that the incidence affected your life in some way? What happened?

Children are very vulnerable, and they do believe in monsters and ghosts when they are very young. Do you think that it is wrong to frighten a child? How was this child's life affected by the insensitivity of an older boy?

Do you think that people, in general, are afraid of the dark? Why?

What is it about the dark that makes people apprehensive?

Why didn't the frightened little boy tell someone about the Sandman?

Have you ever had a frightening experience that you never told anyone about or that you waited a long time before you told someone? What happened and why didn't you tell someone? Or why did you wait so long to tell someone?

The Light Changes Everything

Joy was just 17 and a high school senior. She worked at a drive-in theater not far from her house. It was a four-mile walk to the theater, and that wasn't so far in the daylight. But after the theater closed, that four-mile walk home in the dark seemed like 200 miles, especially one Saturday night.

A friend had promised Joy that he would pick her up after work, about 11:30 pm, but after waiting until almost midnight for him, she decided to walk home. By midnight, most of the businesses along the busy road where the drive-in was located were closed. There were not many cars, and the stillness of the street was frightening. In the daylight, there were lots of activity on this thoroughfare. She had never been afraid to walk this stretch before. It is strange, she thought, how something so commonplace as this street is can become so ominous and seem so unfamiliar by changing the time of day or by changing the lighting or by removing the people and the cars.

She thought about turning around and running back to the theater. "I should have called Mom to come and get me," she thought. She kept walking, not wanting to give in to her fears. "It's just the quiet that seems so strange," she whispered, not because she would disturb anyone, but because she would disturb the quiet. For some reason, she felt that there would be consequences in making noise.

Up ahead though, she did hear something. A bar that she had never noticed before was still open, and as she came closer to it, she could hear music coming from the open door. Just as she passed the door, a man came out of it and started walking behind her. He kept pace with her stride. When she was a good distance from the bar, it was quiet again. She had a number of alleys to cross and instinctively she walked a little faster. She could hear herself breathing. Then the quiet ended. She could hear his footsteps. Joy crossed the road to gain some distance from the man, but he crossed the road too. Not a single car had passed. She was off of the main road, and the blackness of the night pressed against her chest, and she labored each breath. Without command, her legs started running. Without looking, she knew that his legs had too.

"There is a street light ahead. If only I could make it that far. At least I will have some light and can see who I am dealing with," she felt. As she looked back toward the man, he appeared only as a form in the night. He had no face and no eyes. Still there was not a car in sight. She did not know what she would do when she got to the light. "Maybe I will see a weapon like a stick or a rock that I can use against him" she thought.

His steps were getting closer now, and she felt as if his breath were upon her neck. She ran as fast as she could toward the light. "Please God," she cried, "help me." She wanted to scream. She wanted her legs to move faster. Fear paralyzed her voice, and she knew that even if her pursuer caught her that she would not be able to scream. She could neither see nor hear anything now but the light ahead and the man's labored breath. Nothing else mattered. In a moment, she shuddered, it would all be over with.

Finally, her foot touched the curb, and the light shone upon her and upon her deliverance. A voice called out to her, but she was blinded by her fear, by the light, and by the sweat running into her eyes. She could not see where the voice was coming from except that its sound resonated from the light. From out of nowhere, a car with a man and a woman in it had pulled up next to her. A woman had been calling to her from the car window. "I see a man chasing you," she said to Joy. "Hurry, get into the car," she yelled. "We will not harm you."

The elderly couple drove her home and waited until she entered the house. "You are safe now," she heard them say as she opened the door. When she turned to wave good bye, the car had vanished. She could clearly see down both directions of the street from her front door. The couple was no where in sight.

She did not need to know their names nor how nor why they vanished. She knew that she would see them again, for Angels appear in many forms and are always watching, waiting to open a door.

The Light Changes Everything

SOMETHING TO THINK ABOUT

Have you ever been truly afraid, so afraid that you thought that your life was in danger? What was the situation and what happened? Did someone help you?

Have you ever helped someone out of a dangerous situation? What did you do to help?

Have you ever had an encounter that you could not explain?

Many people believe in Angels. Do you? Have you ever seen an Angel, or has anyone in your family ever seen an Angel? What happened? Why were you or someone you know helped by an Angel?

Saving Santa

"Mom, David says there's no such thing as Santa," Aaron said. Aaron and David are friends, and they are both six years old. David has never believed in Santa, only it didn't matter to Aaron until now. "Do you believe there is a Santa?" his mother asked. "I think so, but I'm not sure," thinking about it for a moment before he answered. "Do you believe in Santa?" the little boy asked his mother in almost a whisper as if he were afraid of the answer. "I believe that Santa lives in your heart," she said, "because that is where the spirit of Christmas lives, and there is plenty of room for Santa and his elves, and all the toys." His mother was worried that her son needed more convincing information; "If there is no such thing as Santa, then why do we see so many Christmas decorations of Santa?" "Why are there so many movies about Santa?" "Why do we see Santa at the mall and at the stores?" "Many people must believe in Santa." The mother knew that once the seed of doubt had been planted, it would not be long before Aaron would say goodbye to Santa Claus.

The magical years when a child believes in the Tooth Fairy, the Easter Bunny, Barney, the Fragels (Jim Henson's muppets), and Santa are gone so quickly. And when one goes, the rest soon follow. The mother wanted her son to hang on to the magic a little while longer. He would have the rest of his life to live without the Tooth Fairy and the rest of her friends, and that is a very long time. At six years old, everything should be magical, and good, and safe.

That Christmas, the mother and father did everything to keep Santa alive. They called Santa on the phone, they sent Santa letters, they had Santa make a surprise visit during their annual Christmas party. They had Santa leave footprints leading from the fireplace when he dropped off the presents, and they had Santa rest his reindeer on the roof before he left for the next house. They knew he was resting and they told Aaron to listen. They could hear the bells on the Reindeer and they could hear a lot of noise from their movement on the roof, Christmas Eve. Aaron did not question Santa's existence again for a long time.

The following summer, the family made a trip to Alaska. From Florida, Alaska is very far. Even in the summer, it was very cold, especially near the glaziers. The only ice that Aaron had really ever seen was in the refrigerator freezer, so he was awed by the solid blocks of blue ice that extended for miles and for some even hundreds of miles. All the ice and snow reminded Aaron of the movies he had seen about the North Pole, and he mentioned that Santa must live in Alaska.

It was during their trip to Fairbanks that the family got the opportunity to visit the North Pole. North Pole, Alaska is right outside of Fairbanks. "Santa's house is not far from here," the tour guide told them. She handed the mother a brochure that told all about Santa's house. The brochure said that they would meet Santa, see his reindeer and visit his toy shop. "We have to take Aaron tomorrow to see Santa at the North Pole," she told her husband. "This is a once in a lifetime opportunity. How many children get the chance to visit the North Pole?" she said, not wanting a reply. After they told Aaron, he was so excited that he could not sleep that night. The kid inside of each parent was excited too, and neither of them could sleep as well.

The hours crept by as they waited for the taxi that would take them to the North Pole. "I thought people could only get to the North Pole by sleigh," Aaron said when they got into the taxi that finally arrived four hours after Aaron had gotten dressed. Aaron looked out of the window as the driver got onto the interstate. "I thought that we had to go over the snow and the blue ice to get to his house," he sighed. "We take the interstate in the summer," the driver said. "And we can always get there by car." he added. The mother wished that he had not added the part about the car. "We don't have any blue ice around here," the driver laughed". "But,"

Aaron started to say, then fell silent as the taxi driver and his dad talked about the temperature changes in Fairbanks.

Just like the brochure said, they arrived at the North Pole from Fairbanks within ten minutes. The cab driver pulled up next to a large pole that had been painted with red and white stripes. "See," he said, "that's the North Pole." Then he laughed. The pole had a sign hanging from it that said, "The North Pole". Next to "The Pole" was the post office, and there were houses everywhere. "Over there next to the interstate is Santa's house," he said. The taxi pulled into a parking lot and faced a small shop that had a large sign out front indicating that this was Santa's house. "I'll wait out here for you," the driver said. Mom, Dad, and Aaron sat there in the car and looked at the shop and looked at the driver and looked at the parking lot. The mother tried to find the magic in the situation and said as enthusiastically as possible, "Let's get out and say hello to Santa." The driver unfolded his newspaper and started to read. Aaron watched him unfold the paper before getting out of the car. Aaron's mother knew that her son was thinking that no one should be this cavalier about sitting in front of Santa's house. And then Aaron gave his father a look that suggested something was wrong here at the North Pole.

Before they entered the house, they followed a path that pointed to Santa's reindeer. Aaron ran ahead of his parents, still believing that Santa could be saved. His parents walked slowly down the path. They looked at each other in silence. They knew from experience that there would be no magic down the path, and they grieved for their son who would soon find that out too. They never expected, though, to find what they did. At the end of the path was a small fenced in pen that held captive an old, frail, thin reindeer that had a chain around its neck, securing the deer to the fence. The family stood staring at the pen, the reindeer, and the chain in disbelief. Aaron stared for only a moment, then he returned the way he had come. He walked alone. "That's the most pathetic thing that I have ever seen," said the mother. "It might not be," added the father, "we have not seen inside the house, yet." "It's a shame," the father said, "with all this land in Alaska, this poor animal is trapped." "I think I will give Santa a piece of my mind," he said."

They had to look for Aaron when they entered the house. He was found, sitting on a bench in a corner next to a shelf of toys. "Mom," he said with tears rolling down his cheeks, "I don't think that Santa really lives here." "Why are all the toys for sale?" "Where are all the elves?" Santa's house was nothing more than a gift shop. A sleigh with a Christmas backdrop was featured in one of the three rooms. A camera on a tripod stood in front of the display. "Santa overslept," the photographer said, "he'll be here in a minute."

"Why couldn't she have said that he was feeding his reindeer (heaven knows the reindeer needs food) or anything else other than he overslept?" Aaron's mother said, not to anyone in particular.

While they waited for Santa to get out of bed, Aaron and his father drank hot chocolate. Aaron's mother waited outside. She looked around at the parking lot,   at the interstate, at the abused reindeer, at the gift shop, and finally at the red and white striped pole. When Aaron and his father walked outside with some coffee for her, they found her crying. She said she didn't feel well, but both of them knew the real reason for her tears. She was crying for the magic that her son lost, the magic that was taken away from him. She was crying over his disillusionment, and his disappointment. She was crying for herself and for her husband and for all those parents who have tried to save Santa. And she cried for the reindeer. Her only hope now was that her son would not suffer permanent psychological damage, carrying Santa baggage the rest of his life.

"Mom is taking this pretty hard," Aaron said to his dad. "That's because she loves you," his father answered.

Aaron didn't understand what his father meant by that, but he knew already that growing up was hard and even sad sometimes, not to mention confusing and complicated. He would not mention North Pole, Alaska again. He didn't know why; perhaps it was because he loved his parents, too.

Not long after they had gotten back to Florida, Aaron and his mother were driving on one of Tampa's busiest streets when Aaron questioned his mother about another one of life's mysteries that he and David had been discussing. "David says that aliens do not exist. He says that there are no aliens on earth. I believe that aliens exist," he said. "Do you believe in aliens, Mom?" he asked her.

"Yes, I do," she said, "and I think that there are some here on earth." "Good," Aaron excitedly said, "because there is an alien sitting in that car right next to us."

Quickly, his mother looked over into the car that sat at the light opposite her on the driver's side. Sure enough, something was sitting in the front seat with purple and green spiked hair. It had a ring it is nose, a chain coming out of its tongue, black circles drawn around its eyes, and wearing a dog collar with daggers hanging from it around its neck.

"It sure is," she said.

They drove on, not talking of aliens again. There was no need to. Their existence and appearance here on earth had been confirmed by an actual sighting.

"The magic still exist," the mother thought. "I'm not going to tell him that what he saw was a teenager." "Saving Santa was hard enough."

Saving Santa

SOMETHING TO THINK ABOUT

How did you feel when you learned the truth about Santa? Who told you? How did you find out?
Have you ever tried to protect someone from learning the truth about something that would affect that person's beliefs? What did you do? What was the situation?
Do you feel that it is important for children to believe in magical beings such as the Tooth Fairy and Santa Claus? Why do you or don't you believe that magic is important in a child's life?
Have you ever tried to keep the magic alive for a child? What did you do? Where you successful?

The Race Horse

His father started out selling produce from a shed under a tree. Pop was just a boy, then. During the evening, he watched the place, and during the day, he washed the vegetables in a tub of water. The family did not own a car or a truck because it was the depression, so their produce selection was limited to watermelons and a few vegetables that Uncle Clint delivered to them in his truck.

The second location of the produce market was a better one because it was right across the street from the family's house, and it had a larger area than that afforded by the shed and the space under the tree. This location developed into a real produce market. Although it only had sawdust for floors, it had screen doors that could be locked at night.

Pop had seven brothers and sisters, and each one had an assigned responsibility to make sure that the customers were assisted and that the produce was cleaned and displayed properly. Pop's mother worked in the market too, but she always made time to prepare lunch and dinner. By 11:00 am everyday, she had lunch ready, and by 6:00 pm she had dinner ready for her family of 10. She made cornbread and a deep pan pie and fresh vegetables everyday. And this is how life was for 20 years. Pop's father opened the market at 6:00 am and closed it at 9:00 pm each day, seven days a week.

When they were young men, Pop and two of his brothers opened their own market. His third brother became a minister. His three sisters divided their time between the two markets. The brothers were goodnatured and hard working, so they acquired quite a following of dedicated customers. The three brothers shared their interests in the market until Pop opened his own in the mid-forties.

Of the three, though, Pop was the prankster. Pop knew that the depression had taken its toll on just about everybody, so he invested some of his time in making people smile. And he devoted some of his time to making practical jokes. People from all over the town soon heard about Pop's humor. He had developed quite a reputation for bringing laughter into the hard times. Most people appreciated his humor, but there were some who didn't know quite how to take his wit.

Pop loved to paint. In fact, he painted everything, including his produce. During the Mediterranean Fruit Fly scare of the 1930's, it was unlawful, in Florida, to display citrus fruit outside of a screened enclosure. Pop was a law-abiding citizen and he didn't mean to be disrespectful. He simply thought that the government, sometimes, gets a little too serious and needs to be deflated just a bit. And he liked to stir up a little excitement during the deflation process. He bought 50 rubber balls the sizes of oranges and grapefruits and painted them orange and yellow. He displayed them in front of his market and left them there until he was cited by the Florida Citrus Council for displaying fruit outside of a screen. He convinced the Council that he was cited for displaying rubber balls, so it reduced the sentence to a warning. Some words were exchanged. Pop said that those high government officials were fooled by rubber balls, and they said that he was the fruit and that he still should be cited for being outside of a screen enclosure. This wasn't the only time that Pop got into trouble for painting fruit.

Everyone knows that watermelons are green, so when Pop bought a load of white watermelons from Georgia, he had trouble selling them. There was quite a bit of suspicion surrounding his watermelons of a different color. People really didn't believe that the meat could taste as good as a green melon. Of course, Pop showed the people what he thought of their narrow-minded and inflexible thinking. He painted the whole load yellow, pink, and orange using enamel paint.

His sister lived across the street from the market and she had a son in the first grade. Vernon came home crying from school and told his mother that he had been sent to the principal's office for arguing with his teacher over the color of watermelons. The assignment was to color a picture of fruit the appropriate colors, and Vernon painted his watermelons the color of Easter eggs, hardly appropriate the teacher said. Vernon insisted that watermelons were pink, yellow, and orange. In fact, he cried and insisted that his teacher was wrong in denying that watermelons could be any other color but green. Pop's sister looked out from her front window at Pop's Easter egg colored watermelons and consoled her son, probably for having to live across from his uncle, and called his teacher. Pop's sister convinced the teacher to bring her class to the market on a field trip so they could all see the pink, yellow, and orange watermelons.

When the teacher arrived at the market with her students, she saw that the melons had been painted with enamel paint. The teacher apologized to Pop's nephew. But she tried to explain to him and to all her students that the watermelons weren't really the color of Easter eggs. However, painted or not, the watermelons were pink, yellow, and orange and that is how the children saw them and that is how they colored them at school after their field trip to Pop's market. Pop gave all of the children, including the teacher, an apple and thanked them for coming to visit his store. The teacher said something to Pop on the way out of the market, but he didn't quite catch all of what she said. He felt it best not to ask her to repeat it.

All the children in the neighborhood loved Pop. He always gave each child who came into the store an apple or a banana. Sometimes, as a joke, he would give a child a plantain instead of a banana to eat. Plantains look like bananas but they have to be cooked. The child always spit out the bite and usually threw the plantain on the floor. Pop considered it a bonus if the disbelieving parent took a bite and followed through with the same reaction as the child.

Pop's favorite time to play tricks was on Halloween. He was a very generous man and would leave a bushel of apples and a box of bananas out for the trick-or-treaters to help themselves to. But he always left a bushel of onions or a bushel of cucumbers out with the apples and bananas. He thought that it would be funny when the children got home and dumped out their bag of candy and out rolled an onion or a cucumber. "Who would ever expect a child to come home with an onion in his trick or treat bag?" he would laugh. People in Pop's neighborhood probably expected nothing less, except maybe a cucumber.

Pop loved to make people laugh, and he loved a good joke. Rarely, though, was the joke on him. However, when it was, the joke had to be a powerful one in order to be effective.

Occasionally, Pop delivered Florida citrus fruit to sell at produce markets in Georgia and Alabama. On one particular trip he hauled tangerines and oranges to Birmingham, Alabama. Pop had quite a reputation among the farmers for sensible and knowledgeable produce purchases. He knew what to buy and what to pay. He knew quality produce when he saw it and never argued about the cost when the price was fair. Apparently, though, he didn't know anything about horses.

The produce auction in Birmingham was large and offered a wide variety of fruits and vegetables at a good price to the right bidder. This trip, Pop bought more than what he bargained for and paid more than it was worth. Pop had never seen a horse auctioned at the produce market until now. When the auctioneer opened the bidding at a dollar, Pop was shocked. "How could a whole horse sell for one dollar?" he mumbled. He thought it odd that very few people were interested in the horse, but he raised his hand, and then he raised it again. Within seconds, Pop had bought a horse. "Sold for three dollars," the auctioneer shouted. Pop paid for his purchase and looked at his horse. "I bought a horse for three dollars," he said. The produce that Pop bought was already on his truck, so he loaded the horse on the back of the truck in the remaining space and drove off. Pop had kinfolk in Culman, Alabama, so he decided to visit with them before heading home to Florida. He couldn't wait to show his uncle and cousins his fine horse.

When he pulled up to his uncle's farm, his cousins ran out to greet him. Pop was so proud of his three dollar horse. He told his cousins all about his clever purchase, and they hung on to ever word as if he were the pot mender on his once a year trip through town. Just as Pop got the horse off of the truck, Uncle Lewis walked up. Uncle Lewis owned a livery stable and was a horse trader. Before Pop could even shake his hand, Uncle Lewis started laughing. He laughed loud and long. "I hope no one passed this animal off as a horse," he bellowed. Pop stood before his uncle mortified. One of Pop's cousins yelled from the back of the crowd that had gathered around Pop and his horse, "He paid three whole dollars for that horse." When Uncle Lewis heard that, he bellowed even louder. Pop knew that something was wrong now, and he was afraid to say a word. Uncle Lewis climbed onto the back of the truck and faced the crowd. He looked like an evangelist beckoning the people to wake up and repent their secret sins before it was too late. "This horse is so old that it can no longer stand without leaning on something for support," he said. Pop was hoping that his uncle would stop there, but he continued to point out the animal's finer qualities. "This horse does not have a single tooth left in its mouth, and it is missing an eye." "The only thing of value is the hide, and if you paid more than one dollar for that, you got robbed." All of Pop's kinfolk were laughing by now. And it seemed to Pop that the crowd got larger.

Pop spent the longest night of his life that night. He and his horse were the topic before dinner, during dinner, after dinner and even in the dark when the family went to bed. The next morning, Pop got up early and loaded the horse on the truck. Pop just wanted to get out of there and head home before his kinfolk were finished with their chores and coming in for breakfast. Too late. His aunt was already ringing the breakfast bell as Pop was loading the horse. He knew that it was impolite to leave now that breakfast was ready, so he stayed and endured his uncle's laughter for what he thought was just a few minutes longer.

When he got ready to leave, his uncle and cousins followed him out to the truck. It was extremely cold and a few snow flurries could be seen drifting in the air. Luckily, the cold air prevented a lengthy goodby and shortened the humorous remarks considerably. Pop was glad. He just wanted to drive off into the sunrise with his horse in peace and quiet. Too late. His aunt came running up the drive with a blanket. Pop called out to her that he didn't need a blanket because he had a working heater in the truck. "The blanket is for the horse," she yelled. With that remark, the crowd broke into laughter and continued to laugh while his aunt wrapped the horse and tied the blanket to it. Pop could see them in his rearview mirror still laughing as they watched him drive out of sight.

When Pop got as far as Birmingham, he stopped to rest for a few minutes and to get something to drink. When he came back out to the truck, he noticed a drunk looking under the blanket at the horse. "That's a race horse," Pop said. "I'm taking him back to Florida for the big race." "I'll give you ten dollars for that horse," the drunk said. Pop put the ten dollars in his pocket. "That's the hardest ten dollars I've ever earned," he said. And he watched the man and the horse wobble down the street, sharing the blanket.

Pop had a long ride home, and he knew that Uncle Lewis' letter telling the kinfolk in Florida about his visit with the horse would probably beat him there and that he would have to endure the laughter again.

He patted the ten dollars in his pocket. "That's cheap for a race horse."

The Race Horse

SOMETHING TO THINK ABOUT

Have you ever played a practical joke on someone? What did you do? What was the outcome?

Has anyone ever played a practical joke on you? What happened?

Can you remember your most embarrassing moment? What happened and how did you and others around you react?

Pop was embarrassed in front of his relatives, and he knew that they would talk about him and his horse for a long time. Have you ever done something that you wish your relatives had not found out about because they would talk about it and remind you of the situation for a long time?

Why Cross the Road

Joy and George have a beautiful fenced-in family orchard of twenty-five fruit trees, berry vines, and healthy green grass. There is plenty of sun as well as plenty of shade. They also raise chickens. They are not ordinary chickens. They are problem chickens. These chickens do not like the orchard, so they crawl under the fence or fly over it to get to the front yard. The front yard is a one-half acre paradise of multiple kinds of flowers, trees, and beautiful grass. Still the chickens are not happy. They do not like the front yard either.

But they do like the neighbor's yard. These chickens know that they are not supposed to go into the neighbor's yard, but they do it anyway. They wait until no one is looking and then they run. Yes! They run as fast as they can go to get over the fence before any one sees them.

Joy kept telling her husband that the chickens were doing this, and he found the story a little hard to believe. Most people think that chickens are stupid and incapable of deception*.

Joy suggested to her husband that he trick the chickens by going into the house and watching them from the window. As he walked into the house, he turned and watched them happily destroying Joy's marigolds as they scratched for seeds and bugs. "These chickens are so contented*," he yelled back at his wife. "They like it here, and why shouldn't they," he added, "they have a chicken's paradise. The neighbor's yard is not nearly as nice as ours, and the chickens love your marigolds! The neighbor's yard doesn't even have marigolds," he said.

She urged him to follow through with the plan. "The chickens are watching you out of the corner of their eyes," she said. "Do you think that they are suspicious*?" With that remark, he went inside, now more worried about his wife than about the alleged* chicken escape. She was certain that she saw them turn and watch him enter the house, and as soon as he did, they ran as fast as they could the whole length of the yard to get to the neighbor's yard. George ran out of the house mumbling something about the neighbor's yard not even having marigolds, and that it wasn't nearly as nice as his yard. He thought the neighbor's complaints about the problem chickens were unfounded. He looked around and shook his head. How could they not be contented with all that they had!

"The grass isn't even green on the other side of the fence," he sighed. They both laughed at what he had said.

Because the chickens continued to invade the neighbor's yard, they eventually lost their freedom to explore the family orchard and to flatten the marigolds. The discontented chickens were caged. Just like the chickens, people sometimes think that the grass is greener on the other side of the fence. And just like the chickens, they lose what they have: the family orchard, the marigolds, and the greenest grass in town.

*DECEPTION: lying, deceit, dishonesty
*CONTENTED: fulfilled, happy
*SUSPICIOUS: distrustful, unbelieving
*ALLEGED: supposed, pretended

Why Cross the Road

SOMETHING TO THINK ABOUT

Have you ever looked for something better and discovered that you already had the best?

Did you have to learn the hard way that you should have been content with what you have?

Did you have to lose something in order to appreciate its worth?

How did you change from that experience?

Are you more appreciative of what you have now?

The Acorns

The children were usually on the playground when I picked up my son, Tyler, each day from preschool. When he saw my white Volvo pull onto the circular drive, he came running across the playground as fast as his nearly four year old legs would move. With his arms outstretched and with a smile on his face, he would yell, "Mommy, Mommy, Mommy," as he readied to leap into my arms. There are many moments that a parent freezes in time; these are, indeed, among my most cherished.

Even though I only worked half days, I missed him, and never a minute passed, it seems, when I didn't think of him. He loved school, and he was well cared for. Learning Gate had a barn with pigs, goats, and even a horse named Buckwheat that the children were allowed to ride. The school even had a swimming pool and a large playground that was shaded by large grandfather oaks. His teacher was loving, kind, and gentle, and she had the creative energy of ten mothers. Tyler had such a full schedule and such a wonderful learning and play environment that I was surprised to learn that he thought of me too during the day, and that I was a part of his world even in my absence.

One afternoon as he ran to greet me, I could hear him yell, "I have a surprise for you! Mommy, I have a surprise for you in my pocket." He was so proud and so excited as his tiny hands dug deep into his pocket where he retrieved* the treasure that he clutched in his hand before presenting it to me. As I caught the sparkle in his eyes, he said, "Here, it's a present for you." In his tiny hand he held three acorns. "Thank you. I love these acorns," I said, and I picked him up and kissed him.

As we were examining each acorn, another mother drove up, and we watched as her daughter greeted her, also clutching a treasure in her hand. "I have a present for you, Mommy. It's a pretty leaf," she said. Instantly, the mother scolded the little girl. "I don't want that dirty old leaf," she said. "I have all the leaves I need at home." The child quickly glanced over at Tyler before she silently got into the car. Even at four years old, her face reflected shame and embarrassment.

Why didn't her mommy like the present?" he whispered. How could I explain to my preschooler that the little girl's mother was insensitive*. That she was teaching her child that gifts from the heart should be scorned and discarded. That she was demeaning* the child and destroying her self-esteem. And worst of all, she was teaching her daughter that thinking of her mother during the day and selecting a present for her from her natural environment, the only source available to her, was unacceptable behavior. I have thought about that incident many times since that day.

Tyler is nearly six now, and I have a jar full of acorns sitting on my kitchen cabinet. But I don't see them in the jar. I see him running toward me across the playground with his arms outstretched yelling, "Mommy, I have a present for you. Mommy, I missed you today. Mommy, I love you."

I see the acorns in his pockets, in his shoes, and clutched in his tiny hands until he placed them in my heart where a majestic oak has grown.

*RETRIEVED: found, fetched
*INSENSITIVE: uncaring, thoughtless
*DEMEANING: disgrace, humiliating

The Acorns

SOMETHING TO THINK ABOUT

Have you ever been given a gift from the heart?
Have you ever given a gift from the heart?
How was your gift received?
Have you ever been disappointed when you gave a gift that was not appreciated?
What was your reaction?

From Pop's Perspective: The Wild Man

Pop had a knack for drawing attention to himself. Sometimes he planned it that way, and sometimes it just happened. Pop said this incident happened one morning during the 1930s when a crowd gathered to see the "wild man." Pop was working in a small citrus fruit packing house on the corner of Pierce and Twiggs Street, where the Tampa Court House is now built.

The fruit from Polk County had to be brought into town in screened trucks because of the Mediterranean fruit fly scare. The Mediterranean fruit fly can destroy the citrus industry in Florida, so every precaution was taken to isolate the fly and its damage. The citrus trucks were completely screened in; they even had screen doors on the back of the beds. Most of the trucks had awnings across the top, which made it look like the carnival was in town when the trucks gathered for unloading. Gypsy carnivals could spring up anywhere at anytime, so people thought the fruit trucks signaled a carnival was passing through, and crowds quickly gathered, but the crowds just as quickly dispersed* when the people saw it was only fruit and nothing more.

Pop was a young man back then, and he had been working day and night for nearly a week to get the trucks unloaded. He was dirty, bearded, and had lengthy hair, which was uncommon in those days. After the last truck was unloaded, Pop crawled onto the bed of the truck and fell asleep. While he was sleeping, someone locked the screen door to the back of the truck and hung a large sign on the screen, "BEWARE THE WILD MAN."

When Pop woke up and realized that the screen door was locked, he started yelling, "Let me out! Let me out!" He shook the screen door, and he jumped up and down. Before long, a small crowd gathered, but no one would let him out, so he continued to do the most natural thing: he yelled and he jumped up and down and he pounded on the side of the truck. Before long, a large crowd gathered, and the people just starred at him. "What is the matter with you people?" he cried out. Finally, a police officer came. He took down the sign, he unlocked the door, and he let Pop out. Not many people remembered the fruit fly epidemic*, but everybody remembered the year the carnival brought the "wild man" to town.

*DISPERSED: broke up, scattered
*EPIDEMIC: outbreak, infection

From Pop's Perspective

SOMETHING TO THINK ABOUT

Have you ever played a practical joke on someone, or has someone ever played a practical joke on you?

What prompted the joke, and what was the result?

Can you remember your most embarrassing moment?

Did you attract attention?

Where were you, and what happened to cause you embarrassment?

Betsy's Garden

Steve Hagy

Betsy Gardner felt peculiar. She didn't know why. Usually, a youthful vitality frolicked in her eighty-nine-year-old mind and body, and usually, the beauty and serenity of her garden comforted her loneliness and quelled her longing for Walter, her loving husband, long ago deceased. However, on this day, she felt feeble, alone, and she missed—to tears—she missed Walter.

Her lack of vigor began that morning as the first light of dawn peeked over the stonewall, filtered through the tree branches, and beamed a hearty good morning through her kitchen window. Usually, as she waited for the water to boil for tea, she gazed back at the sunrise, its light diffusing past her eyes, bouncing off her soul, then reflecting back out her eyes as glinting sparks of verve. However, on this day, it glimmered off her tears.

Hearing the whistling kettle, she went to the stove, poured boiling water into her teacup, let the tea bag steep, dunked it a few times, and then swirled in a teaspoon of honey. Usually, she only spooned in one teaspoon; however, on this day, she added one more—the way Walter liked it. Holding her warm cup in both hands, she stepped out the back door and sat in a wooden rocking chair next to a trellis of wide-awake, blue morning glories. Rocking gently in her chair, in the tranquility of daybreak, she sipped her steaming cup of honeyed tea and beheld the awakening of her heavenly garden.

With an invasion of brilliance, rays of sunshine burst forth upon the landscape, brightening the dew-covered blossoms of every genus and color into a floricultural paradise. Doves cooed. Sparrows chirped. Robins trilled. Two white butterflies fluttered in erratic circles while buzzing honeybees gathered pollen. A sleek, red squirrel scurried across the manicured lawn and another up the trunk of a towering pine tree. The entire garden bustled in the sunlight.

Usually, while drinking her tea, Betsy planned the chores and errands of the day. However, on this day, she thought about Walter and the mornings he used to sit in the rocking chair next to her and enjoy his tea. When it was time, he'd charge off to work, but not before he had kissed her on the cheek. He'd then march out the garden gates, up main street, along the stonewall to his office, where, as a family doctor, he had become well acquainted with the insides and outs from the nose to the toes of most of the town folks and the farm folks too.

Memories flowed by Betsy with every sip of the sweet, honeyed tea. She visualized the modest, country school, where she and Walter as small children had played together in the schoolyard and the quaint, little church, where they as teenagers had married. She recalled the years while Walter attended medical school when they lived in a big city far away. The hardships they endured only deepened their devotion to one another. Upon returning to their hometown, their families had helped them purchase a seven-acre parcel on the edge of town with a large, two-story, Victorian home. The forlorn house sat at the center of the barren land with the entire property surrounded by a six-foot-high stonewall. Walter had worked hard, restoring the house while Betsy had toiled, creating a garden. She marveled at how, over time, the small town had grown and their estate had become the heart of the city.

She stopped rocking in her chair and hung her head in sorrow, reflecting on the nearly two decades she had spent, wanting, trying, and praying for a child of their own, but never to be blessed with one. Then, she thought of all the countless babies that Walter had delivered and how she had insisted on going with him to each newborn's first check up. Cuddling the infants, she had silently asked God to bestow a blessing upon them. Thinking about the darling babies, her spirits lifted and she smiled, rocking again in her chair.

With the last sip of her tea, her mind returned to the present. She stepped back into the house, ate a light breakfast, dressed, put on her gardening apron and bonnet, and strode out into her garden.

173

All day long as she gardened, the splendid, summer day treated her especially kind, providing warm rays of bright sunshine as she clipped bouquets of flowers for next Sunday's worship service and sending her a slight, cooling breeze when she had tilled the flowerbeds. Usually, she hummed a hymn as she worked, however, on this day, she raked, hoed, and clipped in silence, lost in her memories of Walter.

At the end of the afternoon, as the fleeing sun slipped behind the gnarled and knotted limbs of the regal old oak tree, she needed to finish one last task.

Down on her hands and knees, she patted the loose dirt firmly around the skinny trunk of a three-foot tall willow tree that she had just transplanted from under its parent tree to an open spot where it could thrive.

With the young tree standing at attention, she raised up on her knees, placed her small shovel in an apron pocket next to the pocket with her clipping shears, and wiped her hands off on a little towel drooped over her apron string. She then stood up and peered down at the junior tree. In her elderly, wavering voice, she spoke softly, yet firmly as if it were her child. "Now, first of all, you tiny tot of a tree, I planted you with love, just like I did with all the plants in my garden, so you belong here; this is your home. Secondly, I planted you in a perfect spot where you've got everything you need to grow into a mighty tree—rich soil, bright sunshine, and refreshing water from the rain and that sprinkler over there. The birds will keep the hungry bugs off you, so you can stretch out them branches, and there's plenty of wigglin' earthworms to keep your soil tilled, so you can reach out them roots. Thirdly, there aren't no weeds in my garden nor them naughty gophers, so none are gonna bully you and don't fear the unruly wind neither 'cause that burly hedge will shelter you from blowin' over until you can hold your ground. Lastly, I expect you to provide a lot of shade someday for the little critters around here and for young lovers who come and picnic under your branches. Just delight in the sunrises and sunsets. Enjoy every sunbeam, raindrop, or snowflake in between, and just like this old gal, you'll do fine."

When she finished her exhortation to the peewee tree, she removed her sunbonnet, slid it into an apron pocket, placed her hands on her hips, and gazed out at the garden all around her. A quiet stillness subdued the garden in the emerging twilight—no tweets from the roosting birds; no buzzing bees, only the whispering, gurgling water, cascading over rocks in the stone fountain.

She glanced at the large, wrought iron gates at the garden's entrance, then looked away, then back again. She thought that she had seen Walter coming through the entrance as he had always done. Nevertheless, no one was there. She began to feel faint as though her knees would collapse. She shuffled a short distance and sat down on a wooden bench. Again, she peered over at the gates, feeling a strange notion that she would see Walter.

Every workday, whether sunny, rainy, windy, or chilly, Walter had come strolling through the gates and into the garden, whistling in the sunshine with his hands in his pockets, pressing his fedora hat down upon his head in the wind or holding an umbrella in the rain. Over almost four decades of living at the estate, on those bright days, she had sat on the bench waiting for him. As he entered, they'd wave to each other and then, he'd march directly toward her, his footsteps clip-clopping on the cobblestones and his whistle-song in the air.

Arriving at the bench, he'd blurt out with a wide and genuine smile, "Now there's the prettiest flower in the garden!"

She'd jump into his arms, stand on her tiptoes, and kiss her tall and handsome prince upon his cheek. Holding hands, they'd walk over to the bench and sit down where she'd always have ice-cold lemonade mixed with sweet tea, exactly how Walter liked it.

She'd listen as he talked about the interesting lives of his patients and he'd listen to her share about her activities in the garden, the quilting circle, and the church. They'd converse until their separate adventures of the day became a part of both and always, before they'd go into the house for supper, they'd pray for those whom her husband was doctoring and ask God to bless her garden.

On this day, alone in her garden, she ignored her silly notions of Walter strolling through the gates. For a moment, in her mind, she relived that night, twenty-five years ago, when shortly after dinner, he had muttered, "Honey, I feel peculiar. I'm goin' on up-stairs to bed. Will you bring me up a seltzer when you come?"

"Sure dear, I'll be right up with it, after I put Kittyrose out."

Holding the glass of fizzing seltzer, she climbed the stairs, entered the bedroom, and found Walter in bed, eyes closed, sitting motionless, propped up on his pillows. Thinking he had already fallen asleep, she softly called out, "Walter." No answer. She moved to his side, sat the glass on the nightstand, and brushing back his hair from his forehead, she whispered, "Walter." There was no awakening him and to her horror, he had stopped breathing. She tried desperately to revive him, but to no avail. Suffering from silent heart disease, her beloved Walter was gone.

Out in the garden, sitting on the bench, she felt feeble, alone, and she missed Walter so that she sobbed into her apron. She tried to stand and go into the house, but felt dizzy and sat back down. She felt peculiar. Her chest felt tight, it seemed difficult to breathe, and she felt pain in her fingers. She decided to lie down for just a minute and rest, placing her hands under her head and curling her knees up on the bench. Though the sun still spied over the stonewall, darkness surrounded her.

"Betsy! Betsy dear!"

She heard her name called out and awoke. She sat up, wondering how long she had slept. Although the sun had dipped below the horizon, a celestial sky of golden clouds illuminated the garden in flaxen light.

"Betsy!"

Hearing her name sung out again and footsteps on the cobblestones, she peered toward the gates and saw a tall man, wearing a fedora hat, walking toward her. She stood up. No dizziness; no labored breath; no pain. She felt euphoric and her joy bubbled into girlish giggles.

He continued strolling toward her; his whistle-song in the air; his face obscured in a silhouette. Her heart raced and her skin tingled with excitement. When the man was but a short distance away, he exclaimed, "Now, there's the prettiest flower in the garden!"

"Walter!" she cried out in a youthful, unfaltering voice. She ran to him and wrapped her arms around him, hugging and kissing him.

He embraced her, enveloping her in his arms, and then held her away from him. "Hold on Bet," he chuckled. "Hold on and let me see you." As he gazed at her angelic face, he whispered, "Truly, sweetie, you are such a lovely flower."

"Oh, Walter," she moaned, seeing that he was but a young man, "you don't want to ogle an old gal like me."

"You're not old Bet," he informed, walking her over to the fountain and its reflecting pool of water, "you're young, just like on our wedding day."

She stared at her youthful reflection and smiled. Walter smiled too. They turned and faced each other, both still grinning when he witnessed her face turn somber.

"What's wrong Bet?" he entreated with tenderness.

"Well, I've been feeling peculiar all day—thinking about you and missing you horribly. This morning as I gazed out the kitchen window at the sunrise—I cried. I sensed your presence, but because we weren't together, I felt lonelier than ever. My longing for you seemed greater than my joy for life. I'm happy now that we're together—but I'm afraid. Walter, are you going away again?"

"No, darling," he said cheerfully, "I've come to take you with me."

"Oh, that's wonderful!" she burst out, then asked solemnly, "But—what about my garden?"

In the faint light of twilight, Walter gazed all around him in awe. "Well, Bet, your garden is a mighty fine garden—the finest. Indeed, it is a piece of Heaven, but it's only a very, small piece. I can't wait to show you the rest of it." He reached out and stretched his arm around her shoulders, hugging her in tight, and said, "Honey, come with me."

She wrapped her arms around his waist, leaned her head on his shoulder, and together, they strolled down the cobblestone walk, stepped off onto the grass, and vanished behind a majestic weeping willow tree.

Betsy's Garden

SOMETHING TO THINK ABOUT

1. Many people believe that loved ones who have passed over can come back to get those who are ready to die.
If you have ever had a near death experience, explain what happened.

2. Explain the significance of Betty's garden to story development. Explain the importance of the garden as the setting for the story.

Mirror Me-Man

Steve Hagy

My life was fairly routine, until three weeks ago, on a Saturday morning, around nine-o-clock. For breakfast, I wolfed down a crispy waffle sopped with maple syrup and gulped down a cup of coffee. My breakfast, however, had nothing to do with my undoing. You see, I am who I am but I am *not* who I am. I do my best *here* as I am certain I do my best *there*, even though, I know—no, *we* know—I am not one but two.

Before you think I'm crazy, hear me out. My name is Adam Twain. I'm thirty-two years old and I don't smoke, do drugs, or booze it up. Okay, once in awhile, I booze it up. I'm five-foot-nine, have brown hair and blue eyes, and I'm fairly in shape. I've been married to my sexy wife, Melanie for ten years whose thrilling hobby is piecing together picture puzzles. I play first base on a city-league softball team and watch a lot of baseball on TV. We have two kids, six-year-old Brandon and four-year-old Brittany who are exceptionally bright except at bedtime when they act like escaped monkeys from the zoo. We live in a small home in Paso Robles, California, we have a terrier named Barky that our neighbors hate, and for my job as a civil engineer, I draw plans for converting stop signs to traffic signals at busy intersections. Believe me, I'm a normal guy. Let me tell you what happened.

On that particular Saturday, while my wife cleaned the kitchen and the kids watched cartoons, I stood in my boxers at my bathroom sink and brushed my teeth. My reflection in the mirror looked rabid with toothpaste foaming out of my mouth. But, I wasn't rabid—remember, I'm not crazy. The bathroom, an extension of our master bedroom, had an enclosed tub and shower, a walk-in closet with a full length mirror hanging on the outside of its door, and a little private cubicle with a toilet and copies of Reader's Digest and Sports Illustrated. Sunlight filtered in between the blinds of a small window. I spit out the toothpaste and rinsed out my mouth, soaked my morning stubble with a hot, wet, wash cloth, slathered on shaving lotion and shaved, grabbed a hand towel hanging next to me, dried my face and hands, and hung the towel back on the rack. I then combed my hair, set the comb down, glanced in the mirror, and turned to leave, but stopped, spun back around, and again faced the mirror. Something had caught my attention. On my forehead, above my right eye, there appeared to be a pea-sized black dot. I leaned over the sink and scrutinized this new addition to my face. My reflection scrutinized me back. I tried to wash off the dot with the washcloth, but the dot remained. I examined it closer and determined the small alien blemish to be a mole. It looked harmless: round and black, not irregular or discolored. I raised up my hand and rubbed the mole with my index finger—but felt no bump. Odd. I looked again; felt again. My finger felt nothing. Bizarre. How could this be? A normal-not-crazy guy like me wakes up one morning with an invading mole that is seen but not felt. I quickly dressed in my weekend, yardworking clothes: a T-shirt, shorts, and grass-stained tennis shoes. I then hustled out of the bathroom, through the master bedroom, past my kids watching TV in the family room, and into the kitchen to see Melanie.

"Sweetie," I said, "will you look at something here on my forehead?"

She leaned over, loaded a dish in the dishwasher, stood up, and replied, "Sure. What is it?"

"Right here," I said, pointing at the spot where I'd seen the mole, "do you see a black mole?"

She stood on her tiptoes, examined my forehead, and muttered, "No hun, I don't see a mole."

"Are you sure?" I asked, pointing again, "Right here?"

She examined my forehead again and stated, "I'm sure of it. There's nothing there. No mole, sweetie."

"Okay. I thought I saw something. Thank you."

I gave her a kiss on her forehead. She grabbed up the waffle iron to clean as I strolled out of the kitchen, past the kids, through the bedroom, and back into the bathroom. I stood in front of the full-length, closet-door mirror and stared at myself. What the hell? There it was—the mole. I drew in close. With my face clenched in concentration, I studied the mole. Again, I felt for a bump. Again, it felt smooth. Engrossed by it, I took a step back, crossed my arms, and pondered it. Surely, my wife could not have *not* seen it. Was the mole there or not?

Since I had a yard to mow and because the summer heat would soon be overbearing, I shrugged my shoulders and turned to leave. As I moved, my mirror image moved, move for move with me, as one would expect of a mirror image, but then, out of the corner of my eye, I noticed as I took a step away from the mirror, my mirror image did *not* move, move for move with me, but moved, move for move a split second behind me. No way. My mind reeled. How, with a reflection, could there be a lapse in synchronization? Inconceivable. I tensed. I breathed hard. I leapt back in front of the mirror. Now, my reflection mirrored me, move for move again. Uniformity returned, but I stared myself down. The seconds ticked by . . . 15 . . . 30 . . . 45 and then, the unbelievable occurred. I—no—not I—but my mirror image sniffed. Not a long, glottal, phlegm-coagulating snort; not a wet sniffle or a lengthy whiff. Just a sniff. Only the mirror me-man with the creepy mole sniffed; sniffed alone on his own. Not just scary, but scary as Hell. I sprung back, startled, never taking my eyes off me. My reflection did as I did as I did it. Our eyes narrowed. Our brows creased. We brooded. How could a reflection do something independent of that which it reflects? Impossible. Cautiously, I stepped up to the mirror; my face so close, my breath condensed on the glass. I glared never blinking. My image glared back never blinking.

"Come on, you me-bastard," I demanded, "do something different!"

As I spoke, he demanded word for word from me.

I waited. The mirror me-man with the mole waited. He was probably wondering who I was: the me-bastard that didn't sniff; the me-he without a mole on his forehead; the me-bro staring him down, challenging him to do something different.

Suddenly, I felt an inexplicable tug toward the mirror. I tried to resist it as my reflection did the same. The tow increased. We both placed our hands on the glass and tried to push away. With all of our combined strength, we could not escape the pull. My face slammed into my reflection's face as both of our bodies hurled up against the glass. Panic gripped us; our eyes darted; our teeth clenched; our faces contorted in horror. The suction grew stronger and just as I thought the mirror would crack, I heard the deafening discord of a congested intersection. Horns blared, motors revved, and brakes squealed mixed with crashing metal, breaking glass, and wailing sirens combined with angry shouts and horrific screams. Blinding red, amber, and green lights of countless traffic signals repeatedly flashed. One of my arms, one of my legs, and half my torso burst through the glass, however, to my astonishment, the mirror didn't break. Then, half my face plunged through with one eye, one nostril, and one ear on one side of the mirror while the other half of my matching set remained on the other side. I quite literally straddled the mirror fifty-fifty. With one eye, I saw on my side of the mirror, my bathroom with vanity, window, tub, and shower. Out of my other eye, I expected to see our shoes, clothes, and storage boxes in the closet, but I saw my bathroom with vanity, window, tub, and shower—but opposite—a mirror image. My skin crawled. My innards twisted. My underwear felt tight. I was not alone. There was I—and there was me, the other I. We were like two drops of water now forming one. Two replicate beings with two feelings, two beating hearts, and two souls with two inner voices having the same reasoning, formulating identical conclusions, and reacting exactly alike, but now, doing so, not in hidden reflective worlds, but at the same time and in the same space, straddling our closet mirror at my house, which also, was my reflection's diametrical house. Two alike people with only one miniscule difference: a mole.

Simultaneously, it became clear to the both of us that we stood at an intersection of two worlds; parallel worlds, like two trains running on the same schedule toward the same destination running side by side on separate tracks. Both worlds usually hidden from the other and separated by a gap; a ribbon of independence; a hint of individuality; a buffer zone that absorbed any and all autonomous quirks and instantaneously converted them back into a perfect reflection. My reflection was not only a reflection of me, but also, I was a reflection of my reflection, who was unequivocally another me and incontestably equal in all aspects. When our side by side worlds drew too close, our mutual awareness of each other caused the gap to narrow dangerously to the point that the two worlds not only touched, like in cases of déjà vu, but the worlds actually crossed and at this crisscross, they mysteriously merged like two trains choo-chooing at the same time on the same track. So there we stood, at the intersection of our worlds, both my reflection and me straddling our closet mirror.

The tug spiked tremendously and propelled me forward casting me out the other side of the mirror. My reflection shot out the opposite side of the mirror as both of us landed onto the bathroom floor. The noise and the flashing lights abruptly stopped. We laid there stunned for a few seconds and then both of us jumped to our feet and scanned the room. We saw the vanity, window, tub and shower, but to our mutual horror, I was on my reflection's side of the mirror and my reflection was on my side. Everything was situated opposite of what we knew in our daily lives. All that had been on my right was now on my left. As for my mirror image, all that had been on his left was now on his right. We both panicked and with the same idea of crossing back over to our respective worlds, we slammed ourselves up against the mirror and mashed ours faces against the glass, trying desperately to squish ourselves back through to our former realm. Nothing happened except an oily face smudge on the mirror. We took a step back, exhaled slowly, gave each other a reassuring look, and with greater force, slammed our bodies into the mirror again. Unfortunately, our worlds had disconnected and the gap between them had widened back to the ribbon of parallelism they had always been, sadly, sealing our fates. Furthermore, our combined impact shattered the mirror sending reflective pieces of our cherished domains crashing to the floor into a jagged mosaic of us looking forlorn. We panicked. He ran one way and I ran the other way. I turned left instead of right out of the bathroom, sped the opposite way through the bedroom, zoomed past my kids and the TV facing the wrong way, and burst into the backward kitchen.

"Melanie! Melanie!" I yelled.

My wife, wiping off the counter top, jumped and exclaimed, "Oh my, Adam, you startled me. What is it? What's the matter?"

Instead of rattling on about my reflection, the me-man with the mole, and the intersection of two parallel worlds, I simply blurted out, "I accidentally broke the closet mirror."

"Are you okay?" she asked with concern and compassion.

"I think so," I said, still trying to calm down and catch my breath.

"Well, come closer. Let me look at you and make sure you're not hurt."

I stepped up to her as she stood on her tiptoes and scrutinized my face.

"Hmmm. That's odd," she said.

"What's odd?" I asked.

"Your forehead."

"What about it?"

Speechless with her hand over her mouth, she shuffled back a step, glared at me with suspicion, and uttered, "You seem strangely different. Besides, you've always had a mole on your forehead, but now—it's gone."

So, you see, I am who I am but I am *not* who I am. I do my best *here* as I am certain I do my best *there*, even though, I know—no, *we* know—I am not one but two.

Mirror Me-Man

SOMETHING TO THINK ABOUT

Have you ever been told that you have a double who looks just like you that someone as seen?
Many famous people have encountered their own doubles or ghosts. Abraham Lincoln saw his own ghost and so did Mary Shelley's husband, Percy Shelley.
Describe an experience that you had with your double (doppelganger).
Explain whether you agree or disagree with some scientists who believe in parallel worlds

The Necklace

Guy De Maupassant
1850–1893

The girl was one of those pretty and charming young creatures who sometimes are born, as if by a slip of fate, into a family of clerks. She had no dowry, no expectations, no way of being known, understood, loved, married by any rich and distinguished man; so she let herself be married to a little clerk of the Ministry of Public Instruction.

She dressed plainly because she could not dress well, but she was unhappy as if she had really fallen from a higher station; since with women there is neither caste nor rank, for beauty, grace and charm take the place of family and birth. Natural ingenuity, instinct for what is elegant, a supple mind are their sole hierarchy, and often make of women of the people the equals of the very greatest ladies.

Mathilde suffered ceaselessly, feeling herself born to enjoy all delicacies and all luxuries. She was distressed at the poverty of her dwelling, at the bareness of the walls, at the shabby chairs, the ugliness of the curtains. All those things, of which another woman of her rank would never even have been conscious, tortured her and made her angry. The sight of the little Breton peasant who did her humble housework aroused in her despairing regrets and bewildering dreams. She thought of silent antechambers hung with Oriental tapestry, illumined by tall bronze candelabra, and of two great footmen in knee breeches who sleep in the big armchairs, made drowsy by the oppressive heat of the stove. She thought of long reception halls hung with ancient silk, of the dainty cabinets containing priceless curiosities and of the little coquettish perfumed reception rooms made for chatting at five o'clock with intimate friends, with men famous and sought after, whom all women envy and whose attention they all desire.

When she sat down to dinner, before the round table covered with a tablecloth in use three days, opposite her husband, who uncovered the soup tureen and declared with a delighted air, "Ah, the good soup! I don't know anything better than that," she thought of dainty dinners, of shining silverware, of tapestry that peopled the walls with ancient personages and with strange birds flying in the midst of a fairy forest; and she thought of delicious dishes served on marvellous plates and of the whispered gallantries to which you listen with a sphinx-like smile while you are eating the pink meat of a trout or the wings of a quail.

She had no gowns, no jewels, nothing. And she loved nothing but that. She felt made for that. She would have liked so much to please, to be envied, to be charming, to be sought after.

She had a friend, a former schoolmate at the convent, who was rich, and whom she did not like to go to see any more because she felt so sad when she came home.

But one evening her husband reached home with a triumphant air and holding a large envelope in his hand.

"There," said he, "there is something for you."

She tore the paper quickly and drew out a printed card which bore these words:

The Minister of Public Instruction and Madame Georges Ramponneau request the honor of M. and Madame Loisel's company at the palace of the Ministry on Monday evening, January 18th.

Instead of being delighted, as her husband had hoped, she threw the invitation on the table crossly, muttering:

"What do you wish me to do with that?"

"Why, my dear, I thought you would be glad. You never go out, and this is such a fine opportunity. I had great trouble to get it. Every one wants to go; it is very select, and they are not giving many invitations to clerks. The whole official world will be there."

She looked at him with an irritated glance and said impatiently:

"And what do you wish me to put on my back?"

He had not thought of that. He stammered:

"Why, the gown you go to the theatre in. It looks very well to me."

He stopped, distracted, seeing that his wife was weeping. Two great tears ran slowly from the corners of her eyes toward the corners of her mouth.

"What's the matter? What's the matter?" he answered.

By a violent effort she conquered her grief and replied in a calm voice, while she wiped her wet cheeks:

"Nothing. Only I have no gown, and, therefore, I can't go to this ball. Give your card to some colleague whose wife is better equipped than I am."

He was in despair. He resumed:

"Come, let us see, Mathilde. How much would it cost, a suitable gown, which you could use on other occasions—something very simple?"

She reflected several seconds, making her calculations and wondering also what sum she could ask without drawing on herself an immediate refusal and a frightened exclamation from the economical clerk.

Finally she replied hesitating:

"I don't know exactly, but I think I could manage it with four hundred francs."

He grew a little pale, because he was laying aside just that amount to buy a gun and treat himself to a little shooting next summer on the plain of Nanterre, with several friends who went to shoot larks there of a Sunday.

But he said:

"Very well. I will give you four hundred francs. And try to have a pretty gown."

The day of the ball drew near and Madame Loisel seemed sad, uneasy, anxious. Her frock was ready, however. Her husband said to her one evening:

"What is the matter? Come, you have seemed very queer these last three days."

And she answered:

"It annoys me not to have a single piece of jewelry, not a single ornament, nothing to put on. I shall look poverty-stricken. I would almost rather not go at all."

"You might wear natural flowers," said her husband. "They're very stylish at this time of year. For ten francs you can get two or three magnificent roses."

She was not convinced.

"No; there's nothing more humiliating than to look poor among other women who are rich."

"How stupid you are!" her husband cried. "Go look up your friend, Madame Forestier, and ask her to lend you some jewels. You're intimate enough with her to do that."

She uttered a cry of joy:

"True! I never thought of it."

The next day she went to her friend and told her of her distress.

Madame Forestier went to a wardrobe with a mirror, took out a large jewel box, brought it back, opened it and said to Madame Loisel:

"Choose, my dear."

She saw first some bracelets, then a pearl necklace, then a Venetian gold cross set with precious stones, of admirable workmanship. She tried on the ornaments before the mirror, hesitated and could not make up her mind to part with them, to give them back. She kept asking:

"Haven't you any more?"

"Why, yes. Look further; I don't know what you like."

Suddenly she discovered, in a black satin box, a superb diamond necklace, and her heart throbbed with an immoderate desire. Her hands trembled as she took it. She fastened it round her throat, outside her high-necked waist, and was lost in ecstasy at her reflection in the mirror.

Then she asked, hesitating, filled with anxious doubt:

"Will you lend me this, only this?"

"Why, yes, certainly."

She threw her arms round her friend's neck, kissed her passionately, then fled with her treasure.

The night of the ball arrived. Madame Loisel was a great success. She was prettier than any other woman present, elegant, graceful, smiling and wild with joy. All the men looked at her, asked her name, sought to be introduced. All the attaches of the Cabinet wished to waltz with her. She was remarked by the minister himself.

She danced with rapture, with passion, intoxicated by pleasure, forgetting all in the triumph of her beauty, in the glory of her success, in a sort of cloud of happiness comprised of all this homage, admiration, these awakened desires and of that sense of triumph which is so sweet to woman's heart.

She left the ball about four o'clock in the morning. Her husband had been sleeping since midnight in a little deserted anteroom with three other gentlemen whose wives were enjoying the ball.

He threw over her shoulders the wraps he had brought, the modest wraps of common life, the poverty of which contrasted with the elegance of the ball dress. She felt this and wished to escape so as not to be remarked by the other women, who were enveloping themselves in costly furs.

Loisel held her back, saying: "Wait a bit. You will catch cold outside. I will call a cab."

But she did not listen to him and rapidly descended the stairs. When they reached the street they could not find a carriage and began to look for one, shouting after the cabmen passing at a distance.

They went toward the Seine in despair, shivering with cold. At last they found on the quay one of those ancient night cabs which, as though they were ashamed to show their shabbiness during the day, are never seen round Paris until after dark.

It took them to their dwelling in the Rue des Martyrs, and sadly they mounted the stairs to their flat. All was ended for her. As to him, he reflected that he must be at the ministry at ten o'clock that morning.

She removed her wraps before the glass so as to see herself once more in all her glory. But suddenly she uttered a cry. She no longer had the necklace around her neck!

"What is the matter with you?" demanded her husband, already half undressed.

She turned distractedly toward him.

"I have—I have—I've lost Madame Forestier's necklace," she cried.

He stood up, bewildered.

"What!—how? Impossible!"

They looked among the folds of her skirt, of her cloak, in her pockets, everywhere, but did not find it.

"You're sure you had it on when you left the ball?" he asked.

"Yes, I felt it in the vestibule of the minister's house."

"But if you had lost it in the street we should have heard it fall. It must be in the cab."

"Yes, probably. Did you take his number?"

"No. And you—didn't you notice it?"

"No."

They looked, thunderstruck, at each other. At last Loisel put on his clothes.

"I shall go back on foot," said he, "over the whole route, to see whether I can find it."

He went out. She sat waiting on a chair in her ball dress, without strength to go to bed, overwhelmed, without any fire, without a thought.

Her husband returned about seven o'clock. He had found nothing.

He went to police headquarters, to the newspaper offices to offer a reward; he went to the cab companies—everywhere, in fact, whither he was urged by the least spark of hope.

She waited all day, in the same condition of mad fear before this terrible calamity.

Loisel returned at night with a hollow, pale face. He had discovered nothing.

"You must write to your friend," said he, "that you have broken the clasp of her necklace and that you are having it mended. That will give us time to turn round."

She wrote at his dictation.

At the end of a week they had lost all hope. Loisel, who had aged five years, declared:

"We must consider how to replace that ornament."

The next day they took the box that had contained it and went to the jeweler whose name was found within. He consulted his books.

"It was not I, madame, who sold that necklace; I must simply have furnished the case."

Then they went from jeweler to jeweler, searching for a necklace like the other, trying to recall it, both sick with chagrin and grief.

They found, in a shop at the Palais Royal, a string of diamonds that seemed to them exactly like the one they had lost. It was worth forty thousand francs. They could have it for thirty-six.

So they begged the jeweler not to sell it for three days yet. And they made a bargain that he should buy it back for thirty-four thousand francs, in case they should find the lost necklace before the end of February.

Loisel possessed eighteen thousand francs which his father had left him. He would borrow the rest.

He did borrow, asking a thousand francs of one, five hundred of another, five louis here, three louis there. He gave notes, took up ruinous obligations, dealt with usurers and all the race of lenders. He compromised all the rest of his life, risked signing a note without even knowing whether he could meet it; and, frightened by the trouble yet to come, by the black misery that was about to fall upon him, by the prospect of all the physical privations and moral tortures that he was to suffer, he went to get the new necklace, laying upon the jeweler's counter thirty-six thousand francs.

When Madame Loisel took back the necklace Madame Forestier said to her with a chilly manner:

"You should have returned it sooner; I might have needed it."

She did not open the case, as her friend had so much feared. If she had detected the substitution, what would she have thought, what would she have said? Would she not have taken Madame Loisel for a thief?

Thereafter Madame Loisel knew the horrible existence of the needy. She bore her part, however, with sudden heroism. That dreadful debt must be paid. She would pay it. They dismissed their servant; they changed their lodgings; they rented a garret under the roof.

She came to know what heavy housework meant and the odious cares of the kitchen. She washed the dishes, using her dainty fingers and rosy nails on greasy pots and pans. She washed the soiled linen, the shirts and the dishcloths, which she dried upon a line; she carried the slops down to the street every morning and carried up the water, stopping for breath at every landing. And dressed like a woman of the people, she went to the fruiterer, the grocer, the butcher, a basket on her arm, bargaining, meeting with impertinence, defending her miserable money, sou by sou.

Every month they had to meet some notes, renew others, obtain more time.

Her husband worked evenings, making up a tradesman's accounts, and late at night he often copied manuscript for five sous a page.

This life lasted ten years.

At the end of ten years they had paid everything, everything, with the rates of usury and the accumulations of the compound interest.

Madame Loisel looked old now. She had become the woman of impoverished households—strong and hard and rough. With frowsy hair, skirts askew and red hands, she talked loud while washing the floor with great swishes of water. But sometimes, when her husband was at the office, she sat down near the window and she thought of that gay evening of long ago, of that ball where she had been so beautiful and so admired.

What would have happened if she had not lost that necklace? Who knows? who knows? How strange and changeful is life! How small a thing is needed to make or ruin us!

But one Sunday, having gone to take a walk in the Champs Elysees to refresh herself after the labors of the week, she suddenly perceived a woman who was leading a child. It was Madame Forestier, still young, still beautiful, still charming.

Madame Loisel felt moved. Should she speak to her? Yes, certainly. And now that she had paid, she would tell her all about it. Why not?

She went up.

"Good-day, Jeanne."

The other, astonished to be familiarly addressed by this plain good-wife, did not recognize her at all and stammered:

"But—madame!—I do not know—You must have mistaken."

"No. I am Mathilde Loisel."

Her friend uttered a cry.

"Oh, my poor Mathilde! How you are changed!"

"Yes, I have had a pretty hard life, since I last saw you, and great poverty—and that because of you!"

"Of me! How so?"

"Do you remember that diamond necklace you lent me to wear at the ministerial ball?"

"Yes. Well?"

"Well, I lost it."

"What do you mean? You brought it back."

"I brought you back another exactly like it. And it has taken us ten years to pay for it. You can understand that it was not easy for us, for us who had nothing. At last it is ended, and I am very glad."

Madame Forestier had stopped.

"You say that you bought a necklace of diamonds to replace mine?"

"Yes. You never noticed it, then! They were very similar."

And she smiled with a joy that was at once proud and ingenuous.

Madame Forestier, deeply moved, took her hands.

"Oh, my poor Mathilde! Why, my necklace was paste! It was worth at most only five hundred francs!"

Rappaccini's Daughter

Nathaniel Hawthorne
1804–1864

A young man, named Giovanni Guasconti, came, very long ago, from the more southern region of Italy, to pursue his studies at the University of Padua. Giovanni, who had but a scanty supply of gold ducats in his pocket, took lodgings in a high and gloomy chamber of an old edifice which looked not unworthy to have been the palace of a Paduan noble, and which, in fact, exhibited over its entrance the armorial bearings of a family long since extinct. The young stranger, who was not unstudied in the great poem of his country, recollected that one of the ancestors of this family, and perhaps an occupant of this very mansion, had been pictured by Dante as a partaker of the immortal agonies of his Inferno. These reminiscences and associations, together with the tendency to heartbreak natural to a young man for the first time out of his native sphere, caused Giovanni to sigh heavily as he looked around the desolate and ill-furnished apartment.

"Holy Virgin, signor!" cried old Dame Lisabetta, who, won by the youth's remarkable beauty of person, was kindly endeavoring to give the chamber a habitable air, "what a sigh was that to come out of a young man's heart! Do you find this old mansion gloomy? For the love of Heaven, then, put your head out of the window, and you will see as bright sunshine as you have left in Naples."

Guasconti mechanically did as the old woman advised, but could not quite agree with her that the Paduan sunshine was as cheerful as that of southern Italy. Such as it was, however, it fell upon a garden beneath the window and expended its fostering influences on a variety of plants, which seemed to have been cultivated with exceeding care.

"Does this garden belong to the house?" asked Giovanni.

"Heaven forbid, signor, unless it were fruitful of better pot herbs than any that grow there now," answered old Lisabetta. "No; that garden is cultivated by the own hands of Signor Giacomo Rappaccini, the famous doctor, who, I warrant him, has been heard of as far as Naples. It is said that he distils these plants into medicines that are as potent as a charm. Oftentimes you may see the signor doctor at work, and perchance the signora, his daughter, too, gathering the strange flowers that grow in the garden."

The old woman had now done what she could for the aspect of the chamber; and, commending the young man to the protection of the saints, took her departure.

Giovanni still found no better occupation than to look down into the garden beneath his window. From its appearance, he judged it to be one of those botanic gardens which were of earlier date in Padua than elsewhere in Italy or in the world. Or, not improbably, it might once have been the pleasure-place of an opulent family; for there was the ruin of a marble fountain in the centre, sculptured with rare art, but so wofully shattered that it was impossible to trace the original design from the chaos of remaining fragments. The water, however, continued to gush and sparkle into the sunbeams as cheerfully as ever. A little gurgling sound ascended to the young man's window, and made him feel as if the fountain were an immortal spirit that sung its song unceasingly and without heeding the vicissitudes around it, while one century imbodied it in marble and another scattered the perishable garniture on the soil. All about the pool into which the water subsided grew various plants, that seemed to require a plentiful supply of moisture for the nourishment of gigantic leaves, and in some instances, flowers gorgeously magnificent. There was one shrub in particular, set in a marble vase in the midst of the pool, that bore a profusion of purple blossoms, each of which had the lustre and richness of a gem; and the whole together made a show so resplendent that it seemed enough to illuminate the garden, even had there been no sunshine. Every portion of the soil was peopled with plants and herbs, which, if less beautiful, still bore tokens of assiduous care, as if all had their individual virtues, known to the scientific mind that fostered them. Some were placed in urns, rich with old carving, and others in common garden pots; some crept serpent-like along the ground or climbed on high, using whatever means of ascent was offered them. One plant had wreathed itself round a statue of Vertumnus, which was thus quite veiled and shrouded in a drapery of hanging foliage, so happily arranged that it might have served a sculptor for a study.

While Giovanni stood at the window he heard a rustling behind a screen of leaves, and became aware that a person was at work in the garden. His figure soon emerged into view, and showed itself to be that of no common laborer, but a tall, emaciated, sallow, and sickly-looking man, dressed in a scholar's garb of black. He was beyond the middle term of life, with gray hair, a thin, gray beard, and a face singularly marked with intellect and cultivation, but which could never, even in his more youthful days, have expressed much warmth of heart.

Nothing could exceed the intentness with which this scientific gardener examined every shrub which grew in his path: it seemed as if he was looking into their inmost nature, making observations in regard to their creative essence, and discovering why one leaf grew in this shape and another in that, and wherefore such and such flowers differed among themselves in hue and perfume. Nevertheless, in spite of this deep intelligence on his part, there was no approach to intimacy between himself and these vegetable existences. On the contrary, he avoided their actual touch or the direct inhaling of their odors with a caution that impressed Giovanni most disagreeably; for the man's demeanor was that of one walking among malignant influences, such as savage beasts, or deadly snakes, or evil spirits, which, should he allow them one moment of license, would wreak upon him some terrible fatality. It was strangely frightful to the young man's imagination to see this air of insecurity in a person cultivating a garden, that most simple and innocent of human toils, and which had been alike the joy and labor of the unfallen parents of the race. Was this garden, then, the Eden of the present world? And this man, with such a perception of harm in what his own hands caused to grow,—was he the Adam?

The distrustful gardener, while plucking away the dead leaves or pruning the too luxuriant growth of the shrubs, defended his hands with a pair of thick gloves. Nor were these his only armor. When, in his walk through the garden, he came to the magnificent plant that hung its purple gems beside the marble fountain, he placed a kind of mask over his mouth and nostrils, as if all this beauty did but conceal a deadlier malice; but, finding his task still too dangerous, he drew back, removed the mask, and called loudly, but in the infirm voice of a person affected with inward disease, "Beatrice! Beatrice!"

"Here am I, my father. What would you?" cried a rich and youthful voice from the window of the opposite house—a voice as rich as a tropical sunset, and which made Giovanni, though he knew not why, think of deep hues of purple or crimson and of perfumes heavily delectable. "Are you in the garden?"

"Yes, Beatrice," answered the gardener, "and I need your help."

Soon there emerged from under a sculptured portal the figure of a young girl, arrayed with as much richness of taste as the most splendid of the flowers, beautiful as the day, and with a bloom so deep and vivid that one shade more would have been too much. She looked redundant with life, health, and energy; all of which attributes were bound down and compressed, as it were and girdled tensely, in their luxuriance, by her virgin zone. Yet Giovanni's fancy must have grown morbid while he looked down into the garden; for the impression which the fair stranger made upon him was as if here were another flower, the human sister of those vegetable ones, as beautiful as they, more beautiful than the richest of them, but still to be touched only with a glove, nor to be approached without a mask. As Beatrice came down the garden path, it was observable that she handled and inhaled the odor of several of the plants which her father had most sedulously avoided.

"Here, Beatrice," said the latter, "see how many needful offices require to be done to our chief treasure. Yet, shattered as I am, my life might pay the penalty of approaching it so closely as circumstances demand. Henceforth, I fear, this plant must be consigned to your sole charge."

"And gladly will I undertake it," cried again the rich tones of the young lady, as she bent towards the magnificent plant and opened her arms as if to embrace it. "Yes, my sister, my splendour, it shall be Beatrice's task to nurse and serve thee; and thou shalt reward her with thy kisses and perfumed breath, which to her is as the breath of life."

Then, with all the tenderness in her manner that was so strikingly expressed in her words, she busied herself with such attentions as the plant seemed to require; and Giovanni, at his lofty window, rubbed his eyes and almost doubted whether it were a girl tending her favorite flower, or one sister performing the duties of affection to another. The scene soon terminated. Whether Dr. Rappaccini had finished his labors in the garden, or that his watchful eye had caught the stranger's face, he now took his daughter's arm and retired. Night was already closing in; oppressive exhalations seemed to proceed from the plants and steal upward past the open window; and Giovanni, closing the lattice, went to his couch and dreamed of a rich flower and beautiful girl. Flower and maiden were different, and yet the same, and fraught with some strange peril in either shape.

But there is an influence in the light of morning that tends to rectify whatever errors of fancy, or even of judgment, we may have incurred during the sun's decline, or among the shadows of the night, or in the less wholesome glow of moonshine. Giovanni's first movement, on starting from sleep, was to throw open the window and gaze down into the garden which his dreams had made so fertile of mysteries. He was surprised and a little ashamed to find how real and matter-of-fact an affair it proved to be, in the first rays of the sun which gilded the dew-drops that hung upon leaf and blossom, and, while giving a brighter beauty to each rare flower, brought everything within the limits of ordinary experience. The young man rejoiced that, in the heart of the barren city, he had the privilege of overlooking this spot of lovely and luxuriant vegetation. It would serve, he said to himself, as a symbolic language to keep him in communion with Nature. Neither the sickly and thoughtworn Dr. Giacomo Rappaccini, it is true, nor his brilliant daughter, were now visible; so that Giovanni could not determine how much of the singularity which he attributed to both was due to their own qualities and how much to his wonder-working fancy; but he was inclined to take a most rational view of the whole matter.

In the course of the day he paid his respects to Signor Pietro Baglioni, professor of medicine in the university, a physician of eminent repute to whom Giovanni had brought a letter of introduction. The professor was an elderly personage, apparently of genial nature, and habits that might almost be called jovial. He kept the young man to dinner, and made himself very agreeable by the freedom and liveliness of his conversation, especially when warmed by a flask or two of Tuscan wine. Giovanni, conceiving that men of science, inhabitants of the same city, must needs be on familiar terms with one another, took an opportunity to mention the name of Dr. Rappaccini. But the professor did not respond with so much cordiality as he had anticipated.

"Ill would it become a teacher of the divine art of medicine," said Professor Pietro Baglioni, in answer to a question of Giovanni, "to withhold due and well-considered praise of a physician so eminently skilled as Rappaccini; but, on the other hand, I should answer it but scantily to my conscience were I to permit a worthy youth like yourself, Signor Giovanni, the son of an ancient friend, to imbibe erroneous ideas respecting a man who might hereafter chance to hold your life and death in his hands. The truth is, our worshipful Dr. Rappaccini has as much science as any member of the faculty—with perhaps one single exception—in Padua, or all Italy; but there are certain grave objections to his professional character."

"And what are they?" asked the young man.

"Has my friend Giovanni any disease of body or heart, that he is so inquisitive about physicians?" said the professor, with a smile. "But as for Rappaccini, it is said of him—and I, who know the man well, can answer for its truth—that he cares infinitely more for science than for mankind. His patients are interesting to him only as subjects for some new experiment. He would sacrifice human life, his own among the rest, or whatever else was dearest to him, for the sake of adding so much as a grain of mustard seed to the great heap of his accumulated knowledge."

"Methinks he is an awful man indeed," remarked Guasconti, mentally recalling the cold and purely intellectual aspect of Rappaccini. "And yet, worshipful professor, is it not a noble spirit? Are there many men capable of so spiritual a love of science?"

"God forbid," answered the professor, somewhat testily; "at least, unless they take sounder views of the healing art than those adopted by Rappaccini. It is his theory that all medicinal virtues are comprised within those substances which we term vegetable poisons. These he cultivates with his own hands, and is said even to have produced new varieties of poison, more horribly deleterious than Nature, without the assistance of this learned person, would ever have plagued the world withal. That the signor doctor does less mischief than might be expected with such dangerous substances is undeniable. Now and then, it must be owned, he has effected, or seemed to effect, a marvellous cure; but, to tell you my private mind, Signor Giovanni, he should receive little credit for such instances of success,—they being probably the work of chance,—but should be held strictly accountable for his failures, which may justly be considered his own work."

The youth might have taken Baglioni's opinions with many grains of allowance had he known that there was a professional warfare of long continuance between him and Dr. Rappaccini, in which the latter was generally thought to have gained the advantage. If the reader be inclined to judge for himself, we refer him to certain black-letter tracts on both sides, preserved in the medical department of the University of Padua.

"I know not, most learned professor," returned Giovanni, after musing on what had been said of Rappaccini's exclusive zeal for science,—"I know not how dearly this physician may love his art; but surely there is one object more dear to him. He has a daughter."

"Aha!" cried the professor, with a laugh. "So now our friend Giovanni's secret is out. You have heard of this daughter, whom all the young men in Padua are wild about, though not half a dozen have ever had the good hap to see her face. I know little of the Signora Beatrice save that Rappaccini is said to have instructed her deeply in his science, and that, young and beautiful as fame reports her, she is already qualified to fill a professor's chair. Perchance her father destines her for mine! Other absurd rumors there be, not worth talking about or listening to. So now, Signor Giovanni, drink off your glass of lachryma."

Guasconti returned to his lodgings somewhat heated with the wine he had quaffed, and which caused his brain to swim with strange fantasies in reference to Dr. Rappaccini and the beautiful Beatrice. On his way, happening to pass by a florist's, he bought a fresh bouquet of flowers.

Ascending to his chamber, he seated himself near the window, but within the shadow thrown by the depth of the wall, so that he could look down into the garden with little risk of being discovered. All beneath his eye was a solitude. The strange plants were basking in the sunshine, and now and then nodding gently to one another, as if in acknowledgment of sympathy and kindred. In the midst, by the shattered fountain, grew the magnificent shrub, with its purple gems clustering all over it; they glowed in the air, and gleamed back again out of the depths of the pool, which thus seemed to overflow with colored radiance from the rich reflection that was steeped in it. At first, as we have said, the garden was a solitude. Soon, however,—as Giovanni had half hoped, half feared, would be the case,—a figure appeared beneath the antique sculptured portal, and came down between the rows of plants, inhaling their various perfumes as if she were one of those beings of old classic fable that lived upon sweet odors. On again beholding Beatrice, the young man was even startled to perceive how much her beauty exceeded his recollection of it; so brilliant, so vivid, was its character, that she glowed amid the sunlight, and, as Giovanni whispered to himself, positively illuminated the more shadowy intervals of the garden path. Her face being now more revealed than on the former occasion, he was struck by its expression of simplicity and sweetness,—qualities that had not entered into his idea of her character, and which made him ask anew what manner of mortal she might be. Nor did he fail again to observe, or imagine, an analogy between the beautiful girl and the gorgeous shrub that hung its gemlike flowers over the fountain,—a resemblance which Beatrice seemed to have indulged a fantastic humor in heightening, both by the arrangement of her dress and the selection of its hues.

Approaching the shrub, she threw open her arms, as with a passionate ardor, and drew its branches into an intimate embrace—so intimate that her features were hidden in its leafy bosom and her glistening ringlets all intermingled with the flowers.

"Give me thy breath, my sister," exclaimed Beatrice; "for I am faint with common air. And give me this flower of thine, which I separate with gentlest fingers from the stem and place it close beside my heart."

With these words the beautiful daughter of Rappaccini plucked one of the richest blossoms of the shrub, and was about to fasten it in her bosom. But now, unless Giovanni's draughts of wine had bewildered his senses, a singular incident occurred. A small orange-colored reptile, of the lizard or chameleon species, chanced to be creeping along the path, just at the feet of Beatrice. It appeared to Giovanni,—but, at the distance from which he gazed, he could scarcely have seen anything so minute,—it appeared to him, however, that a drop or two of moisture from the broken stem of the flower descended upon the lizard's head. For an instant the reptile contorted itself violently, and then lay motionless in the sunshine. Beatrice observed this remarkable phenomenon and crossed herself, sadly, but without surprise; nor did she therefore hesitate to arrange the fatal flower in her bosom. There it blushed, and almost glimmered with the dazzling effect of a precious stone, adding to her dress and aspect the one appropriate charm which nothing else in the world could have supplied. But Giovanni, out of the shadow of his window, bent forward and shrank back, and murmured and trembled.

"Am I awake? Have I my senses?" said he to himself. "What is this being? Beautiful shall I call her, or inexpressibly terrible?"

Beatrice now strayed carelessly through the garden, approaching closer beneath Giovanni's window, so that he was compelled to thrust his head quite out of its concealment in order to gratify the intense and painful curiosity which she excited. At this moment there came a beautiful insect over the garden wall; it had, perhaps, wandered through the city, and found no flowers or verdure among those antique haunts of men until the heavy perfumes of Dr. Rappaccini's shrubs had lured it from afar. Without alighting on the flowers, this winged brightness seemed to be attracted by Beatrice, and lingered in the air and fluttered about her head. Now, here it could not be but that Giovanni Guasconti's eyes deceived him. Be that as it might, he fancied that, while Beatrice was gazing at the insect with childish delight, it grew faint and fell at her feet; its bright wings shivered; it was dead—from no cause that he could discern, unless it were the atmosphere of her breath. Again Beatrice crossed herself and sighed heavily as she bent over the dead insect.

An impulsive movement of Giovanni drew her eyes to the window. There she beheld the beautiful head of the young man—rather a Grecian than an Italian head, with fair, regular features, and a glistening of gold among his ringlets—gazing down upon her like a being that hovered in mid air. Scarcely knowing what he did, Giovanni threw down the bouquet which he had hitherto held in his hand.

"Signora," said he, "there are pure and healthful flowers. Wear them for the sake of Giovanni Guasconti."

"Thanks, signor," replied Beatrice, with her rich voice, that came forth as it were like a gush of music, and with a mirthful expression half childish and half woman-like. "I accept your gift, and would fain recompense it with this precious purple flower; but if I toss it into the air it will not reach you. So Signor Guasconti must even content himself with my thanks."

She lifted the bouquet from the ground, and then, as if inwardly ashamed at having stepped aside from her maidenly reserve to respond to a stranger's greeting, passed swiftly homeward through the garden. But few as the moments were, it seemed to Giovanni, when she was on the point of vanishing beneath the sculptured portal, that his beautiful bouquet was already beginning to wither in her grasp. It was an idle thought; there could be no possibility of distinguishing a faded flower from a fresh one at so great a distance.

For many days after this incident the young man avoided the window that looked into Dr. Rappaccini's garden, as if something ugly and monstrous would have blasted his eyesight had he been betrayed into a glance. He felt conscious of having put himself, to a certain extent, within the influence of an unintelligible power by the communication which he had opened with Beatrice. The wisest course would have been, if his heart were in any real danger, to quit his lodgings and Padua itself at once; the next wiser, to have accustomed himself, as far as possible, to the familiar and daylight view of Beatrice—thus bringing her rigidly and systematically within the limits of ordinary experience. Least of all, while avoiding her sight, ought Giovanni to have remained so near this extraordinary being that the proximity and possibility even of intercourse should give a kind of substance and reality to the wild vagaries which his imagination ran riot continually in producing. Guasconti had not a deep heart—or, at all events, its depths were not sounded now; but he had a quick fancy, and an ardent southern temperament, which rose every instant to a higher fever pitch. Whether or no Beatrice possessed those terrible attributes, that fatal breath, the affinity with those so beautiful and deadly flowers which were indicated by what Giovanni had witnessed, she had at least instilled a fierce and subtle poison into his system. It was not love, although her rich beauty was a madness to him; nor horror, even while he fancied her spirit to be imbued with the same baneful essence that seemed to pervade her physical frame; but a wild offspring of both love and horror that had each parent in it, and burned like one and shivered like the other. Giovanni knew not what to dread; still less did he know what to hope; yet hope and dread kept a continual warfare in his breast, alternately vanquishing one another and starting up afresh to renew the contest. Blessed are all simple emotions, be they dark or bright! It is the lurid intermixture of the two that produces the illuminating blaze of the infernal regions.

Sometimes he endeavored to assuage the fever of his spirit by a rapid walk through the streets of Padua or beyond its gates: his footsteps kept time with the throbbings of his brain, so that the walk was apt to accelerate itself to a race. One day he found himself arrested; his arm was seized by a portly personage, who had turned back on recognizing the young man and expended much breath in overtaking him.

"Signor Giovanni! Stay, my young friend!" cried he. "Have you forgotten me? That might well be the case if I were as much altered as yourself."

It was Baglioni, whom Giovanni had avoided ever since their first meeting, from a doubt that the professor's sagacity would look too deeply into his secrets. Endeavoring to recover himself, he stared forth wildly from his inner world into the outer one and spoke like a man in a dream.

"Yes; I am Giovanni Guasconti. You are Professor Pietro Baglioni. Now let me pass!"

"Not yet, not yet, Signor Giovanni Guasconti," said the professor, smiling, but at the same time scrutinizing the youth with an earnest glance. "What! did I grow up side by side with your father? and shall his son pass me like a stranger in these old streets of Padua? Stand still, Signor Giovanni; for we must have a word or two before we part."

"Speedily, then, most worshipful professor, speedily," said Giovanni, with feverish impatience. "Does not your worship see that I am in haste?"

Now, while he was speaking there came a man in black along the street, stooping and moving feebly like a person in inferior health. His face was all overspread with a most sickly and sallow hue, but yet so pervaded with an expression of piercing and active intellect that an observer might easily have overlooked the merely physical attributes and have seen only this wonderful energy. As he passed, this person exchanged a cold and distant salutation with Baglioni, but fixed his eyes upon Giovanni with an intentness that seemed to bring out whatever was within him worthy of notice. Nevertheless, there was a peculiar quietness in the look, as if taking merely a speculative, not a human interest, in the young man.

"It is Dr. Rappaccini!" whispered the professor when the stranger had passed. "Has he ever seen your face before?"

"Not that I know," answered Giovanni, starting at the name.

"He HAS seen you! he must have seen you!" said Baglioni, hastily. "For some purpose or other, this man of science is making a study of you. I know that look of his! It is the same that coldly illuminates his face as he bends over a bird, a mouse, or a butterfly, which, in pursuance of some experiment, he has killed by the perfume of a flower; a look as deep as Nature itself, but without Nature's warmth of love. Signor Giovanni, I will stake my life upon it, you are the subject of one of Rappaccini's experiments!"

"Will you make a fool of me?" cried Giovanni, passionately. "THAT, signor professor, were an untoward experiment."

"Patience! patience!" replied the imperturbable professor. "I tell thee, my poor Giovanni, that Rappaccini has a scientific interest in thee. Thou hast fallen into fearful hands! And the Signora Beatrice,—what part does she act in this mystery?"

But Guasconti, finding Baglioni's pertinacity intolerable, here broke away, and was gone before the professor could again seize his arm. He looked after the young man intently and shook his head.

"This must not be," said Baglioni to himself. "The youth is the son of my old friend, and shall not come to any harm from which the arcana of medical science can preserve him. Besides, it is too insufferable an impertinence in Rappaccini, thus to snatch the lad out of my own hands, as I may say, and make use of him for his infernal experiments. This daughter of his! It shall be looked to. Perchance, most learned Rappaccini, I may foil you where you little dream of it!"

Meanwhile Giovanni had pursued a circuitous route, and at length found himself at the door of his lodgings. As he crossed the threshold he was met by old Lisabetta, who smirked and smiled, and was evidently desirous to attract his attention; vainly, however, as the ebullition of his feelings had momentarily subsided into a cold and dull vacuity. He turned his eyes full upon the withered face that was puckering itself into a smile, but seemed to behold it not. The old dame, therefore, laid her grasp upon his cloak.

"Signor! signor!" whispered she, still with a smile over the whole breadth of her visage, so that it looked not unlike a grotesque carving in wood, darkened by centuries. "Listen, signor! There is a private entrance into the garden!"

"What do you say?" exclaimed Giovanni, turning quickly about, as if an inanimate thing should start into feverish life. "A private entrance into Dr. Rappaccini's garden?"

"Hush! hush! not so loud!" whispered Lisabetta, putting her hand over his mouth. "Yes; into the worshipful doctor's garden, where you may see all his fine shrubbery. Many a young man in Padua would give gold to be admitted among those flowers."

Giovanni put a piece of gold into her hand.

"Show me the way," said he.

A surmise, probably excited by his conversation with Baglioni, crossed his mind, that this interposition of old Lisabetta might perchance be connected with the intrigue, whatever were its nature, in which the professor seemed to suppose that Dr. Rappaccini was involving him. But such a suspicion, though it disturbed Giovanni, was inadequate to restrain him. The instant that he was aware of the possibility of approaching Beatrice, it seemed an absolute necessity of his existence to do so. It mattered not whether she were angel or demon; he was irrevocably within her sphere, and must obey the law that whirled him onward, in ever-lessening circles, towards a result which he did not attempt to foreshadow; and yet, strange to say, there came across him a sudden doubt whether this intense interest on his part were not delusory; whether it were really of so deep and positive a nature as to justify him in now thrusting himself into an incalculable position; whether it were not merely the fantasy of a young man's brain, only slightly or not at all connected with his heart.

He paused, hesitated, turned half about, but again went on. His withered guide led him along several obscure passages, and finally undid a door, through which, as it was opened, there came the sight and sound of rustling leaves, with the broken sunshine glimmering among them. Giovanni stepped forth, and, forcing himself through the entanglement of a shrub that wreathed its tendrils over the hidden entrance, stood beneath his own window in the open area of Dr. Rappaccini's garden.

How often is it the case that, when impossibilities have come to pass and dreams have condensed their misty substance into tangible realities, we find ourselves calm, and even coldly self-possessed, amid circumstances which it would have been a delirium of joy or agony to anticipate! Fate delights to thwart us thus. Passion will choose his own time to rush upon the scene, and lingers sluggishly behind when an appropriate adjustment of events would seem to summon his appearance. So was it now with Giovanni. Day after day his pulses had throbbed with feverish blood at the improbable idea of an interview with Beatrice, and of standing with her, face to face, in this very garden, basking in the Oriental sunshine of her beauty, and snatching from her full gaze the mystery which he deemed the riddle of his own existence. But now there was a singular and untimely equanimity within his breast. He threw a glance around the garden to discover if Beatrice or her father were present, and, perceiving that he was alone, began a critical observation of the plants.

The aspect of one and all of them dissatisfied him; their gorgeousness seemed fierce, passionate, and even unnatural. There was hardly an individual shrub which a wanderer, straying by himself through a forest, would not have been startled to find growing wild, as if an unearthly face had glared at him out of the thicket. Several also would have shocked a delicate instinct by an appearance of artificialness indicating that there had been such commixture, and, as it were, adultery, of various vegetable species, that the production was no longer of God's making, but the monstrous offspring of man's depraved fancy, glowing with only an evil mockery of beauty. They were probably the result of experiment, which in one or two cases had succeeded in mingling plants individually lovely into a compound possessing the questionable and ominous character that distinguished the whole growth of the garden. In fine, Giovanni recognized but two or three plants in the collection, and those of a kind that he well knew to be poisonous. While busy with these contemplations he heard the rustling of a silken garment, and, turning, beheld Beatrice emerging from beneath the sculptured portal.

Giovanni had not considered with himself what should be his deportment; whether he should apologize for his intrusion into the garden, or assume that he was there with the privity at least, if not by the desire, of Dr. Rappaccini or his daughter; but Beatrice's manner placed him at his ease, though leaving him still in doubt by what agency he had gained admittance. She came lightly along the path and met him near the broken fountain. There was surprise in her face, but brightened by a simple and kind expression of pleasure.

"You are a connoisseur in flowers, signor," said Beatrice, with a smile, alluding to the bouquet which he had flung her from the window. "It is no marvel, therefore, if the sight of my father's rare collection has tempted you to take a nearer view. If he were here, he could tell you many strange and interesting facts as to the nature and habits of these shrubs; for he has spent a lifetime in such studies, and this garden is his world."

"And yourself, lady," observed Giovanni, "if fame says true,—you likewise are deeply skilled in the virtues indicated by these rich blossoms and these spicy perfumes. Would you deign to be my instructress, I should prove an apter scholar than if taught by Signor Rappaccini himself."

"Are there such idle rumors?" asked Beatrice, with the music of a pleasant laugh. "Do people say that I am skilled in my father's science of plants? What a jest is there! No; though I have grown up among these flowers, I know no more of them than their hues and perfume; and sometimes methinks I would fain rid myself of even that small knowledge. There are many flowers here, and those not the least brilliant, that shock and offend me when they meet my eye. But pray, signor, do not believe these stories about my science. Believe nothing of me save what you see with your own eyes."

"And must I believe all that I have seen with my own eyes?" asked Giovanni, pointedly, while the recollection of former scenes made him shrink. "No, signora; you demand too little of me. Bid me believe nothing save what comes from your own lips."

It would appear that Beatrice understood him. There came a deep flush to her cheek; but she looked full into Giovanni's eyes, and responded to his gaze of uneasy suspicion with a queenlike haughtiness.

"I do so bid you, signor," she replied. "Forget whatever you may have fancied in regard to me. If true to the outward senses, still it may be false in its essence; but the words of Beatrice Rappaccini's lips are true from the depths of the heart outward. Those you may believe."

A fervor glowed in her whole aspect and beamed upon Giovanni's consciousness like the light of truth itself; but while she spoke there was a fragrance in the atmosphere around her, rich and delightful, though evanescent, yet which the young man, from an indefinable reluctance, scarcely dared to draw into his lungs. It might be the odor of the flowers. Could it be Beatrice's breath which thus embalmed her words with a strange richness, as if by steeping them in her heart? A faintness passed like a shadow over Giovanni and flitted away; he seemed to gaze through the beautiful girl's eyes into her transparent soul, and felt no more doubt or fear.

The tinge of passion that had colored Beatrice's manner vanished; she became gay, and appeared to derive a pure delight from her communion with the youth not unlike what the maiden of a lonely island might have felt conversing with a voyager from the civilized world. Evidently her experience of life had been confined within the limits of that garden. She talked now about matters as simple as the daylight or summer clouds, and now asked questions in reference to the city, or Giovanni's distant home, his friends, his mother, and his sisters—questions indicating such seclusion, and such lack of familiarity with modes and forms, that Giovanni responded as if to an infant. Her spirit gushed out before him like a fresh rill that was just catching its first glimpse of the sunlight and wondering at the reflections of earth and sky which were flung into its bosom. There came thoughts, too, from a deep source, and fantasies of a gemlike brilliancy, as if diamonds and rubies sparkled upward among the bubbles of the fountain. Ever and anon there gleamed across the young man's mind a sense of wonder that he should be walking side by side with the being who had so wrought upon his imagination, whom he had idealized in such hues of terror, in whom he had positively witnessed such manifestations of dreadful attributes,—that he should be conversing with Beatrice like a brother, and should find her so human and so maidenlike. But such reflections were only momentary; the effect of her character was too real not to make itself familiar at once.

In this free intercourse they had strayed through the garden, and now, after many turns among its avenues, were come to the shattered fountain, beside which grew the magnificent shrub, with its treasury of glowing blossoms. A fragrance was diffused from it which Giovanni recognized as identical with that which he had attributed to Beatrice's breath, but incomparably more powerful. As her eyes fell upon it, Giovanni beheld her press her hand to her bosom as if her heart were throbbing suddenly and painfully.

"For the first time in my life," murmured she, addressing the shrub, "I had forgotten thee."

"I remember, signora," said Giovanni, "that you once promised to reward me with one of these living gems for the bouquet which I had the happy boldness to fling to your feet. Permit me now to pluck it as a memorial of this interview."

He made a step towards the shrub with extended hand; but Beatrice darted forward, uttering a shriek that went through his heart like a dagger. She caught his hand and drew it back with the whole force of her slender figure. Giovanni felt her touch thrilling through his fibres.

"Touch it not!" exclaimed she, in a voice of agony. "Not for thy life! It is fatal!"

Then, hiding her face, she fled from him and vanished beneath the sculptured portal. As Giovanni followed her with his eyes, he beheld the emaciated figure and pale intelligence of Dr. Rappaccini, who had been watching the scene, he knew not how long, within the shadow of the entrance.

No sooner was Guasconti alone in his chamber than the image of Beatrice came back to his passionate musings, invested with all the witchery that had been gathering around it ever since his first glimpse of her, and now likewise imbued with a tender warmth of girlish womanhood. She was human; her nature was endowed with all gentle and feminine qualities; she was worthiest to be worshipped; she was capable, surely, on her part, of the height and heroism of love. Those tokens which he had hitherto considered as proofs of a frightful peculiarity in her physical and moral system were now either forgotten, or, by the subtle sophistry of passion transmitted into a golden crown of enchantment, rendering Beatrice the more admirable by so much as she was the more unique. Whatever had looked ugly was now beautiful; or, if incapable of such a change, it stole away and hid itself among those shapeless half ideas which throng the dim region beyond the daylight of our perfect consciousness. Thus did he spend the night, nor fell asleep until the dawn had begun to awake the slumbering flowers in Dr. Rappaccini's garden, whither Giovanni's dreams doubtless led him. Up rose the sun in his due season, and, flinging his beams upon the young man's eyelids, awoke him to a sense of pain. When thoroughly aroused, he became sensible of a burning and tingling agony in his hand—in his right hand—the very hand which Beatrice had grasped in her own when he was on the point of plucking one of the gemlike flowers. On the back of that hand there was now a purple print like that of four small fingers, and the likeness of a slender thumb upon his wrist.

Oh, how stubbornly does love,—or even that cunning semblance of love which flourishes in the imagination, but strikes no depth of root into the heart,—how stubbornly does it hold its faith until the moment comes when it is doomed to vanish into thin mist! Giovanni wrapped a handkerchief about his hand and wondered what evil thing had stung him, and soon forgot his pain in a reverie of Beatrice.

After the first interview, a second was in the inevitable course of what we call fate. A third; a fourth; and a meeting with Beatrice in the garden was no longer an incident in Giovanni's daily life, but the whole space in which he might be said to live; for the anticipation and memory of that ecstatic hour made up the remainder. Nor was it otherwise with the daughter of Rappaccini. She watched for the youth's appearance, and flew to his side with confidence as unreserved as if they had been playmates from early infancy—as if they were such playmates still. If, by any unwonted chance, he failed to come at the appointed moment, she stood beneath the window and sent up the rich sweetness of her tones to float around him in his chamber and echo and reverberate throughout his heart: "Giovanni! Giovanni! Why tarriest thou? Come down!" And down he hastened into that Eden of poisonous flowers.

But, with all this intimate familiarity, there was still a reserve in Beatrice's demeanor, so rigidly and invariably sustained that the idea of infringing it scarcely occurred to his imagination. By all appreciable signs, they loved; they had looked love with eyes that conveyed the holy secret from the depths of one soul into the depths of the other, as if it were too sacred to be whispered by the way; they had even spoken love in those gushes of passion when their spirits darted forth in articulated breath like tongues of long-hidden flame; and yet there had been no seal of lips, no clasp of hands, nor any slightest caress such as love claims and hallows. He had never touched one of the gleaming ringlets of her hair; her garment—so marked was the physical barrier between them—had never been waved against him by a breeze. On the few occasions when Giovanni had seemed tempted to overstep the limit, Beatrice grew so sad, so stern, and withal wore such a look of desolate separation, shuddering at itself, that not a spoken word was requisite to repel him. At such times he was startled at the horrible suspicions that rose, monster-like, out of the caverns of his heart and stared him in the face; his love grew thin and faint as the morning mist, his doubts alone had substance. But, when Beatrice's face brightened again after the momentary shadow, she was transformed at once from the mysterious, questionable being whom he had watched with so much awe and horror; she was now the beautiful and unsophisticated girl whom he felt that his spirit knew with a certainty beyond all other knowledge.

A considerable time had now passed since Giovanni's last meeting with Baglioni. One morning, however, he was disagreeably surprised by a visit from the professor, whom he had scarcely thought of for whole weeks, and would willingly have forgotten still longer. Given up as he had long been to a pervading excitement, he could tolerate no companions except upon condition of their perfect sympathy with his present state of feeling. Such sympathy was not to be expected from Professor Baglioni.

The visitor chatted carelessly for a few moments about the gossip of the city and the university, and then took up another topic.

"I have been reading an old classic author lately," said he, "and met with a story that strangely interested me. Possibly you may remember it. It is of an Indian prince, who sent a beautiful woman as a present to Alexander the Great. She was as lovely as the dawn and gorgeous as the sunset; but what especially distinguished her was a certain rich perfume in her breath—richer than a garden of Persian roses. Alexander, as was natural to a youthful conqueror, fell in love at first sight with this magnificent stranger; but a certain sage physician, happening to be present, discovered a terrible secret in regard to her."

"And what was that?" asked Giovanni, turning his eyes downward to avoid those of the professor.

"That this lovely woman," continued Baglioni, with emphasis, "had been nourished with poisons from her birth upward, until her whole nature was so imbued with them that she herself had become the deadliest poison in existence. Poison was her element of life. With that rich perfume of her breath she blasted the very air. Her love would have been poison—her embrace death. Is not this a marvellous tale?"

"A childish fable," answered Giovanni, nervously starting from his chair. "I marvel how your worship finds time to read such nonsense among your graver studies."

"By the by," said the professor, looking uneasily about him, "what singular fragrance is this in your apartment? Is it the perfume of your gloves? It is faint, but delicious; and yet, after all, by no means agreeable. Were I to breathe it long, methinks it would make me ill. It is like the breath of a flower; but I see no flowers in the chamber."

"Nor are there any," replied Giovanni, who had turned pale as the professor spoke; "nor, I think, is there any fragrance except in your worship's imagination. Odors, being a sort of element combined of the sensual and the spiritual, are apt to deceive us in this manner. The recollection of a perfume, the bare idea of it, may easily be mistaken for a present reality."

"Ay; but my sober imagination does not often play such tricks," said Baglioni; "and, were I to fancy any kind of odor, it would be that of some vile apothecary drug, wherewith my fingers are likely enough to be imbued. Our worshipful friend Rappaccini, as I have heard, tinctures his medicaments with odors richer than those of Araby. Doubtless, likewise, the fair and learned Signora Beatrice would minister to her patients with draughts as sweet as a maiden's breath; but woe to him that sips them!"

Giovanni's face evinced many contending emotions. The tone in which the professor alluded to the pure and lovely daughter of Rappaccini was a torture to his soul; and yet the intimation of a view of her character opposite to his own, gave instantaneous distinctness to a thousand dim suspicions, which now grinned at him like so many demons. But he strove hard to quell them and to respond to Baglioni with a true lover's perfect faith.

"Signor professor," said he, "you were my father's friend; perchance, too, it is your purpose to act a friendly part towards his son. I would fain feel nothing towards you save respect and deference; but I pray you to observe, signor, that there is one subject on which we must not speak. You know not the Signora Beatrice. You cannot, therefore, estimate the wrong—the blasphemy, I may even say—that is offered to her character by a light or injurious word."

"Giovanni! my poor Giovanni!" answered the professor, with a calm expression of pity, "I know this wretched girl far better than yourself. You shall hear the truth in respect to the poisoner Rappaccini and his poisonous daughter; yes, poisonous as she is beautiful. Listen; for, even should you do violence to my gray hairs, it shall not silence me. That old fable of the Indian woman has become a truth by the deep and deadly science of Rappaccini and in the person of the lovely Beatrice."

Giovanni groaned and hid his face

"Her father," continued Baglioni, "was not restrained by natural affection from offering up his child in this horrible manner as the victim of his insane zeal for science; for, let us do him justice, he is as true a man of science as ever distilled his own heart in an alembic. What, then, will be your fate? Beyond a doubt you are selected as the material of some new experiment. Perhaps the result is to be death; perhaps a fate more awful still. Rappaccini, with what he calls the interest of science before his eyes, will hesitate at nothing."

"It is a dream," muttered Giovanni to himself; "surely it is a dream."

"But," resumed the professor, "be of good cheer, son of my friend. It is not yet too late for the rescue. Possibly we may even succeed in bringing back this miserable child within the limits of ordinary nature, from which her father's madness has estranged her. Behold this little silver vase! It was wrought by the hands of the renowned Benvenuto Cellini, and is well worthy to be a love gift to the fairest dame in Italy. But its contents are invaluable. One little sip of this antidote would have rendered the most virulent poisons of the Borgias innocuous. Doubt not that it will be as efficacious against those of Rappaccini. Bestow the vase, and the precious liquid within it, on your Beatrice, and hopefully await the result."

Baglioni laid a small, exquisitely wrought silver vial on the table and withdrew, leaving what he had said to produce its effect upon the young man's mind.

"We will thwart Rappaccini yet," thought he, chuckling to himself, as he descended the stairs; "but, let us confess the truth of him, he is a wonderful man—a wonderful man indeed; a vile empiric, however, in his practice, and therefore not to be tolerated by those who respect the good old rules of the medical profession."

Throughout Giovanni's whole acquaintance with Beatrice, he had occasionally, as we have said, been haunted by dark surmises as to her character; yet so thoroughly had she made herself felt by him as a simple, natural, most affectionate, and guileless creature, that the image now held up by Professor Baglioni looked as strange and incredible as if it were not in accordance with his own original conception. True, there were ugly recollections connected with his first glimpses of the beautiful girl; he could not quite forget the bouquet that withered in her grasp, and the insect that perished amid the sunny air, by no ostensible agency save the fragrance of her breath. These incidents, however, dissolving in the pure light of her character, had no longer the efficacy of facts, but were acknowledged as mistaken fantasies, by whatever testimony of the senses they might appear to be substantiated. There is something truer and more real than what we can see with the eyes and touch with the finger. On such better evidence had Giovanni founded his confidence in Beatrice, though rather by the necessary force of her high attributes than by any deep and generous faith on his part. But now his spirit was incapable of sustaining itself at the height to which the early enthusiasm of passion had exalted it; he fell down, grovelling among earthly doubts, and defiled therewith the pure whiteness of Beatrice's image. Not that he gave her up; he did but distrust. He resolved to institute some decisive test that should satisfy him, once for all, whether there were those dreadful peculiarities in her physical nature which could not be supposed to exist without some corresponding monstrosity of soul. His eyes, gazing down afar, might have deceived him as to the lizard, the insect, and the flowers; but if he could witness, at the distance of a few paces, the sudden blight of one fresh and healthful flower in Beatrice's hand, there would be room for no further question. With this idea he hastened to the florist's and purchased a bouquet that was still gemmed with the morning dew-drops.

It was now the customary hour of his daily interview with Beatrice. Before descending into the garden, Giovanni failed not to look at his figure in the mirror,—a vanity to be expected in a beautiful young man, yet, as displaying itself at that troubled and feverish moment, the token of a certain shallowness of feeling and insincerity of character. He did gaze, however, and said to himself that his features had never before possessed so rich a grace, nor his eyes such vivacity, nor his cheeks so warm a hue of superabundant life.

"At least," thought he, "her poison has not yet insinuated itself into my system. I am no flower to perish in her grasp."

With that thought he turned his eyes on the bouquet, which he had never once laid aside from his hand. A thrill of indefinable horror shot through his frame on perceiving that those dewy flowers were already beginning to droop; they wore the aspect of things that had been fresh and lovely yesterday. Giovanni grew white as marble, and stood motionless before the mirror, staring at his own reflection there as at the likeness of something frightful. He remembered Baglioni's remark about the fragrance that seemed to pervade the chamber. It must have been the poison in his breath! Then he shuddered—shuddered at himself. Recovering from his stupor, he began to watch with curious eye a spider that was busily at work hanging its web from the antique cornice of the apartment, crossing and recrossing the artful system of interwoven lines—as vigorous and active a spider as ever dangled from an old ceiling. Giovanni bent towards the insect, and emitted a deep, long breath. The spider suddenly ceased its toil; the web vibrated with a tremor originating in the body of the small artisan. Again Giovanni sent forth a breath, deeper, longer, and imbued with a venomous feeling out of his heart: he knew not whether he were wicked, or only desperate. The spider made a convulsive gripe with his limbs and hung dead across the window.

"Accursed! accursed!" muttered Giovanni, addressing himself. "Hast thou grown so poisonous that this deadly insect perishes by thy breath?"

At that moment a rich, sweet voice came floating up from the garden.

"Giovanni! Giovanni! It is past the hour! Why tarriest thou? Come down!"

"Yes," muttered Giovanni again. "She is the only being whom my breath may not slay! Would that it might!"

He rushed down, and in an instant was standing before the bright and loving eyes of Beatrice. A moment ago his wrath and despair had been so fierce that he could have desired nothing so much as to wither her by a glance; but with her actual presence there came influences which had too real an existence to be at once shaken off: recollections of the delicate and benign power of her feminine nature, which had so often enveloped him in a religious calm; recollections of many a holy and passionate outgush of her heart, when the pure fountain had been unsealed from its depths and made visible in its transparency to his mental eye; recollections which, had Giovanni known how to estimate them, would have assured him that all this ugly mystery was but an earthly illusion, and that, whatever mist of evil might seem to have gathered over her, the real Beatrice was a heavenly angel. Incapable as he was of such high faith, still her presence had not utterly lost its magic. Giovanni's rage was quelled into an aspect of sullen insensibility. Beatrice, with a quick spiritual sense, immediately felt that there was a gulf of blackness between them which neither he nor she could pass. They walked on together, sad and silent, and came thus to the marble fountain and to its pool of water on the ground, in the midst of which grew the shrub that bore gem-like blossoms. Giovanni was affrighted at the eager enjoyment—the appetite, as it were—with which he found himself inhaling the fragrance of the flowers.

"Beatrice," asked he, abruptly, "whence came this shrub?"

"My father created it," answered she, with simplicity.

"Created it! created it!" repeated Giovanni. "What mean you, Beatrice?"

"He is a man fearfully acquainted with the secrets of Nature," replied Beatrice; "and, at the hour when I first drew breath, this plant sprang from the soil, the offspring of his science, of his intellect, while I was but his earthly child. Approach it not!" continued she, observing with terror that Giovanni was drawing nearer to the shrub. "It has qualities that you little dream of. But I, dearest Giovanni,—I grew up and blossomed with the plant and was nourished with its breath. It was my sister, and I loved it with a human affection; for, alas!—hast thou not suspected it?—there was an awful doom."

Here Giovanni frowned so darkly upon her that Beatrice paused and trembled. But her faith in his tenderness reassured her, and made her blush that she had doubted for an instant.

"There was an awful doom," she continued, "the effect of my father's fatal love of science, which estranged me from all society of my kind. Until Heaven sent thee, dearest Giovanni, oh, how lonely was thy poor Beatrice!"

"Was it a hard doom?" asked Giovanni, fixing his eyes upon her.

"Only of late have I known how hard it was," answered she, tenderly. "Oh, yes; but my heart was torpid, and therefore quiet."

Giovanni's rage broke forth from his sullen gloom like a lightning flash out of a dark cloud.

"Accursed one!" cried he, with venomous scorn and anger. "And, finding thy solitude wearisome, thou hast severed me likewise from all the warmth of life and enticed me into thy region of unspeakable horror!"

"Giovanni!" exclaimed Beatrice, turning her large bright eyes upon his face. The force of his words had not found its way into her mind; she was merely thunderstruck.

"Yes, poisonous thing!" repeated Giovanni, beside himself with passion. "Thou hast done it! Thou hast blasted me! Thou hast filled my veins with poison! Thou hast made me as hateful, as ugly, as loathsome and deadly a creature as thyself—a world's wonder of hideous monstrosity! Now, if our breath be happily as fatal to ourselves as to all others, let us join our lips in one kiss of unutterable hatred, and so die!"

"What has befallen me?" murmured Beatrice, with a low moan out of her heart. "Holy Virgin, pity me, a poor heart-broken child!"

"Thou,—dost thou pray?" cried Giovanni, still with the same fiendish scorn. "Thy very prayers, as they come from thy lips, taint the atmosphere with death. Yes, yes; let us pray! Let us to church and dip our fingers in the holy water at the portal! They that come after us will perish as by a pestilence! Let us sign crosses in the air! It will be scattering curses abroad in the likeness of holy symbols!"

"Giovanni," said Beatrice, calmly, for her grief was beyond passion, "why dost thou join thyself with me thus in those terrible words? I, it is true, am the horrible thing thou namest me. But thou,—what hast thou to do, save with one other shudder at my hideous misery to go forth out of the garden and mingle with thy race, and forget there ever crawled on earth such a monster as poor Beatrice?"

"Dost thou pretend ignorance?" asked Giovanni, scowling upon her. "Behold! this power have I gained from the pure daughter of Rappaccini."

There was a swarm of summer insects flitting through the air in search of the food promised by the flower odors of the fatal garden. They circled round Giovanni's head, and were evidently attracted towards him by the same influence which had drawn them for an instant within the sphere of several of the shrubs. He sent forth a breath among them, and smiled bitterly at Beatrice as at least a score of the insects fell dead upon the ground.

"I see it! I see it!" shrieked Beatrice. "It is my father's fatal science! No, no, Giovanni; it was not I! Never! never! I dreamed only to love thee and be with thee a little time, and so to let thee pass away, leaving but thine image in mine heart; for, Giovanni, believe it, though my body be nourished with poison, my spirit is God's creature, and craves love as its daily food. But my father,—he has united us in this fearful sympathy. Yes; spurn me, tread upon me, kill me! Oh, what is death after such words as thine? But it was not I. Not for a world of bliss would I have done it."

Giovanni's passion had exhausted itself in its outburst from his lips. There now came across him a sense, mournful, and not without tenderness, of the intimate and peculiar relationship between Beatrice and himself. They stood, as it were, in an utter solitude, which would be made none the less solitary by the densest throng of human life. Ought not, then, the desert of humanity around them to press this insulated pair closer together? If they should be cruel to one another, who was there to be kind to them? Besides, thought Giovanni, might there not still be a hope of his returning within the limits of ordinary nature, and leading Beatrice, the redeemed Beatrice, by the hand? O, weak, and selfish, and unworthy spirit, that could dream of an earthly union and earthly happiness as possible, after such deep love had been so bitterly wronged as was Beatrice's love by Giovanni's blighting words! No, no; there could be no such hope. She must pass heavily, with that broken heart, across the borders of Time—she must bathe her hurts in some fount of paradise, and forget her grief in the light of immortality, and THERE be well.

But Giovanni did not know it.

"Dear Beatrice," said he, approaching her, while she shrank away as always at his approach, but now with a different impulse, "dearest Beatrice, our fate is not yet so desperate. Behold! there is a medicine, potent, as a wise physician has assured me, and almost divine in its efficacy. It is composed of ingredients the most opposite to those by which thy awful father has brought this calamity upon thee and me. It is distilled of blessed herbs. Shall we not quaff it together, and thus be purified from evil?"

"Give it me!" said Beatrice, extending her hand to receive the little silver vial which Giovanni took from his bosom. She added, with a peculiar emphasis, "I will drink; but do thou await the result."

She put Baglioni's antidote to her lips; and, at the same moment, the figure of Rappaccini emerged from the portal and came slowly towards the marble fountain. As he drew near, the pale man of science seemed to gaze with a triumphant expression at the beautiful youth and maiden, as might an artist who should spend his life in achieving a picture or a group of statuary and finally be satisfied with his success. He paused; his bent form grew erect with conscious power; he spread out his hands over them in the attitude of a father imploring a blessing upon his children; but those were the same hands that had thrown poison into the stream of their lives. Giovanni trembled. Beatrice shuddered nervously, and pressed her hand upon her heart.

"My daughter," said Rappaccini, "thou art no longer lonely in the world. Pluck one of those precious gems from thy sister shrub and bid thy bridegroom wear it in his bosom. It will not harm him now. My science and the sympathy between thee and him have so wrought within his system that he now stands apart from common men, as thou dost, daughter of my pride and triumph, from ordinary women. Pass on, then, through the world, most dear to one another and dreadful to all besides!"

"My father," said Beatrice, feebly,—and still as she spoke she kept her hand upon her heart,—"wherefore didst thou inflict this miserable doom upon thy child?"

"Miserable!" exclaimed Rappaccini. "What mean you, foolish girl? Dost thou deem it misery to be endowed with marvellous gifts against which no power nor strength could avail an enemy—misery, to be able to quell the mightiest with a breath—misery, to be as terrible as thou art beautiful? Wouldst thou, then, have preferred the condition of a weak woman, exposed to all evil and capable of none?"

"I would fain have been loved, not feared," murmured Beatrice, sinking down upon the ground. "But now it matters not. I am going, father, where the evil which thou hast striven to mingle with my being will pass away like a dream-like the fragrance of these poisonous flowers, which will no longer taint my breath among the flowers of Eden. Farewell, Giovanni! Thy words of hatred are like lead within my heart; but they, too, will fall away as I ascend. Oh, was there not, from the first, more poison in thy nature than in mine?"

To Beatrice,—so radically had her earthly part been wrought upon by Rappaccini's skill,—as poison had been life, so the powerful antidote was death; and thus the poor victim of man's ingenuity and of thwarted nature, and of the fatality that attends all such efforts of perverted wisdom, perished there, at the feet of her father and Giovanni. Just at that moment Professor Pietro Baglioni looked forth from the window, and called loudly, in a tone of triumph mixed with horror, to the thunderstricken man of science, "Rappaccini! Rappaccini! and is THIS the upshot of your experiment!"

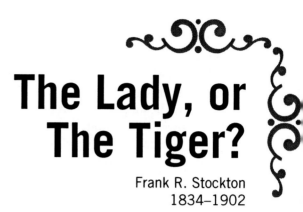

The Lady, or The Tiger?

Frank R. Stockton
1834–1902

In the very olden time there lived a semi-barbaric king, whose ideas, though somewhat polished and sharpened by the progressiveness of distant Latin neighbors, were still large, florid, and untrammeled, as became the half of him which was barbaric. He was a man of exuberant fancy, and, withal, of an authority so irresistible that, at his will, he turned his varied fancies into facts. He was greatly given to self-communing, and, when he and himself agreed upon anything, the thing was done. When every member of his domestic and political systems moved smoothly in its appointed course, his nature was bland and genial; but, whenever there was a little hitch, and some of his orbs got out of their orbits, he was blander and more genial still, for nothing pleased him so much as to make the crooked straight and crush down uneven places.

Among the borrowed notions by which his barbarism had become semified was that of the public arena, in which, by exhibitions of manly and beastly valor, the minds of his subjects were refined and cultured.

But even here the exuberant and barbaric fancy asserted itself. The arena of the king was built, not to give the people an opportunity of hearing the rhapsodies of dying gladiators, nor to enable them to view the inevitable conclusion of a conflict between religious opinions and hungry jaws, but for purposes far better adapted to widen and develop the mental energies of the people. This vast amphitheater, with its encircling galleries, its mysterious vaults, and its unseen passages, was an agent of poetic justice, in which crime was punished, or virtue rewarded, by the decrees of an impartial and incorruptible chance.

When a subject was accused of a crime of sufficient importance to interest the king, public notice was given that on an appointed day the fate of the accused person would be decided in the king's arena, a structure which well deserved its name, for, although its form and plan were borrowed from afar, its purpose emanated solely from the brain of this man, who, every barleycorn a king, knew no tradition to which he owed more allegiance than pleased his fancy, and who ingrafted on every adopted form of human thought and action the rich growth of his barbaric idealism.

When all the people had assembled in the galleries, and the king, surrounded by his court, sat high up on his throne of royal state on one side of the arena, he gave a signal, a door beneath him opened, and the accused subject stepped out into the amphitheater. Directly opposite him, on the other side of the inclosed space, were two doors, exactly alike and side by side. It was the duty and the privilege of the person on trial to walk directly to these doors and open one of them. He could open either door he pleased; he was subject to no guidance or influence but that of the aforementioned impartial and incorruptible chance. If he opened the one, there came out of it a hungry tiger, the fiercest and most cruel that could be procured, which immediately sprang upon him and tore him to pieces as a punishment for his guilt. The moment that the case of the criminal was thus decided, doleful iron bells were clanged, great wails went up from the hired mourners posted on the outer rim of the arena, and the vast audience, with bowed heads and downcast hearts, wended slowly their homeward way, mourning greatly that one so young and fair, or so old and respected, should have merited so dire a fate.

But, if the accused person opened the other door, there came forth from it a lady, the most suitable to his years and station that his majesty could select among his fair subjects, and to this lady he was immediately married, as a reward of his innocence. It mattered not that he might already possess a wife and family, or that his affections might be engaged upon an object of his own selection; the king allowed no such subordinate arrangements to interfere with his great scheme of retribution and reward. The exercises, as in the other instance, took place immediately, and in the arena. Another door opened beneath the king, and a priest, followed by a band of choristers, and dancing maidens blowing joyous airs on golden horns and treading an epithalamic measure, advanced to where the pair stood, side by side, and the wedding was promptly and cheerily solemnized. Then the gay brass bells rang forth their merry peals, the people shouted glad hurrahs, and the innocent man, preceded by children strewing flowers on his path, led his bride to his home.

This was the king's semi-barbaric method of administering justice. Its perfect fairness is obvious. The criminal could not know out of which door would come the lady; he opened either he pleased, without having the slightest idea whether, in the next instant, he was to be devoured or married. On some occasions the tiger came out of one door, and on some out of the other. The decisions of this tribunal were not only fair, they were positively determinate: the accused person was instantly punished if he found himself guilty, and, if innocent, he was rewarded on the spot, whether he liked it or not. There was no escape from the judgments of the king's arena.

The institution was a very popular one. When the people gathered together on one of the great trial days, they never knew whether they were to witness a bloody slaughter or a hilarious wedding. This element of uncertainty lent an interest to the occasion which it could not otherwise have attained. Thus, the masses were entertained and pleased, and the thinking part of the community could bring no charge of unfairness against this plan, for did not the accused person have the whole matter in his own hands?

This semi-barbaric king had a daughter as blooming as his most florid fancies, and with a soul as fervent and imperious as his own. As is usual in such cases, she was the apple of his eye, and was loved by him above all humanity. Among his courtiers was a young man of that fineness of blood and lowness of station common to the conventional heroes of romance who love royal maidens. This royal maiden was well satisfied with her lover, for he was handsome and brave to a degree unsurpassed in all this kingdom, and she loved him with an ardor that had enough of barbarism in it to make it exceedingly warm and strong. This love affair moved on happily for many months, until one day the king happened to discover its existence. He did not hesitate nor waver in regard to his duty in the premises. The youth was immediately cast into prison, and a day was appointed for his trial in the king's arena. This, of course, was an especially important occasion, and his majesty, as well as all the people, was greatly interested in the workings and development of this trial. Never before had such a case occurred; never before had a subject dared to love the daughter of the king. In after years such things became commonplace enough, but then they were in no slight degree novel and startling.

The tiger-cages of the kingdom were searched for the most savage and relentless beasts, from which the fiercest monster might be selected for the arena; and the ranks of maiden youth and beauty throughout the land were carefully surveyed by competent judges in order that the young man might have a fitting bride in case fate did not determine for him a different destiny. Of course, everybody knew that the deed with which the accused was charged had been done. He had loved the princess, and neither he, she, nor any one else, thought of denying the fact; but the king would not think of allowing any fact of this kind to interfere with the workings of the tribunal, in which he took such great delight and satisfaction. No matter how the affair turned out, the youth would be disposed of, and the king would take an aesthetic pleasure in watching the course of events, which would determine whether or not the young man had done wrong in allowing himself to love the princess.

The appointed day arrived. From far and near the people gathered, and thronged the great galleries of the arena, and crowds, unable to gain admittance, massed themselves against its outside walls. The king and his court were in their places, opposite the twin doors, those fateful portals, so terrible in their similarity.

All was ready. The signal was given. A door beneath the royal party opened, and the lover of the princess walked into the arena. Tall, beautiful, fair, his appearance was greeted with a low hum of admiration and anxiety. Half the audience had not known so grand a youth had lived among them. No wonder the princess loved him! What a terrible thing for him to be there!

As the youth advanced into the arena he turned, as the custom was, to bow to the king, but he did not think at all of that royal personage. His eyes were fixed upon the princess, who sat to the right of her father. Had it not been for the moiety of barbarism in her nature it is probable that lady would not have been there, but her intense and fervid soul would not allow her to be absent on an occasion in which she was so terribly interested. From the moment that the decree had gone forth that her lover should decide his fate in the king's arena, she had thought of nothing, night or day, but this great event and the various subjects connected with it. Possessed of more power, influence, and force of character than any one who had ever before been interested in such a case, she had done what no other person had done,—she had possessed herself of the secret of the doors. She knew in which of the two rooms, that lay behind those doors, stood the cage of the tiger, with its open front, and in which waited the lady. Through these thick doors, heavily curtained with skins on the inside, it was impossible that any noise or suggestion should come from within to the person who should approach to raise the latch of one of them. But gold, and the power of a woman's will, had brought the secret to the princess.

And not only did she know in which room stood the lady ready to emerge, all blushing and radiant, should her door be opened, but she knew who the lady was. It was one of the fairest and loveliest of the damsels of the court who had been selected as the reward of the accused youth, should he be proved innocent of the crime of aspiring to one so far above him; and the princess hated her. Often had she seen, or imagined that she had seen, this fair creature throwing glances of admiration upon the person of her lover, and sometimes she thought these glances were perceived, and even returned. Now and then she had seen them talking together; it was but for a moment or two, but much can be said in a brief space; it may have been on most unimportant topics, but how could she know that? The girl was lovely, but she had dared to raise her eyes to the loved one of the princess; and, with all the intensity of the savage blood transmitted to her through long lines of wholly barbaric ancestors, she hated the woman who blushed and trembled behind that silent door.

When her lover turned and looked at her, and his eye met hers as she sat there, paler and whiter than any one in the vast ocean of anxious faces about her, he saw, by that power of quick perception which is given to those whose souls are one, that she knew behind which door crouched the tiger, and behind which stood the lady. He had expected her to know it. He understood her nature, and his soul was assured that she would never rest until she had made plain to herself this thing, hidden to all other lookers-on, even to the king. The only hope for the youth in which there was any element of certainty was based upon the success of the princess in discovering this mystery; and the moment he looked upon her, he saw she had succeeded, as in his soul he knew she would succeed.

Then it was that his quick and anxious glance asked the question: "Which?" It was as plain to her as if he shouted it from where he stood. There was not an instant to be lost. The question was asked in a flash; it must be answered in another.

Her right arm lay on the cushioned parapet before her. She raised her hand, and made a slight, quick movement toward the right. No one but her lover saw her. Every eye but his was fixed on the man in the arena.

He turned, and with a firm and rapid step he walked across the empty space. Every heart stopped beating, every breath was held, every eye was fixed immovably upon that man. Without the slightest hesitation, he went to the door on the right, and opened it.

Now, the point of the story is this: Did the tiger come out of that door, or did the lady?

The more we reflect upon this question, the harder it is to answer. It involves a study of the human heart which leads us through devious mazes of passion, out of which it is difficult to find our way. Think of it, fair reader, not as if the decision of the question depended upon yourself, but upon that hot-blooded, semi-barbaric princess, her soul at a white heat beneath the combined fires of despair and jealousy. She had lost him, but who should have him?

How often, in her waking hours and in her dreams, had she started in wild horror, and covered her face with her hands as she thought of her lover opening the door on the other side of which waited the cruel fangs of the tiger!

But how much oftener had she seen him at the other door! How in her grievous reveries had she gnashed her teeth, and torn her hair, when she saw his start of rapturous delight as he opened the door of the lady! How her soul had burned in agony when she had seen him rush to meet that woman, with her flushing cheek and sparkling eye of triumph; when she had seen him lead her forth, his whole frame kindled with the joy of recovered life; when she had heard the glad shouts from the multitude, and the wild ringing of the happy bells; when she had seen the priest, with his joyous followers, advance to the couple, and make them man and wife before her very eyes; and when she had seen them walk away together upon their path of flowers, followed by the tremendous shouts of the hilarious multitude, in which her one despairing shriek was lost and drowned!

Would it not be better for him to die at once, and go to wait for her in the blessed regions of semi-barbaric futurity?

And yet, that awful tiger, those shrieks, that blood!

Her decision had been indicated in an instant, but it had been made after days and nights of anguished deliberation. She had known she would be asked, she had decided what she would answer, and, without the slightest hesitation, she had moved her hand to the right.

The question of her decision is one not to be lightly considered, and it is not for me to presume to set myself up as the one person able to answer it. And so I leave it with all of you: Which came out of the opened door,—the lady, or the tiger?

The Masque of the Red Death

Edgar Allan Poe
1808–1849

The "Red Death" had long devastated the country. No pestilence had ever been so fatal, or so hideous. Blood was its Avatar and its seal—the redness and the horror of blood. There were sharp pains, and sudden dizziness, and then profuse bleeding at the pores, with dissolution. The scarlet stains upon the body and especially upon the face of the victim, were the pest ban which shut him out from the aid and from the sympathy of his fellow-men. And the whole seizure, progress and termination of the disease, were the incidents of half an hour.

But the Prince Prospero was happy and dauntless and sagacious. When his dominions were half depopulated, he summoned to his presence a thousand hale and light-hearted friends from among the knights and dames of his court, and with these retired to the deep seclusion of one of his castellated abbeys. This was an extensive and magnificent structure, the creation of the prince's own eccentric yet august taste. A strong and lofty wall girdled it in. This wall had gates of iron. The courtiers, having entered, brought furnaces and massy hammers and welded the bolts. They resolved to leave means neither of ingress nor egress to the sudden impulses of despair or of frenzy from within. The abbey was amply provisioned. With such precautions the courtiers might bid defiance to contagion. The external world could take care of itself. In the meantime it was folly to grieve, or to think. The prince had provided all the appliances of pleasure. There were buffoons, there were improvisatori, there were ballet-dancers, there were musicians, there was Beauty, there was wine. All these and security were within. Without was the "Red Death".

It was towards the close of the fifth or sixth month of his seclusion, and while the pestilence raged most furiously abroad, that the Prince Prospero entertained his thousand friends at a masked ball of the most unusual magnificence.

It was a voluptuous scene, that masquerade. But first let me tell of the rooms in which it was held. These were seven—an imperial suite. In many palaces, however, such suites form a long and straight vista, while the folding doors slide back nearly to the walls on either hand, so that the view of the whole extent is scarcely impeded. Here the case was very different, as might have been expected from the duke's love of the *bizarre*. The apartments were so irregularly disposed that the vision embraced but little more than one at a time. There was a sharp turn at every twenty or thirty yards, and at each turn a novel effect. To the right and left, in the middle of each wall, a tall and narrow Gothic window looked out upon a closed corridor which pursued the windings of the suite. These windows were of stained glass whose colour varied in accordance with the prevailing hue of the decorations of the chamber into which it opened. That at the eastern extremity was hung, for example in blue—and vividly blue were its windows. The second chamber was purple in its ornaments and tapestries, and here the panes were purple. The third was green throughout, and so were the casements. The fourth was furnished and lighted with orange—the fifth with white—the sixth with violet. The seventh apartment was closely shrouded in black velvet tapestries that hung all over the ceiling and down the walls, falling in heavy folds upon a carpet of the same material and hue. But in this chamber only, the colour of the windows failed to correspond with the decorations. The panes here were scarlet—a deep blood colour. Now in no one of the seven apartments was there any lamp or candelabrum, amid the profusion of golden ornaments that lay scattered to and fro or depended from the roof. There was no light of any kind emanating from lamp or candle within the suite of chambers. But in the corridors that followed the suite, there stood, opposite to each window, a heavy tripod, bearing a brazier of fire, that projected its rays through the tinted glass and so glaringly illuminated the room. And thus were produced a multitude of gaudy and fantastic appearances. But in the western or black

205

chamber the effect of the fire-light that streamed upon the dark hangings through the blood-tinted panes, was ghastly in the extreme, and produced so wild a look upon the countenances of those who entered, that there were few of the company bold enough to set foot within its precincts at all.

It was in this apartment, also, that there stood against the western wall, a gigantic clock of ebony. Its pendulum swung to and fro with a dull, heavy, monotonous clang; and when the minute-hand made the circuit of the face, and the hour was to be stricken, there came from the brazen lungs of the clock a sound which was clear and loud and deep and exceedingly musical, but of so peculiar a note and emphasis that, at each lapse of an hour, the musicians of the orchestra were constrained to pause, momentarily, in their performance, to harken to the sound; and thus the waltzers perforce ceased their evolutions; and there was a brief disconcert of the whole gay company; and, while the chimes of the clock yet rang, it was observed that the giddiest grew pale, and the more aged and sedate passed their hands over their brows as if in confused revery or meditation. But when the echoes had fully ceased, a light laughter at once pervaded the assembly; the musicians looked at each other and smiled as if at their own nervousness and folly, and made whispering vows, each to the other, that the next chiming of the clock should produce in them no similar emotion; and then, after the lapse of sixty minutes, (which embrace three thousand and six hundred seconds of the Time that flies,) there came yet another chiming of the clock, and then were the same disconcert and tremulousness and meditation as before.

But, in spite of these things, it was a gay and magnificent revel. The tastes of the duke were peculiar. He had a fine eye for colours and effects. He disregarded the *decora* of mere fashion. His plans were bold and fiery, and his conceptions glowed with barbaric lustre. There are some who would have thought him mad. His followers felt that he was not. It was necessary to hear and see and touch him to be *sure* that he was not.

He had directed, in great part, the movable embellishments of the seven chambers, upon occasion of this great *fête*; and it was his own guiding taste which had given character to the masqueraders. Be sure they were grotesque. There were much glare and glitter and piquancy and phantasm—much of what has been since seen in "Hernani". There were arabesque figures with unsuited limbs and appointments. There were delirious fancies such as the madman fashions. There were much of the beautiful, much of the wanton, much of the *bizarre*, something of the terrible, and not a little of that which might have excited disgust. To and fro in the seven chambers there stalked, in fact, a multitude of dreams. And these—the dreams—writhed in and about taking hue from the rooms, and causing the wild music of the orchestra to seem as the echo of their steps. And, anon, there strikes the ebony clock which stands in the hall of the velvet. And then, for a moment, all is still, and all is silent save the voice of the clock. The dreams are stiff-frozen as they stand. But the echoes of the chime die away—they have endured but an instant—and a light, half-subdued laughter floats after them as they depart. And now again the music swells, and the dreams live, and writhe to and fro more merrily than ever, taking hue from the many tinted windows through which stream the rays from the tripods. But to the chamber which lies most westwardly of the seven, there are now none of the maskers who venture; for the night is waning away; and there flows a ruddier light through the blood-coloured panes; and the blackness of the sable drapery appals; and to him whose foot falls upon the sable carpet, there comes from the near clock of ebony a muffled peal more solemnly emphatic than any which reaches *their* ears who indulged in the more remote gaieties of the other apartments.

But these other apartments were densely crowded, and in them beat feverishly the heart of life. And the revel went whirlingly on, until at length there commenced the sounding of midnight upon the clock. And then the music ceased, as I have told; and the evolutions of the waltzers were quieted; and there was an uneasy cessation of all things as before. But now there were twelve strokes to be sounded by the bell of the clock; and thus it happened, perhaps, that more of thought crept, with more of time, into the meditations of the thoughtful among those who revelled. And thus too, it happened, perhaps, that before the last echoes of the last chime had utterly sunk into silence, there were many individuals in the crowd who had found leisure to become aware of the presence of a masked figure which had arrested the attention of no single individual before. And the rumour of this new presence having spread itself whisperingly around, there arose at length from the whole company a buzz, or murmur, expressive of disapprobation and surprise—then, finally, of terror, of horror, and of disgust.

In an assembly of phantasms such as I have painted, it may well be supposed that no ordinary appearance could have excited such sensation. In truth the masquerade licence of the night was nearly unlimited; but the figure in question had out-Heroded Herod, and gone beyond the bounds of even the prince's indefinite decorum. There are chords in the hearts of the most reckless which cannot be touched without emotion. Even with the utterly lost, to whom life and death are equally jests, there are matters of which no jest can be made. The whole company, indeed, seemed now deeply to feel that in the costume and bearing of the stranger neither wit nor propriety existed. The figure was tall and gaunt, and shrouded from head to foot in the habiliments of the grave. The mask which concealed the visage was made so nearly to resemble the countenance of a stiffened corpse that the closest scrutiny must have had difficulty in detecting the cheat. And yet all this might have been endured, if not approved, by the mad revellers around. But the mummer had gone so far as to assume the type of the Red Death. His vesture was dabbled in *blood*—and his broad brow, with all the features of the face, was besprinkled with the scarlet horror.

When the eyes of the Prince Prospero fell upon this spectral image (which, with a slow and solemn movement, as if more fully to sustain its role, stalked to and fro among the waltzers) he was seen to be convulsed, in the first moment with a strong shudder either of terror or distaste; but, in the next, his brow reddened with rage.

"Who dares,"—he demanded hoarsely of the courtiers who stood near him—"who dares insult us with this blasphemous mockery? Seize him and unmask him—that we may know whom we have to hang, at sunrise, from the battlements!"

It was in the eastern or blue chamber in which stood the Prince Prospero as he uttered these words. They rang throughout the seven rooms loudly and clearly, for the prince was a bold and robust man, and the music had become hushed at the waving of his hand.

It was in the blue room where stood the prince, with a group of pale courtiers by his side. At first, as he spoke, there was a slight rushing movement of this group in the direction of the intruder, who at the moment was also near at hand, and now, with deliberate and stately step, made closer approach to the speaker. But from a certain nameless awe with which the mad assumptions of the mummer had inspired the whole party, there were found none who put forth hand to seize him; so that, unimpeded, he passed within a yard of the prince's person; and, while the vast assembly, as if with one impulse, shrank from the centres of the rooms to the walls, he made his way uninterruptedly, but with the same solemn and measured step which had distinguished him from the first, through the blue chamber to the purple—through the purple to the green—through the green to the orange—through this again to the white—and even thence to the violet, ere a decided movement had been made to arrest him. It was then, however, that the Prince Prospero, maddening with rage and the shame of his own momentary cowardice, rushed hurriedly through the six chambers, while none followed him on account of a deadly terror that had seized upon all. He bore aloft a drawn dagger, and had approached, in rapid impetuosity, to within three or four feet of the retreating figure, when the latter, having attained the extremity of the velvet apartment, turned suddenly and confronted his pursuer. There was a sharp cry—and the dagger dropped gleaming upon the sable carpet, upon which, instantly afterwards, fell prostrate in death the Prince Prospero. Then, summoning the wild courage of despair, a throng of the revellers at once threw themselves into the black apartment, and, seizing the mummer, whose tall figure stood erect and motionless within the shadow of the ebony clock, gasped in unutterable horror at finding the grave cerements and corpse-like mask, which they handled with so violent a rudeness, untenanted by any tangible form.

And now was acknowledged the presence of the Red Death. He had come like a thief in the night. And one by one dropped the revellers in the blood-bedewed halls of their revel, and died each in the despairing posture of his fall. And the life of the ebony clock went out with that of the last of the gay. And the flames of the tripods expired. And Darkness and Decay and the Red Death held illimitable dominion over all.

The Monkey's Paw (1902)

W.W. Jacobs
1863–1943

I.

WITHOUT, the night was cold and wet, but in the small parlour of Laburnam Villa the blinds were drawn and the fire burned brightly. Father and son were at chess, the former, who possessed ideas about the game involving radical changes, putting his king into such sharp and unnecessary perils that it even provoked comment from the white-haired old lady knitting placidly by the fire.

"Hark at the wind," said Mr. White, who, having seen a fatal mistake after it was too late, was amiably desirous of preventing his son from seeing it.

"I'm listening," said the latter, grimly surveying the board as he stretched out his hand. "Check."

"I should hardly think that he'd come to-night," said his father, with his hand poised over the board.

"Mate," replied the son.

"That's the worst of living so far out," bawled Mr. White, with sudden and unlooked-for violence; "of all the beastly, slushy, out-of-the-way places to live in, this is the worst. Pathway's a bog, and the road's a torrent. I don't know what people are thinking about. I suppose because only two houses on the road are let, they think it doesn't matter."

"Never mind, dear," said his wife soothingly; "perhaps you'll win the next one."

Mr. White looked up sharply, just in time to intercept a knowing glance between mother and son. The words died away on his lips, and he hid a guilty grin in his thin grey beard.

"There he is," said Herbert White, as the gate banged to loudly and heavy footsteps came toward the door.

The old man rose with hospitable haste, and opening the door, was heard condoling with the new arrival. The new arrival also condoled with himself, so that Mrs. White said, "Tut, tut!" and coughed gently as her husband entered the room, followed by a tall burly man, beady of eye and rubicund of visage.

"Sergeant-Major Morris," he said, introducing him.

The sergeant-major shook hands, and taking the proffered seat by the fire, watched contentedly while his host got out whisky and tumblers and stood a small copper kettle on the fire.

At the third glass his eyes got brighter, and he began to talk, the little family circle regarding with eager interest this visitor from distant parts, as he squared his broad shoulders in the chair and spoke of strange scenes and doughty deeds; of wars and plagues and strange peoples.

"Twenty-one years of it," said Mr. White, nodding at his wife and son. "When he went away he was a slip of a youth in the warehouse. Now look at him."

"He don't look to have taken much harm," said Mrs. White, politely.

"I'd like to go to India myself," said the old man, "just to look round a bit, you know."

"Better where you are," said the sergeant-major, shaking his head. He put down the empty glass, and sighing softly, shook it again.

"I should like to see those old temples and fakirs and jugglers," said the old man. "What was that you started telling me the other day about a monkey's paw or something, Morris?"

"Nothing," said the soldier hastily. "Leastways, nothing worth hearing."

"Monkey's paw?" said Mrs. White curiously.

"Well, it's just a bit of what you might call magic, perhaps," said the sergeant-major off-handedly.

His three listeners leaned forward eagerly. The visitor absentmindedly put his empty glass to his lips and then set it down again. His host filled it for him.

"To look at," said the sergeant-major, fumbling in his pocket, "it's just an ordinary little paw, dried to a mummy."

He took something out of his pocket and proffered it. Mrs. White drew back with a grimace, but her son, taking it, examined it curiously.

"And what is there special about it?" inquired Mr. White, as he took it from his son and, having examined it, placed it upon the table.

"It had a spell put on it by an old fakir," said the sergeant-major, "a very holy man. He wanted to show that fate ruled people's lives, and that those who interfered with it did so to their sorrow. He put a spell on it so that three separate men could each have three wishes from it."

His manner was so impressive that his hearers were conscious that their light laughter jarred somewhat.

"Well, why don't you have three, sir?" said Herbert White cleverly.

The soldier regarded him in the way that middle age is wont to regard presumptuous youth. "I have," he said quietly, and his blotchy face whitened.

"And did you really have the three wishes granted?" asked Mrs. White.

"I did," said the sergeant-major, and his glass tapped against his strong teeth.

"And has anybody else wished?" inquired the old lady.

"The first man had his three wishes, yes," was the reply. "I don't know what the first two were, but the third was for death. That's how I got the paw."

His tones were so grave that a hush fell upon the group.

"If you've had your three wishes, it's no good to you now, then, Morris," said the old man at last. "What do you keep it for?"

The soldier shook his head. "Fancy, I suppose," he said slowly.

"If you could have another three wishes," said the old man, eyeing him keenly, "would you have them?"

"I don't know," said the other. "I don't know."

He took the paw, and dangling it between his front finger and thumb, suddenly threw it upon the fire. White, with a slight cry, stooped down and snatched it off.

"Better let it burn," said the soldier solemnly.

"If you don't want it, Morris," said the old man, "give it to me."

"I won't," said his friend doggedly. "I threw it on the fire. If you keep it, don't blame me for what happens. Pitch it on the fire again, like a sensible man."

The other shook his head and examined his new possession closely. "How do you do it?" he inquired.

"Hold it up in your right hand and wish aloud,' said the sergeant-major, "but I warn you of the consequences."

"Sounds like the *Arabian Nights*," said Mrs White, as she rose and began to set the supper. "Don't you think you might wish for four pairs of hands for me?"

Her husband drew the talisman from his pocket and then all three burst into laughter as the sergeant-major, with a look of alarm on his face, caught him by the arm.

"If you must wish," he said gruffly, "wish for something sensible."

Mr. White dropped it back into his pocket, and placing chairs, motioned his friend to the table. In the business of supper the talisman was partly forgotten, and afterward the three sat listening in an enthralled fashion to a second instalment of the soldier's adventures in India.

"If the tale about the monkey paw is not more truthful than those he has been telling us," said Herbert, as the door closed behind their guest, just in time for him to catch the last train, "we shan't make much out of it."

"Did you give him anything for it, father?" inquired Mrs. White, regarding her husband closely.

"A trifle," said he, colouring slightly. "He didn't want it, but I made him take it. And he pressed me again to throw it away."

"Likely," said Herbert, with pretended horror. "Why, we're going to be rich, and famous, and happy. Wish to be an emperor, father, to begin with; then you can't be henpecked."

He darted round the table, pursued by the maligned Mrs. White armed with an antimacassar.

Mr. White took the paw from his pocket and eyed it dubiously. "I don't know what to wish for, and that's a fact," he said slowly. "It seems to me I've got all I want."

"If you only cleared the house, you'd be quite happy, wouldn't you?" said Herbert, with his hand on his shoulder. "Well, wish for two hundred pounds, then; that'll just do it."

His father, smiling shamefacedly at his own credulity, held up the talisman, as his son, with a solemn face somewhat marred by a wink at his mother, sat down at the piano and struck a few impressive chords.

"I wish for two hundred pounds," said the old man distinctly.

A fine crash from the piano greeted the words, interrupted by a shuddering cry from the old man. His wife and son ran toward him.

"It moved, he cried, with a glance of disgust at the object as it lay on the floor. "As I wished it twisted in my hands like a snake."

"Well, I don't see the money," said his son, as he picked it up and placed it on the table, "and I bet I never shall."

"It must have been your fancy, father," said his wife, regarding him anxiously.

He shook his head. "Never mind, though; there's no harm done, but it gave me a shock all the same."

They sat down by the fire again while the two men finished their pipes. Outside, the wind was higher than ever, and the old man started nervously at the sound of a door banging upstairs. A silence unusual and depressing settled upon all three, which lasted until the old couple rose to retire for the night.

"I expect you'll find the cash tied up in a big bag in the middle of your bed," said Herbert, as he bade them good-night, "and something horrible squatting up on top of the wardrobe watching you as you pocket your ill-gotten gains."

He sat alone in the darkness, gazing at the dying fire, and seeing faces in it. The last face was so horrible and so simian that he gazed at it in amazement. It got so vivid that, with a little uneasy laugh, he felt on the table for a glass containing a little water to throw over it. His hand grasped the monkey's paw, and with a little shiver he wiped his hand on his coat and went up to bed.

II.

IN the brightness of the wintry sun next morning as it streamed over the breakfast table Herbert laughed at his fears. There was an air of prosaic wholesomeness about the room which it had lacked on the previous night, and the dirty, shrivelled little paw was pitched on the sideboard with a carelessness which betokened no great belief in its virtues.

"I suppose all old soldiers are the same," said Mrs White. "The idea of our listening to such nonsense! How could wishes be granted in these days? And if they could, how could two hundred pounds hurt you, father?"

"Might drop on his head from the sky," said the frivolous Herbert.

"Morris said the things happened so naturally," said his father, "that you might if you so wished attribute it to coincidence."

"Well, don't break into the money before I come back," said Herbert, as he rose from the table. "I'm afraid it'll turn you into a mean, avaricious man, and we shall have to disown you."

His mother laughed, and following him to the door, watched him down the road, and returning to the breakfast table, was very happy at the expense of her husband's credulity. All of which did not prevent her from scurrying to the door at the postman's knock, nor prevent her from referring somewhat shortly to retired sergeant-majors of bibulous habits when she found that the post brought a tailor's bill.

"Herbert will have some more of his funny remarks, I expect, when he comes home," she said, as they sat at dinner.

"I dare say," said Mr. White, pouring himself out some beer; "but for all that, the thing moved in my hand; that I'll swear to."

"You thought it did," said the old lady soothingly.

"I say it did," replied the other. "There was no thought about it; I had just—What's the matter?"

His wife made no reply. She was watching the mysterious movements of a man outside, who, peering in an undecided fashion at the house, appeared to be trying to make up his mind to enter. In mental connection with the two hundred pounds, she noticed that the stranger was well dressed and wore a silk hat of glossy newness. Three times he paused at the gate, and then walked on again. The fourth time he stood with his hand upon it, and then with sudden resolution flung it open and walked up the path. Mrs. White at the same moment placed her hands behind her, and hurriedly unfastening the strings of her apron, put that useful article of apparel beneath the cushion of her chair.

She brought the stranger, who seemed ill at ease, into the room. He gazed at her furtively, and listened in a preoccupied fashion as the old lady apologized for the appearance of the room, and her husband's coat, a garment which he usually reserved for the garden. She then waited as patiently as her sex would permit, for him to broach his business, but he was at first strangely silent.

"I—was asked to call," he said at last, and stooped and picked a piece of cotton from his trousers. "I come from Maw and Meggins."

The old lady started. "Is anything the matter?" she asked breathlessly. "Has anything happened to Herbert? What is it? What is it?"

Her husband interposed. "There, there, mother," he said hastily. "Sit down, and don't jump to conclusions. You've not brought bad news, I'm sure, sir" and he eyed the other wistfully.

"I'm sorry—" began the visitor.

"Is he hurt?" demanded the mother.

The visitor bowed in assent. "Badly hurt," he said quietly, "but he is not in any pain."

"Oh, thank God!" said the old woman, clasping her hands. "Thank God for that! Thank—"

She broke off suddenly as the sinister meaning of the assurance dawned upon her and she saw the awful confirmation of her fears in the other's averted face. She caught her breath, and turning to her slower-witted husband, laid her trembling old hand upon his. There was a long silence.

"He was caught in the machinery," said the visitor at length, in a low voice.

"Caught in the machinery," repeated Mr. White, in a dazed fashion, "yes."

He sat staring blankly out at the window, and taking his wife's hand between his own, pressed it as he had been wont to do in their old courting days nearly forty years before.

"He was the only one left to us," he said, turning gently to the visitor. "It is hard."

The other coughed, and rising, walked slowly to the window. "The firm wished me to convey their sincere sympathy with you in your great loss," he said, without looking round. "I beg that you will understand I am only their servant and merely obeying orders."

There was no reply; the old woman's face was white, her eyes staring, and her breath inaudible; on the husband's face was a look such as his friend the sergeant might have carried into his first action.

"I was to say that Maw and Meggins disclaim all responsibility," continued the other. "They admit no liability at all, but in consideration of your son's services they wish to present you with a certain sum as compensation."

Mr. White dropped his wife's hand, and rising to his feet, gazed with a look of horror at his visitor. His dry lips shaped the words, "How much?"

"Two hundred pounds," was the answer.

Unconscious of his wife's shriek, the old man smiled faintly, put out his hands like a sightless man, and dropped, a senseless heap, to the floor.

III.

IN the huge new cemetery, some two miles distant, the old people buried their dead, and came back to a house steeped in shadow and silence. It was all over so quickly that at first they could hardly realize it, and remained in a state of expectation as though of something else to happen–something else which was to lighten this load, too heavy for old hearts to bear.

But the days passed, and expectation gave place to resignation–the hopeless resignation of the old, sometimes miscalled, apathy. Sometimes they hardly exchanged a word, for now they had nothing to talk about, and their days were long to weariness.

It was about a week after that that the old man, waking suddenly in the night, stretched out his hand and found himself alone. The room was in darkness, and the sound of subdued weeping came from the window. He raised himself in bed and listened.

"Come back," he said tenderly. "You will be cold."

"It is colder for my son," said the old woman, and wept afresh.

The sound of her sobs died away on his ears. The bed was warm, and his eyes heavy with sleep. He dozed fitfully, and then slept until a sudden wild cry from his wife awoke him with a start.

"*The paw!*" she cried wildly. "The monkey's paw!"

He started up in alarm. "Where? Where is it? What's the matter?"

She came stumbling across the room toward him. "I want it," she said quietly. "You've not destroyed it?"

"It's in the parlour, on the bracket," he replied, marvelling. "Why?"

She cried and laughed together, and bending over, kissed his cheek.

"I only just thought of it," she said hysterically. "Why didn't I think of it before? Why didn't *you* think of it?"

"Think of what?" he questioned.

"The other two wishes," she replied rapidly. "We've only had one."

"Was not that enough?" he demanded fiercely.

"No," she cried, triumphantly; "we'll have one more. Go down and get it quickly, and wish our boy alive again."

The man sat up in bed and flung the bedclothes from his quaking limbs. "Good God, you are mad!" he cried aghast.

"Get it," she panted; "get it quickly, and wish— Oh, my boy, my boy!"

Her husband struck a match and lit the candle. "Get back to bed," he said, unsteadily. "You don't know what you are saying."

"We had the first wish granted," said the old woman, feverishly; "why not the second."

"A coincidence," stammered the old man.

"Go and get it and wish," cried the old woman, quivering with excitement.

The old man turned and regarded her, and his voice shook. "He has been dead ten days, and besides he–I would not tell you else, but–I could only recognize him by his clothing. If he was too terrible for you to see then, how now?"

"Bring him back," cried the old woman, and dragged him toward the door. "Do you think I fear the child I have nursed?"

He went down in the darkness, and felt his way to the parlour, and then to the mantelpiece. The talisman was in its place, and a horrible fear that the unspoken wish might bring his mutilated son before him ere he could escape from the room seized upon him, and he caught his breath as he found that he had lost the direction of the door. His brow cold with sweat, he felt his way round the table, and groped along the wall until he found himself in the small passage with the unwholesome thing in his hand.

Even his wife's face seemed changed as he entered the room. It was white and expectant, and to his fears seemed to have an unnatural look upon it. He was afraid of her.

"*Wish!*" she cried, in a strong voice.

"It is foolish and wicked," he faltered.

"*Wish!*" repeated his wife.

He raised his hand. "I wish my son alive again."

The talisman fell to the floor, and he regarded it fearfully. Then he sank trembling into a chair as the old woman, with burning eyes, walked to the window and raised the blind.

He sat until he was chilled with the cold, glancing occasionally at the figure of the old woman peering through the window. The candle end, which had burnt below the rim of the china candlestick, was throwing pulsating shadows on the ceiling and walls, until, with a flicker larger than the rest, it expired. The old man, with an unspeakable sense of relief at the failure of the talisman, crept back to his bed, and a minute or two afterward the old woman came silently and apathetically beside him.

Neither spoke, but both lay silently listening to the ticking of the clock. A stair creaked, and a squeaky mouse scurried noisily through the wall. The darkness was oppressive, and after lying for some time screwing up his courage, the husband took the box of matches, and striking one, went downstairs for a candle.

At the foot of the stairs the match went out, and he paused to strike another, and at the same moment a knock, so quiet and stealthy as to be scarcely audible, sounded on the front door.

The matches fell from his hand. He stood motionless, his breath suspended until the knock was repeated. Then he turned and fled swiftly back to his room, and closed the door behind him. A third knock sounded through the house.

"*What's that?*" cried the old woman, starting up.

"A rat," said the old man, in shaking tones–"a rat. It passed me on the stairs."

His wife sat up in bed listening. A loud knock resounded through the house.

"It's Herbert!" she screamed. "It's Herbert!"

She ran to the door, but her husband was before her, and catching her by the arm, held her tightly.

"What are you going to do?" he whispered hoarsely.

"It's my boy; it's Herbert!" she cried, struggling mechanically. "I forgot it was two miles away. What are you holding me for? Let go. I must open the door."

"For God's sake, don't let it in," cried the old man trembling.

"You're afraid of your own son," she cried, struggling. "Let me go. I'm coming, Herbert; I'm coming."

There was another knock, and another. The old woman with a sudden wrench broke free and ran from the room. Her husband followed to the landing, and called after her appealingly as she hurried downstairs. He heard the chain rattle back and the bottom bolt drawn slowly and stiffly from the socket. Then the old woman's voice, strained and panting.

"The bolt," she cried loudly. "Come down. I can't reach it."

But her husband was on his hands and knees groping wildly on the floor in search of the paw. If he could only find it before the thing outside got in. A perfect fusillade of knocks reverberated through the house, and he heard the scraping of a chair as his wife put it down in the passage against the door. He heard the creaking of the bolt as it came slowly back, and at the same moment he found the monkey's paw, and frantically breathed his third and last wish.

The knocking ceased suddenly, although the echoes of it were still in the house. He heard the chair drawn back and the door opened. A cold wind rushed up the staircase, and a long loud wail of disappointment and misery from his wife gave him courage to run down to her side, and then to the gate beyond. The street lamp flickering opposite shone on a quiet and deserted road.

(End.)

The Story of An Hour

Kate Chopin
1894

Knowing that Mrs. Mallard was afflicted with a heart trouble, great care was taken to break to her as gently as possible the news of her husband's death.

It was her sister Josephine who told her, in broken sentences; veiled hints that revealed in half concealing. Her husband's friend Richards was there, too, near her. It was he who had been in the newspaper office when intelligence of the railroad disaster was received, with Brently Mallard's name leading the list of "killed." He had only taken the time to assure himself of its truth by a second telegram, and had hastened to forestall any less careful, less tender friend in bearing the sad message.

She did not hear the story as many women have heard the same, with a paralyzed inability to accept its significance. She wept at once, with sudden, wild abandonment, in her sister's arms. When the storm of grief had spent itself she went away to her room alone. She would have no one follow her.

There stood, facing the open window, a comfortable, roomy armchair. Into this she sank, pressed down by a physical exhaustion that haunted her body and seemed to reach into her soul.

She could see in the open square before her house the tops of trees that were all aquiver with the new spring life. The delicious breath of rain was in the air. In the street below a peddler was crying his wares. The notes of a distant song which some one was singing reached her faintly, and countless sparrows were twittering in the eaves.

There were patches of blue sky showing here and there through the clouds that had met and piled one above the other in the west facing her window.

She sat with her head thrown back upon the cushion of the chair, quite motionless, except when a sob came up into her throat and shook her, as a child who has cried itself to sleep continues to sob in its dreams.

She was young, with a fair, calm face, whose lines bespoke repression and even a certain strength. But now there was a dull stare in her eyes, whose gaze was fixed away off yonder on one of those patches of blue sky. It was not a glance of reflection, but rather indicated a suspension of intelligent thought.

There was something coming to her and she was waiting for it, fearfully. What was it? She did not know; it was too subtle and elusive to name. But she felt it, creeping out of the sky, reaching toward her through the sounds, the scents, the color that filled the air.

Now her bosom rose and fell tumultuously. She was beginning to recognize this thing that was approaching to possess her, and she was striving to beat it back with her will--as powerless as her two white slender hands would have been. When she abandoned herself a little whispered word escaped her slightly parted lips. She said it over and over under hte breath: "free, free, free!" The vacant stare and the look of terror that had followed it went from her eyes. They stayed keen and bright. Her pulses beat fast, and the coursing blood warmed and relaxed every inch of her body.

She did not stop to ask if it were or were not a monstrous joy that held her. A clear and exalted perception enabled her to dismiss the suggestion as trivial. She knew that she would weep again when she saw the kind, tender hands folded in death; the face that had never looked save with love upon her, fixed and gray and dead. But she saw beyond that bitter moment a long procession of years to come that would belong to her absolutely. And she opened and spread her arms out to them in welcome.

There would be no one to live for during those coming years; she would live for herself. There would be no powerful will bending hers in that blind persistence with which men and women believe they have a right to impose a private will upon a fellow-creature. A kind intention or a cruel intention made the act seem no less a crime as she looked upon it in that brief moment of illumination.

And yet she had loved him--sometimes. Often she had not. What did it matter! What could love, the unsolved mystery, count for in the face of this possession of self-assertion which she suddenly recognized as the strongest impulse of her being!

"Free! Body and soul free!" she kept whispering.

Josephine was kneeling before the closed door with her lips to the keyhole, imploring for admission. "Louise, open the door! I beg; open the door--you will make yourself ill. What are you doing, Louise? For heaven's sake open the door."

"Go away. I am not making myself ill." No; she was drinking in a very elixir of life through that open window.

Her fancy was running riot along those days ahead of her. Spring days, and summer days, and all sorts of days that would be her own. She breathed a quick prayer that life might be long. It was only yesterday she had thought with a shudder that life might be long.

She arose at length and opened the door to her sister's importunities. There was a feverish triumph in her eyes, and she carried herself unwittingly like a goddess of Victory. She clasped her sister's waist, and together they descended the stairs. Richards stood waiting for them at the bottom.

Some one was opening the front door with a latchkey. It was Brently Mallard who entered, a little travel-stained, composedly carrying his grip-sack and umbrella. He had been far from the scene of the accident, and did not even know there had been one. He stood amazed at Josephine's piercing cry; at Richards' quick motion to screen him from the view of his wife.

When the doctors came they said she had died of heart disease--of the joy that kills.

Trifles

Susan Glaspell
1876–1948

First performed by the Provincetown Players at the Wharf Theatre, Provincetown, Mass., August 8, 1916.

GEORGE HENDERSON (County Attorney)
HENRY PETERS (Sheriff)
LEWIS HALE, A neighboring farmer
MRS PETERS
MRS HALE

SCENE: *The kitchen is the now abandoned farmhouse of* JOHN WRIGHT, *a gloomy kitchen, and left without having been put in order—unwashed pans under the sink, a loaf of bread outside the bread-box, a dish-towel on the table—other signs of incompleted work. At the rear the outer door opens and the SHERIFF comes in followed by the* COUNTY ATTORNEY *and* HALE. *The* SHERIFF *and* HALE *are men in middle life, the* COUNTY ATTORNEY *is a young man; all are much bundled up and go at once to the stove. They are followed by the two women—the* SHERIFF's *wife first; she is a slight wiry woman, a thin nervous face.* MRS HALE *is larger and would ordinarily be called more comfortable looking, but she is disturbed now and looks fearfully about as she enters. The women have come in slowly, and stand close together near the door.*

COUNTY ATTORNEY: (*rubbing his hands*) This feels good. Come up to the fire, ladies.

MRS PETERS: (*after taking a step forward*) I'm not—cold.

SHERIFF: (*unbuttoning his overcoat and stepping away from the stove as if to mark the beginning of official business*) Now, Mr Hale, before we move things about, you explain to Mr Henderson just what you saw when you came here yesterday morning.

COUNTY ATTORNEY: By the way, has anything been moved? Are things just as you left them yesterday?

SHERIFF: (*looking about*) It's just the same. When it dropped below zero last night I thought I'd better send Frank out this morning to make a fire for us—no use getting pneumonia with a big case on, but I told him not to touch anything except the stove—and you know Frank.

COUNTY ATTORNEY: Somebody should have been left here yesterday.

SHERIFF: Oh—yesterday. When I had to send Frank to Morris Center for that man who went crazy—I want you to know I had my hands full yesterday. I knew you could get back from Omaha by today and as long as I went over everything here myself—

COUNTY ATTORNEY: Well, Mr Hale, tell just what happened when you came here yesterday morning.

HALE: Harry and I had started to town with a load of potatoes. We came along the road from my place and as I got here I said, 'I'm going to see if I can't get John Wright to go in with me on a party telephone.' I spoke to Wright about it once before and he put me off, saying folks talked too much anyway, and all he asked was peace and quiet—I guess you know about how much he talked himself; but I thought maybe if I went to the house and talked about it before his wife, though I said to Harry that I didn't know as what his wife wanted made much difference to John—

COUNTY ATTORNEY: Let's talk about that later, Mr Hale. I do want to talk about that, but tell now just what happened when you got to the house.

HALE: I didn't hear or see anything; I knocked at the door, and still it was all quiet inside. I knew they must be up, it was past eight o'clock. So I knocked again, and I thought I heard somebody say, 'Come in.' I wasn't sure, I'm not sure yet, but I opened the door—this door (*indicating the door by which the two women are still standing*) and there in that rocker—(*pointing to it*) sat Mrs Wright.

(*They all look at the rocker.*)

COUNTY ATTORNEY: What—was she doing?
HALE: She was rockin' back and forth. She had her apron in her hand and was kind of—pleating it.
COUNTY ATTORNEY: And how did she—look?
HALE: Well, she looked queer.
COUNTY ATTORNEY: How do you mean—queer?
HALE: Well, as if she didn't know what she was going to do next. And kind of done up.
COUNTY ATTORNEY: How did she seem to feel about your coming?
HALE: Why, I don't think she minded—one way or other. She didn't pay much attention. I said, 'How do, Mrs Wright it's cold, ain't it?' And she said, 'Is it?'—and went on kind of pleating at her apron. Well, I was surprised; she didn't ask me to come up to the stove, or to set down, but just sat there, not even looking at me, so I said, 'I want to see John.' And then she—laughed. I guess you would call it a laugh. I thought of Harry and the team outside, so I said a little sharp: 'Can't I see John?' 'No', she says, kind o' dull like. 'Ain't he home?' says I. 'Yes', says she, 'he's home'. 'Then why can't I see him?' I asked her, out of patience. ''Cause he's dead', says she. ‹*Dead*?' says I. She just nodded her head, not getting a bit excited, but rockin' back and forth. 'Why—where is he?' says I, not knowing what to say. She just pointed upstairs—like that (*himself pointing to the room above*) I got up, with the idea of going up there. I walked from there to here—then I says, 'Why, what did he die of?' 'He died of a rope round his neck', says she, and just went on pleatin' at her apron. Well, I went out and called Harry. I thought I might—need help. We went upstairs and there he was lyin'—
COUNTY ATTORNEY: I think I'd rather have you go into that upstairs, where you can point it all out. Just go on now with the rest of the story.
HALE: Well, my first thought was to get that rope off. It looked ... (*stops, his face twitches*) ... but Harry, he went up to him, and he said, 'No, he's dead all right, and we'd better not touch anything.' So we went back down stairs. She was still sitting that same way. 'Has anybody been notified?' I asked. 'No', says she uncon- cerned. 'Who did this, Mrs Wright?' said Harry. He said it business-like—and she stopped pleatin' of her apron. 'I don't know', she says. 'You don't *know*?' says Harry. 'No', says she. 'Weren't you sleepin' in the bed with him?' says Harry. 'Yes', says she, 'but I was on the inside'. 'Somebody slipped a rope round his neck and strangled him and you didn't wake up?' says Harry. 'I didn't wake up', she said after him. We must 'a looked as if we didn't see how that could be, for after a minute she said, 'I sleep sound'. Harry was going to ask her more questions but I said maybe we ought to let her tell her story first to the coroner, or the sheriff, so Harry went fast as he could to Rivers' place, where there's a telephone.
COUNTY ATTORNEY: And what did Mrs Wright do when she knew that you had gone for the coroner?
HALE: She moved from that chair to this one over here (*pointing to a small chair in the corner*) and just sat there with her hands held together and looking down. I got a feeling that I ought to make some conversation, so I said I had come in to see if John wanted to put in a telephone, and at that she started to laugh, and then she stopped and looked at me—scared, (*the* COUNTY ATTORNEY, *who has had his notebook out, makes a note*) I dunno, maybe it wasn't scared. I wouldn't like to say it was. Soon Harry got back, and then Dr Lloyd came, and you, Mr Peters, and so I guess that's all I know that you don't.
COUNTY ATTORNEY: (*looking around*) I guess we'll go upstairs first—and then out to the barn and around there, (*to the* SHERIFF) You›re convinced that there was nothing important here—nothing that would point to any motive.
SHERIFF: Nothing here but kitchen things.

(*The* COUNTY ATTORNEY, *after again looking around the kitchen, opens the door of a cupboard closet. He gets up on a chair and looks on a shelf. Pulls his hand away, sticky.*)

COUNTY ATTORNEY: Here's a nice mess.

(*The women draw nearer.*)

MRS PETERS: (*to the other woman*) Oh, her fruit; it did freeze, (*to the* LAWYER) She worried about that when it turned so cold. She said the fire›d go out and her jars would break.

SHERIFF: Well, can you beat the women! Held for murder and worryin› about her preserves.

COUNTY ATTORNEY: I guess before we›re through she may have something more serious than preserves to worry about.

HALE: Well, women are used to worrying over trifles.

(*The two women move a little closer together.*)

COUNTY ATTORNEY: (*with the gallantry of a young politician*) And yet, for all their worries, what would we do without the ladies? (*the women do not unbend. He goes to the sink, takes a dipperful of water from the pail and pouring it into a basin, washes his hands. Starts to wipe them on the roller-towel, turns it for a cleaner place*) Dirty towels! (*kicks his foot against the pans under the sink*) Not much of a housekeeper, would you say, ladies?

MRS HALE: (*stiffly*) There's a great deal of work to be done on a farm.

COUNTY ATTORNEY: To be sure. And yet (*with a little bow to her*) I know there are some Dickson county farmhouses which do not have such roller towels. (*He gives it a pull to expose its length again.*)

MRS HALE: Those towels get dirty awful quick. Men's hands aren't always as clean as they might be.

COUNTY ATTORNEY: Ah, loyal to your sex, I see. But you and Mrs Wright were neighbors. I suppose you were friends, too.

MRS HALE: (*shaking her head*) I've not seen much of her of late years. I've not been in this house—it's more than a year.

COUNTY ATTORNEY: And why was that? You didn't like her?

MRS HALE: I liked her all well enough. Farmers' wives have their hands full, Mr Henderson. And then—

COUNTY ATTORNEY: Yes—?

MRS HALE: (*looking about*) It never seemed a very cheerful place.

COUNTY ATTORNEY: No—it's not cheerful. I shouldn't say she had the homemaking instinct.

MRS HALE: Well, I don't know as Wright had, either.

COUNTY ATTORNEY: You mean that they didn't get on very well?

MRS HALE: No, I don't mean anything. But I don't think a place'd be any cheerfuller for John Wright's being in it.

COUNTY ATTORNEY: I'd like to talk more of that a little later. I want to get the lay of things upstairs now. (*He goes to the left, where three steps lead to a stair door.*)

SHERIFF: I suppose anything Mrs Peters does'll be all right. She was to take in some clothes for her, you know, and a few little things. We left in such a hurry yesterday.

COUNTY ATTORNEY: Yes, but I would like to see what you take, Mrs Peters, and keep an eye out for anything that might be of use to us.

MRS PETERS: Yes, Mr Henderson.

(*The women listen to the men's steps on the stairs, then look about the kitchen.*)

MRS HALE: I'd hate to have men coming into my kitchen, snooping around and criticising.

(*She arranges the pans under sink which the* LAWYER *had shoved out of place.*)

MRS PETERS: Of course it's no more than their duty.

MRS HALE: Duty's all right, but I guess that deputy sheriff that came out to make the fire might have got a little of this on. (*gives the roller towel a pull*) Wish I'd thought of that sooner. Seems mean to talk about her for not having things slicked up when she had to come away in such a hurry.

MRS PETERS: (*who has gone to a small table in the left rear corner of the room, and lifted one end of a towel that covers a pan*) She had bread set. (*Stands still.*)

MRS HALE: (*eyes fixed on a loaf of bread beside the bread-box, which is on a low shelf at the other side of the room. Moves slowly toward it*) She was going to put this in there, (*picks up loaf, then abruptly drops it. In a manner of returning to familiar things*) It's a shame about her fruit. I wonder if it's all gone. (*gets up on the chair and looks*) I think there's some here that's all right, Mrs Peters. Yes—here; (*holding it toward the window*) this is cherries, too. (*looking again*) I declare I believe that's the only one. (*gets down, bottle in her hand. Goes to the sink and wipes it off on the outside*) She'll feel awful bad after all her hard work in the hot weather. I remember the afternoon I put up my cherries last summer.

(*She puts the bottle on the big kitchen table, center of the room. With a sigh, is about to sit down in the rocking-chair. Before she is seated realizes what chair it is; with a slow look at it, steps back. The chair which she has touched rocks back and forth.*)

MRS PETERS: Well, I must get those things from the front room closet, (*she goes to the door at the right, but after looking into the other room, steps back*) You coming with me, Mrs Hale? You could help me carry them.

(*They go in the other room; reappear, MRS PETERS carrying a dress and skirt, MRS HALE following with a pair of shoes.*)

MRS PETERS: My, it's cold in there.

(*She puts the clothes on the big table, and hurries to the stove.*)

MRS HALE: (*examining the skirt*) Wright was close. I think maybe that's why she kept so much to herself. She didn't even belong to the Ladies Aid. I suppose she felt she couldn't do her part, and then you don't enjoy things when you feel shabby. She used to wear pretty clothes and be lively, when she was Minnie Foster, one of the town girls singing in the choir. But that—oh, that was thirty years ago. This all you was to take in?

MRS PETERS: She said she wanted an apron. Funny thing to want, for there isn't much to get you dirty in jail, goodness knows. But I suppose just to make her feel more natural. She said they was in the top drawer in this cupboard. Yes, here. And then her little shawl that always hung behind the door. (*opens stair door and looks*) Yes, here it is.

(*Quickly shuts door leading upstairs.*)

MRS HALE: (*abruptly moving toward her*) Mrs Peters?
MRS PETERS: Yes, Mrs Hale?
MRS HALE: Do you think she did it?
MRS PETERS: (*in a frightened voice*) Oh, I don't know.
MRS HALE: Well, I don't think she did. Asking for an apron and her little shawl. Worrying about her fruit.
MRS PETERS: (*starts to speak, glances up, where footsteps are heard in the room above. In a low voice*) Mr Peters says it looks bad for her. Mr Henderson is awful sarcastic in a speech and he'll make fun of her sayin' she didn't wake up.
MRS HALE: Well, I guess John Wright didn't wake when they was slipping that rope under his neck.
MRS PETERS: No, it's strange. It must have been done awful crafty and still. They say it was such a—funny way to kill a man, rigging it all up like that.
MRS HALE: That's just what Mr Hale said. There was a gun in the house. He says that's what he can't understand.
MRS PETERS: Mr Henderson said coming out that what was needed for the case was a motive; something to show anger, or—sudden feeling.
MRS HALE: (*who is standing by the table*) Well, I don't see any signs of anger around here, (*she puts her hand on the dish towel which lies on the table, stands looking down at table, one half of which is clean, the other half messy*) It's wiped to here, (*makes a move as if to finish work, then turns and looks at loaf of bread outside the breadbox. Drops towel. In that voice of coming back to familiar things.*) Wonder how they are finding things upstairs. I hope she had it a little more red-up up there. You know, it seems kind of sneaking. Locking her up in town and then coming out here and trying to get her own house to turn against her!
MRS PETERS: But Mrs Hale, the law is the law.
MRS HALE: I s'pose 'tis, (*unbuttoning her coat*) Better loosen up your things, Mrs Peters. You won't feel them when you go out.

(*MRS PETERS takes off her fur tippet, goes to hang it on hook at back of room, stands looking at the under part of the small corner table.*)

MRS PETERS: She was piecing a quilt. (*She brings the large sewing basket and they look at the bright pieces.*)
MRS HALE: It's log cabin pattern. Pretty, isn't it? I wonder if she was goin' to quilt it or just knot it?

(*Footsteps have been heard coming down the stairs. The* SHERIFF *enters followed by* HALE *and the* COUNTY ATTORNEY.)

SHERIFF: They wonder if she was going to quilt it or just knot it! (*The men laugh, the women look abashed.*)

COUNTY ATTORNEY: (*rubbing his hands over the stove*) Frank's fire didn't do much up there, did it? Well, let's go out to the barn and get that cleared up. (*The men go outside.*)

MRS HALE: (*resentfully*) I don't know as there's anything so strange, our takin' up our time with little things while we're waiting for them to get the evidence. (*she sits down at the big table smoothing out a block with decision*) I don't see as it's anything to laugh about.

MRS PETERS: (*apologetically*) Of course they've got awful important things on their minds.

(*Pulls up a chair and joins* MRS HALE *at the table.*)

MRS HALE: (*examining another block*) Mrs Peters, look at this one. Here, this is the one she was working on, and look at the sewing! All the rest of it has been so nice and even. And look at this! It's all over the place! Why, it looks as if she didn't know what she was about!

(*After she has said this they look at each other, then start to glance back at the door. After an instant* MRS HALE *has pulled at a knot and ripped the sewing.*)

MRS PETERS: Oh, what are you doing, Mrs Hale?

MRS HALE: (*mildly*) Just pulling out a stitch or two that's not sewed very good. (*threading a needle*) Bad sewing always made me fidgety.

MRS PETERS: (nervously) I don't think we ought to touch things.

MRS HALE: I'll just finish up this end. (*suddenly stopping and leaning forward*) Mrs Peters?

MRS PETERS: Yes, Mrs Hale?

MRS HALE: What do you suppose she was so nervous about?

MRS PETERS: Oh—I don't know. I don't know as she was nervous. I sometimes sew awful queer when I'm just tired. (MRS HALE *starts to say something, looks at* MRS PETERS, *then goes on sewing*) Well I must get these things wrapped up. They may be through sooner than we think, (*putting apron and other things together*) I wonder where I can find a piece of paper, and string.

MRS HALE: In that cupboard, maybe.

MRS PETERS: (*looking in cupboard*) Why, here's a bird-cage, (*holds it up*) Did she have a bird, Mrs Hale?

MRS HALE: Why, I don't know whether she did or not—I've not been here for so long. There was a man around last year selling canaries cheap, but I don't know as she took one; maybe she did. She used to sing real pretty herself.

MRS PETERS: (*glancing around*) Seems funny to think of a bird here. But she must have had one, or why would she have a cage? I wonder what happened to it.

MRS HALE: I s'pose maybe the cat got it.

MRS PETERS: No, she didn't have a cat. She's got that feeling some people have about cats—being afraid of them. My cat got in her room and she was real upset and asked me to take it out.

MRS HALE: My sister Bessie was like that. Queer, ain't it?

MRS PETERS: (*examining the cage*) Why, look at this door. It's broke. One hinge is pulled apart.

MRS HALE: (*looking too*) Looks as if someone must have been rough with it.

MRS PETERS: Why, yes.

(*She brings the cage forward and puts it on the table.*)

MRS HALE: I wish if they're going to find any evidence they'd be about it. I don't like this place.

MRS PETERS: But I'm awful glad you came with me, Mrs Hale. It would be lonesome for me sitting here alone.

MRS HALE: It would, wouldn't it? (*dropping her sewing*) But I tell you what I do wish, Mrs Peters. I wish I had come over sometimes when *she* was here. I—(*looking around the room*)—wish I had.

MRS PETERS: But of course you were awful busy, Mrs Hale—your house and your children.

MRS HALE: I could've come. I stayed away because it weren't cheerful—and that's why I ought to have come. I—I've never liked this place. Maybe because it's down in a hollow and you don't see the road. I dunno what it is, but it's a lonesome place and always was. I wish I had come over to see Minnie Foster sometimes. I can see now—(*shakes her head*)

MRS PETERS: Well, you mustn't reproach yourself, Mrs Hale. Somehow we just don't see how it is with other folks until—something comes up.

MRS HALE: Not having children makes less work—but it makes a quiet house, and Wright out to work all day, and no company when he did come in. Did you know John Wright, Mrs Peters?

MRS PETERS: Not to know him; I've seen him in town. They say he was a good man.

MRS HALE: Yes—good; he didn't drink, and kept his word as well as most, I guess, and paid his debts. But he was a hard man, Mrs Peters. Just to pass the time of day with him—(*shivers*) Like a raw wind that gets to the bone, (*pauses, her eye falling on the cage*) I should think she would 'a wanted a bird. But what do you suppose went with it?

MRS PETERS: I don't know, unless it got sick and died.

(*She reaches over and swings the broken door, swings it again, both women watch it.*)

MRS HALE: You weren't raised round here, were you? (*MRS PETERS shakes her head*) You didn't know—her?

MRS PETERS: Not till they brought her yesterday.

MRS HALE: She—come to think of it, she was kind of like a bird herself—real sweet and pretty, but kind of timid and—fluttery. How—she—did—change. (*silence; then as if struck by a happy thought and relieved to get back to everyday things*) Tell you what, Mrs Peters, why don't you take the quilt in with you? It might take up her mind.

MRS PETERS: Why, I think that's a real nice idea, Mrs Hale. There couldn't possibly be any objection to it, could there? Now, just what would I take? I wonder if her patches are in here—and her things.

(*They look in the sewing basket.*)

MRS HALE: Here's some red. I expect this has got sewing things in it. (*brings out a fancy box*) What a pretty box. Looks like something somebody would give you. Maybe her scissors are in here. (*Opens box. Suddenly puts her hand to her nose*) Why—(MRS PETERS *bends nearer, then turns her face away*) There's something wrapped up in this piece of silk.

MRS PETERS: Why, this isn't her scissors.

MRS HALE: (*lifting the silk*) Oh, Mrs Peters—it's—

(MRS PETERS *bends closer.*)

MRS PETERS: It's the bird.

MRS HALE: (*jumping up*) But, Mrs Peters—look at it! It's neck! Look at its neck!
It's all—other side *to.*

MRS PETERS: Somebody—wrung—its—neck.

(*Their eyes meet. A look of growing comprehension, of horror. Steps are heard outside.* MRS HALE *slips box under quilt pieces, and sinks into her chair. Enter* SHERIFF *and* COUNTY ATTORNEY. MRS PETERS *rises.*)

COUNTY ATTORNEY: (*as one turning from serious things to little pleasantries*) Well ladies, have you decided whether she was going to quilt it or knot it?

MRS PETERS: We think she was going to—knot it.

COUNTY ATTORNEY: Well, that's interesting, I'm sure. (*seeing the birdcage*) Has the bird flown?

MRS HALE: (*putting more quilt pieces over the box*) We think the—cat got it.

COUNTY ATTORNEY: (*preoccupied*) Is there a cat?

(MRS HALE *glances in a quick covert way at* MRS PETERS.)

MRS PETERS: Well, not now. They›re superstitious, you know. They leave.

COUNTY ATTORNEY: (*to* SHERIFF PETERS, *continuing an interrupted conversation*) No sign at all of anyone having come from the outside. Their own rope. Now let's go up again and go over it piece by piece. (*they start upstairs*) It would have to have been someone who knew just the—

(MRS PETERS *sits down. The two women sit there not looking at one another, but as if peering into something and at the same time holding back. When they talk now it is in the manner of feeling their way over strange ground, as if afraid of what they are saying, but as if they can not help saying it.*)

MRS HALE: She liked the bird. She was going to bury it in that pretty box.

MRS PETERS: (*in a whisper*) When I was a girl—my kitten—there was a boy took a hatchet, and before my eyes—and before I could get there—(*covers her face an instant*) If they hadn't held me back I would have—(*catches herself, looks upstairs where steps are heard, falters weakly*)—hurt him.

MRS HALE: (*with a slow look around her*) I wonder how it would seem never to have had any children around, (*pause*) No, Wright wouldn't like the bird—a thing that sang. She used to sing. He killed that, too.

MRS PETERS: (*moving uneasily*) We don't know who killed the bird.

MRS HALE: I knew John Wright.

MRS PETERS: It was an awful thing was done in this house that night, Mrs Hale. Killing a man while he slept, slipping a rope around his neck that choked the life out of him.

MRS HALE: His neck. Choked the life out of him.

(*Her hand goes out and rests on the bird-cage.*)

MRS PETERS: (*with rising voice*) We don't know who killed him. We don't *know*.

MRS HALE: (*her own feeling not interrupted*) If there'd been years and years of nothing, then a bird to sing to you, it would be awful—still, after the bird was still.

MRS PETERS: (*something within her speaking*) I know what stillness is. When we homesteaded in Dakota, and my first baby died—after he was two years old, and me with no other then—

MRS HALE: (*moving*) How soon do you suppose they'll be through, looking for the evidence?

MRS PETERS: I know what stillness is. (*pulling herself back*) The law has got to punish crime, Mrs Hale.

MRS HALE: (*not as if answering that*) I wish you'd seen Minnie Foster when she wore a white dress with blue ribbons and stood up there in the choir and sang. (*a look around the room*) Oh, I wish I'd come over here once in a while! That was a crime! That was a crime! Who's going to punish that?

MRS PETERS: (*looking upstairs*) We mustn't—take on.

MRS HALE: I might have known she needed help! I know how things can be—for women. I tell you, it's queer, Mrs Peters. We live close together and we live far apart. We all go through the same things—it's all just a different kind of the same thing, (*brushes her eyes, noticing the bottle of fruit, reaches out for it*) If I was you, I wouldn't tell her her fruit was gone. Tell her it ain't. Tell her it's all right. Take this in to prove it to her. She—she may never know whether it was broke or not.

MRS PETERS: (*takes the bottle, looks about for something to wrap it in; takes petticoat from the clothes brought from the other room, very nervously begins winding this around the bottle. In a false voice*) My, it's a good thing the men couldn't hear us. Wouldn't they just laugh! Getting all stirred up over a little thing like a—dead canary. As if that could have anything to do with—with—wouldn't they *laugh*!

(*The men are heard coming down stairs.*)

MRS HALE: (*under her breath*) Maybe they would—maybe they wouldn't.

COUNTY ATTORNEY: No, Peters, it's all perfectly clear except a reason for doing it. But you know juries when it comes to women. If there was some definite thing. Something to show—something to make a story about—a thing that would connect up with this strange way of doing it—

(*The women's eyes meet for an instant. Enter HALE from outer door.*)

HALE: Well, I've got the team around. Pretty cold out there.

COUNTY ATTORNEY: I'm going to stay here a while by myself, (*to the* SHERIFF) You can send Frank out for me, can›t you? I want to go over everything. I›m not satisfied that we can›t do better.

SHERIFF: Do you want to see what Mrs Peters is going to take in?

(*The* LAWYER *goes to the table, picks up the apron, laughs.*)

COUNTY ATTORNEY: Oh, I guess they're not very dangerous things the ladies have picked out. (*Moves a few things about, disturbing the quilt pieces which cover the box. Steps back*) No, Mrs Peters doesn't need supervising. For that matter, a sheriff's wife is married to the law. Ever think of it that way, Mrs Peters?

MRS PETERS: Not—just that way.

SHERIFF: (*chuckling*) Married to the law. (*moves toward the other room*) I just want you to come in here a minute, George. We ought to take a look at these windows.

COUNTY ATTORNEY: (*scoffingly*) Oh, windows!

SHERIFF: We'll be right out, Mr Hale.

(HALE *goes outside. The* SHERIFF *follows the* COUNTY ATTORNEY *into the other room. Then* MRS HALE *rises, hands tight together, looking intensely at* MRS PETERS, *whose eyes make a slow turn, finally meeting* MRS HALE's. *A moment* MRS HALE *holds her, then her own eyes point the way to where the box is concealed. Suddenly* MRS PETERS *throws back quilt pieces and tries to put the box in the bag she is wearing. It is too big. She opens box, starts to take bird out, cannot touch it, goes to pieces, stands there helpless. Sound of a knob turning in the other room.* MRS HALE *snatches the box and puts it in the pocket of her big coat. Enter* COUNTY ATTORNEY *and* SHERIFF.)

COUNTY ATTORNEY: (*facetiously*) Well, Henry, at least we found out that she was not going to quilt it. She was going to—what is it you call it, ladies?

MRS HALE: (*her hand against her pocket*) We call it—knot it, Mr Henderson.

The Legend of Sleepy Hollow

Washington Irving
1783–1859

FOUND AMONG THE PAPERS OF THE LATE DIEDRICH KNICKERBOCKER

A pleasing land of drowsy head it was,
Of dreams that wave before the half-shut eye;
And of gay castles in the clouds that pass,
For ever flushing round a summer sky.

CASTLE OF INDOLENCE.

IN the bosom of one of those spacious coves which indent the eastern shore of the Hudson, at that broad expansion of the river denominated by the ancient Dutch navigators the Tappan Zee, and where they always prudently shortened sail, and implored the protection of St. Nicholas when they crossed, there lies a small market-town or rural port, which by some is called Greensburgh, but which is more generally and properly known by the name of Tarry Town. This name was given, we are told, in former days, by the good housewives of the adjacent country, from the inveterate propensity of their husbands to linger about the village tavern on market days. Be that as it may, I do not vouch for the fact, but merely advert to it, for the sake of being precise and authentic. Not far from this village, perhaps about two miles, there is a little valley, or rather lap of land, among high hills, which is one of the quietest places in the whole world. A small brook glides through it, with just murmur enough to lull one to repose; and the occasional whistle of a quail, or tapping of a woodpecker, is almost the only sound that ever breaks in upon the uniform tranquillity.

I recollect that, when a stripling, my first exploit in squirrel-shooting was in a grove of tall walnut-trees that shades one side of the valley. I had wandered into it at noon time, when all nature is peculiarly quiet, and was startled by the roar of my own gun, as it broke the Sabbath stillness around, and was prolonged and reverberated by the angry echoes. If ever I should wish for a retreat, whither I might steal from the world and its distractions, and dream quietly away the remnant of a troubled life, I know of none more promising than this little valley.

From the listless repose of the place, and the peculiar character of its inhabitants, who are descendants from the original Dutch settlers, this sequestered glen has long been known by the name of SLEEPY HOLLOW, and its rustic lads are called the Sleepy Hollow Boys throughout all the neighboring country. A drowsy, dreamy influence seems to hang over the land, and to pervade the very atmosphere. Some say that the place was bewitched by a high German doctor, during the early days of the settlement; others, that an old Indian chief, the prophet or wizard of his tribe, held his pow-wows there before the country was discovered by Master Hendrick Hudson. Certain it is, the place still continues under the sway of some witching power, that holds a spell over the minds of the good people, causing them to walk in a continual reverie. They are given to all kinds of marvellous beliefs; are subject to trances and visions; and frequently see strange sights, and hear music and voices in the air. The whole neighborhood abounds with local tales, haunted spots, and twilight superstitions; stars shoot and meteors glare oftener across the valley than in any other part of the country, and the nightmare, with her whole nine fold, seems to make it the favorite scene of her gambols.

The dominant spirit, however, that haunts this enchanted region, and seems to be commander-in-chief of all the powers of the air, is the apparition of a figure on horseback without a head. It is said by some to be the ghost of a Hessian trooper, whose head had been carried away by a cannon-ball, in some nameless battle

225

during the revolutionary war; and who is ever and anon seen by the country folk hurrying along in the gloom of night, as if on the wings of the wind. His haunts are not confined to the valley, but extend at times to the adjacent roads, and especially to the vicinity of a church at no great distance. Indeed, certain of the most authentic historians of those parts, who have been careful in collecting and collating the floating facts concerning this spectre, allege that the body of the trooper, having been buried in the church-yard, the ghost rides forth to the scene of battle in nightly quest of his head; and that the rushing speed with which he sometimes passes along the Hollow, like a midnight blast, is owing to his being belated, and in a hurry to get back to the church-yard before daybreak.

Such is the general purport of this legendary superstition, which has furnished materials for many a wild story in that region of shadows; and the spectre is known, at all the country firesides, by the name of the Headless Horseman of Sleepy Hollow.

It is remarkable that the visionary propensity I have mentioned is not confined to the native inhabitants of the valley, but is unconsciously imbibed by every one who resides there for a time. However wide awake they may have been before they entered that sleepy region, they are sure, in a little time, to inhale the witching influence of the air, and begin to grow imaginative—to dream dreams, and see apparitions.

I mention this peaceful spot with all possible laud; for it is in such little retired Dutch valleys, found here and there embosomed in the great State of New-York, that population, manners, and customs, remain fixed; while the great torrent of migration and improvement, which is making such incessant changes in other parts of this restless country, sweeps by them unobserved. They are like those little nooks of still water which border a rapid stream; where we may see the straw and bubble riding quietly at anchor, or slowly revolving in their mimic harbor, undisturbed by the rush of the passing current. Though many years have elapsed since I trod the drowsy shades of Sleepy Hollow, yet I question whether I should not still find the same trees and the same families vegetating in its sheltered bosom.

In this by-place of nature, there abode, in a remote period of American history, that is to say, some thirty years since, a worthy wight of the name of Ichabod Crane; who sojourned, or, as he expressed it, "tarried," in Sleepy Hollow, for the purpose of instructing the children of the vicinity. He was a native of Connecticut; a State which supplies the Union with pioneers for the mind as well as for the forest, and sends forth yearly its legions of frontier woodsmen and country schoolmasters. The cognomen of Crane was not inapplicable to his person. He was tall, but exceedingly lank, with narrow shoulders, long arms and legs, hands that dangled a mile out of his sleeves, feet that might have served for shovels, and his whole frame most loosely hung together. His head was small, and flat at top, with huge ears, large green glassy eyes, and a long snipe nose, so that it looked like a weather-cock, perched upon his spindle neck, to tell which way the wind blew. To see him striding along the profile of a hill on a windy day, with his clothes bagging and fluttering about him one might have mistaken him for the genius of famine descending upon the earth, or some scarecrow eloped from a cornfield.

His school-house was a low building of one large room, rudely constructed of logs; the windows partly glazed, and partly patched with leaves of old copy-books. It was most ingeniously secured at vacant hours, by a withe twisted in the handle of the door, and stakes set against the window shutters; so that, though a thief might get in with perfect ease, he would find some embarrassment in getting out; an idea most probably borrowed by the architect, Yost Van Houton, from the mystery of an eel-pot. The school-house stood in a rather lonely but pleasant situation just at the foot of a woody hill, with a brook running close by, and a formidable birch tree growing at one end of it. From hence the low murmur of his pupils' voices, conning over their lessons, might be heard in a drowsy summer's day, like the hum of a bee-hive; interrupted now and then by the authoritative voice of the master, in the tone of menace or command; or, peradventure, by the appalling sound of the birch, as he urged some tardy loiterer along the flowery path of knowledge. Truth to say, he was a conscientious man, and ever bore in mind the golden maxim, "Spare the rod and spoil the child."—Ichabod Crane's scholars certainly were not spoiled.

I would not have it imagined, however, that he was one of those cruel potentates of the school, who joy in the smart of their subjects; on the contrary, he administered justice with discrimination rather than severity; taking the burthen off the backs of the weak, and laying it on those of the strong. Your mere puny stripling, that winced at the least flourish of the rod, was passed by with indulgence; but the claims of justice were satisfied by inflicting a double portion on some little, tough, wrong-headed, broad-skirted Dutch urchin, who sulked and swelled and grew dogged and sullen beneath the birch. All this he called "doing his duty by their parents;" and he never inflicted a chastisement without following it by the assurance, so consolatory to the smarting urchin, that "he would remember it, and thank him for it the longest day he had to live."

When school hours were over, he was even the companion and playmate of the larger boys; and on holiday afternoons would convoy some of the smaller ones home, who happened to have pretty sisters, or good house-wives for mothers, noted for the comforts of the cupboard. Indeed it behooved him to keep on good terms with his pupils. The revenue arising from his school was small, and would have been scarcely sufficient to furnish him with daily bread, for he was a huge feeder, and though lank, had the dilating powers of an anaconda; but to help out his maintenance, he was, according to country custom in those parts, boarded and lodged at the houses of the farmers, whose children he instructed. With these he lived successively a week at a time; thus going the rounds of the neighborhood, with all his worldly effects tied up in a cotton handkerchief.

That all this might not be too onerous on the purses of his rustic patrons, who are apt to consider the costs of schooling a grievous burden, and schoolmasters as mere drones, he had various ways of rendering himself both useful and agreeable. He assisted the farmers occasionally in the lighter labors of their farms; helped to make hay; mended the fences; took the horses to water; drove the cows from pasture; and cut wood for the winter fire. He laid aside, too, all the dominant dignity and absolute sway with which he lorded it in his little empire, the school, and became wonderfully gentle and ingratiating. He found favor in the eyes of the mothers, by petting the children, particularly the youngest; and like the lion bold, which whilom so magnanimously the lamb did hold, he would sit with a child on one knee, and rock a cradle with his foot for whole hours together.

In addition to his other vocations, he was the singing-master of the neighborhood, and picked up many bright shillings by instructing the young folks in psalmody. It was a matter of no little vanity to him, on Sundays, to take his station in front of the church gallery, with a band of chosen singers; where, in his own mind, he completely carried away the palm from the parson. Certain it is, his voice resounded far above all the rest of the congregation; and there are peculiar quavers still to be heard in that church, and which may even be heard half a mile off, quite to the opposite side of the mill-pond, on a still Sunday morning, which are said to be legitimately descended from the nose of Ichabod Crane. Thus, by divers little make-shifts in that ingenious way which is commonly denominated "by hook and by crook," the worthy pedagogue got on tolerably enough, and was thought, by all who understood nothing of the labor of headwork, to have a wonderfully easy life of it.

The schoolmaster is generally a man of some importance in the female circle of a rural neighborhood; being considered a kind of idle gentlemanlike personage, of vastly superior taste and accomplishments to the rough country swains, and, indeed, inferior in learning only to the parson. His appearance, therefore, is apt to occasion some little stir at the tea-table of a farmhouse, and the addition of a supernumerary dish of cakes or sweetmeats, or, peradventure, the parade of a silver tea-pot. Our man of letters, therefore, was peculiarly happy in the smiles of all the country damsels. How he would figure among them in the churchyard, between services on Sundays! gathering grapes for them from the wild vines that overrun the surrounding trees; reciting for their amusement all the epitaphs on the tombstones; or sauntering, with a whole bevy of them, along the banks of the adjacent mill-pond; while the more bashful country bumpkins hung sheepishly back, envying his superior elegance and address.

From his half itinerant life, also, he was a kind of travelling gazette, carrying the whole budget of local gossip from house to house; so that his appearance was always greeted with satisfaction. He was, moreover, esteemed by the women as a man of great erudition, for he had read several books quite through, and was a perfect master of Cotton Mather's history of New England Witchcraft, in which, by the way, he most firmly and potently believed.

He was, in fact, an odd mixture of small shrewdness and simple credulity. His appetite for the marvellous, and his powers of digesting it, were equally extraordinary; and both had been increased by his residence in this spellbound region. No tale was too gross or monstrous for his capacious swallow. It was often his delight, after his school was dismissed in the afternoon, to stretch himself on the rich bed of clover, bordering the little brook that whimpered by his school-house, and there con over old Mather's direful tales, until the gathering dusk of the evening made the printed page a mere mist before his eyes. Then, as he wended his way, by swamp and stream and awful woodland, to the farmhouse where he happened to be quartered, every sound of nature, at that witching hour, fluttered his excited imagination: the moan of the whip-poor-will 1 from the hill-side; the boding cry of the tree-toad, that harbinger of storm; the dreary hooting of the screech-owl, or the sudden rustling in the thicket of birds frightened from their roost. The fire-flies, too, which sparkled most vividly in the darkest places, now and then startled him, as one of uncommon brightness would stream across his path; and if, by chance, a huge blockhead of a beetle came winging his blundering flight against him, the poor varlet was ready to give up the ghost, with the idea that he was struck with a witch's token. His only resource on such occasions, either to drown thought, or drive away evil spirits, was to sing psalm tunes;—and the good people of Sleepy Hollow, as they sat by their doors of an evening, were often filled with awe, at hearing his nasal melody, "in linked sweetness long drawn out," floating from the distant hill, or along the dusky road.

Another of his sources of fearful pleasure was, to pass long winter evenings with the old Dutch wives, as they sat spinning by the fire, with a row of apples roasting and spluttering along the hearth, and listen to their marvellous tales of ghosts and goblins, and haunted fields, and haunted brooks, and haunted bridges, and haunted houses, and particularly of the headless horseman, or galloping Hessian of the Hollow, as they sometimes called him. He would delight them equally by his anecdotes of witchcraft, and of the direful omens and portentous sights and sounds in the air, which prevailed in the earlier times of Connecticut; and would frighten them wofully with speculations upon comets and shooting stars; and with the alarming fact that the world did absolutely turn round, and that they were half the time topsy-turvy!

But if there was a pleasure in all this, while snugly cuddling in the chimney corner of a chamber that was all of a ruddy glow from the crackling wood fire, and where, of course, no spectre dared to show his face, it was dearly purchased by the terrors of his subsequent walk homewards. What fearful shapes and shadows beset his path amidst the dim and ghastly glare of a snowy night!—With what wistful look did he eye every trembling ray of light streaming across the waste fields from some distant window!—How often was he appalled by some shrub covered with snow, which, like a sheeted spectre, beset his very path!—How often did he shrink with curdling awe at the sound of his own steps on the frosty crust beneath his feet; and dread to look over his shoulder, lest he should behold some uncouth being tramping close behind him!—and how often was he thrown into complete dismay by some rushing blast, howling among the trees, in the idea that it was the Galloping Hessian on one of his nightly scourings!

All these, however, were mere terrors of the night, phantoms of the mind that walk in darkness; and though he had seen many spectres in his time, and been more than once beset by Satan in divers shapes, in his lonely perambulations, yet daylight put an end to all these evils; and he would have passed a pleasant life of it, in despite of the devil and all his works, if his path had not been crossed by a being that causes more perplexity to mortal man than ghosts, goblins, and the whole race of witches put together, and that was—a woman.

Among the musical disciples who assembled, one evening in each week, to receive his instructions in psalmody, was Katrina Van Tassel, the daughter and only child of a substantial Dutch farmer. She was a blooming lass of fresh eighteen; plump as a partridge; ripe and melting and rosy cheeked as one of her father's peaches, and universally famed, not merely for her beauty, but her vast expectations. She was withal a little of a coquette, as might be perceived even in her dress, which was a mixture of ancient and modern fashions, as most suited to set off her charms. She wore the ornaments of pure yellow gold, which her great-great-grandmother had brought over from Saardam, the tempting stomacher of the olden time; and withal a provokingly short petticoat, to display the prettiest foot and ankle in the country round.

Ichabod Crane had a soft and foolish heart towards the sex; and it is not to be wondered at, that so tempting a morsel soon found favor in his eyes; more especially after he had visited her in her paternal mansion. Old Baltus Van Tassel was a perfect picture of a thriving, contented, liberal-hearted farmer. He seldom, it is true, sent either his eyes or his thoughts beyond the boundaries of his own farm; but within those every thing was snug, happy, and well-conditioned. He was satisfied with his wealth, but not proud of it; and piqued himself upon the hearty abundance, rather than the style in which he lived. His stronghold was situated on the banks of the Hudson, in one of those green, sheltered, fertile nooks, in which the Dutch farmers are so fond of nestling. A great elm-tree spread its broad branches over it; at the foot of which bubbled up a spring of the softest and sweetest water, in a little well, formed of a barrel; and then stole sparkling away through the grass, to a neighboring brook, that bubbled along among alders and dwarf willows. Hard by the farmhouse was a vast barn, that might have served for a church; every window and crevice of which seemed bursting forth with the treasures of the farm; the flail was busily resounding within it from morning to night; swallows and martins skimmed twittering about the eaves; and rows of pigeons, some with one eye turned up, as if watching the weather, some with their heads under their wings, or buried in their bosoms, and others swelling, and cooing, and bowing about their dames, were enjoying the sunshine on the roof. Sleek unwieldy porkers were grunting in the repose and abundance of their pens; whence sallied forth, now and then, troops of sucking pigs, as if to snuff the air. A stately squadron of snowy geese were riding in an adjoining pond, convoying whole fleets of ducks; regiments of turkeys were gobbling through the farmyard, and guinea fowls fretting about it, like ill-tempered housewives, with their peevish discontented cry. Before the barn door strutted the gallant cock, that pattern of a husband, a warrior, and a fine gentleman, clapping his burnished wings, and crowing in the pride and gladness of his heart—sometimes tearing up the earth with his feet, and then generously calling his ever-hungry family of wives and children to enjoy the rich morsel which he had discovered.

The pedagogue's mouth watered, as he looked upon this sumptuous promise of luxurious winter fare. In his devouring mind's eye, he pictured to himself every roasting-pig running about with a pudding in his belly, and an apple in his mouth; the pigeons were snugly put to bed in a comfortable pie, and tucked in with a coverlet of crust; the geese were swimming in their own gravy; and the ducks pairing cosily in dishes, like snug married couples, with a decent competency of onion sauce. In the porkers he saw carved out the future sleek side of bacon, and juicy relishing ham; not a turkey but he beheld daintily trussed up, with its gizzard under its wing, and, peradventure, a necklace of savory sausages; and even bright chanticleer himself lay sprawling on his back, in a side-dish, with uplifted claws, as if craving that quarter which his chivalrous spirit disdained to ask while living.

As the enraptured Ichabod fancied all this, and as he rolled his great green eyes over the fat meadow-lands, the rich fields of wheat, of rye, of buckwheat, and Indian corn, and the orchards burthened with ruddy fruit, which surrounded the warm tenement of Van Tassel, his heart yearned after the damsel who was to inherit these domains, and his imagination expanded with the idea, how they might be readily turned into cash, and the money invested in immense tracts of wild land, and shingle palaces in the wilderness. Nay, his busy fancy already realized his hopes, and presented to him the blooming Katrina, with a whole family of children, mounted on the top of a wagon loaded with household trumpery, with pots and kettles dangling beneath; and he beheld himself bestriding a pacing mare, with a colt at her heels, setting out for Kentucky, Tennessee, or the Lord knows where.

When he entered the house the conquest of his heart was complete. It was one of those spacious farm-houses, with high-ridged, but lowly-sloping roofs, built in the style handed down from the first Dutch settlers; the low projecting eaves forming a piazza along the front, capable of being closed up in bad weather. Under this were hung flails, harness, various utensils of husbandry, and nets for fishing in the neighboring river. Benches were built along the sides for summer use; and a great spinning-wheel at one end, and a churn at the other, showed the various uses to which this important porch might be devoted. From this piazza the wondering Ichabod entered the hall, which formed the centre of the mansion and the place of usual residence. Here, rows of resplendent pewter, ranged on a long dresser, dazzled his eyes. In one corner stood a huge bag of wool ready to be spun; in another a quantity of linsey-woolsey just from the loom; ears of Indian corn, and strings of dried apples and peaches, hung in gay festoons along the walls, mingled with the gaud of red peppers; and a door left ajar gave him a peep into the best parlor, where the claw-footed chairs, and dark mahogany tables, shone like mirrors; and irons, with their accompanying shovel and tongs, glistened from their covert of asparagus tops; mock-oranges and conch-shells decorated the mantelpiece; strings of various colored birds' eggs were suspended above it: a great ostrich egg was hung from the centre of the room, and a corner cupboard, knowingly left open, displayed immense treasures of old silver and well-mended china.

From the moment Ichabod laid his eyes upon these regions of delight, the peace of his mind was at an end, and his only study was how to gain the affections of the peerless daughter of Van Tassel. In this enterprise, however, he had more real difficulties than generally fell to the lot of a knight-errant of yore, who seldom had any thing but giants, enchanters, fiery dragons, and such like easily-conquered adversaries, to contend with; and had to make his way merely through gates of iron and brass, and walls of adamant, to the castle keep, where the lady of his heart was confined; all which he achieved as easily as a man would carve his way to the centre of a Christmas pie; and then the lady gave him her hand as a matter of course. Ichabod, on the contrary, had to win his way to the heart of a country coquette, beset with a labyrinth of whims and caprices, which were for ever presenting new difficulties and impediments; and he had to encounter a host of fearful adversaries of real flesh and blood, the numerous rustic admirers, who beset every portal to her heart; keeping a watchful and angry eye upon each other, but ready to fly out in the common cause against any new competitor.

Among these the most formidable was a burly, roaring, roystering blade, of the name of Abraham, or, according to the Dutch abbreviation, Brom Van Brunt, the hero of the country round, which rang with his feats of strength and hardihood. He was broad-shouldered and double-jointed, with short curly black hair, and a bluff, but not unpleasant countenance, having a mingled air of fun and arrogance. From his Herculean frame and great powers of limb, he had received the nickname of BROM BONES, by which he was universally known. He was famed for great knowledge and skill in horsemanship, being as dexterous on horseback as a Tartar.

He was foremost at all races and cock-fights; and, with the ascendency which bodily strength acquires in rustic life, was the umpire in all disputes, setting his hat on one side, and giving his decisions with an air and tone admitting of no gainsay or appeal. He was always ready for either a fight or a frolic; but had more mischief than ill-will in his composition; and, with all his overbearing roughness, there was a strong dash of waggish good humor at bottom. He had three or four boon companions, who regarded him as their model, and at the head of whom he scoured the country, attending every scene of feud or merriment for miles round. In cold weather he was distinguished by a fur cap, surmounted with a flaunting fox's tail; and when the folks at a country gathering descried this well-known crest at a distance, whisking about among a squad of hard riders, they always stood by for a squall. Sometimes his crew would be heard dashing along past the farmhouses at midnight, with whoop and halloo, like a troop of Don Cossacks; and the old dames, startled out of their sleep, would listen for a moment till the hurry-scurry had clattered by, and then exclaim, "Ay, there goes Brom Bones and his gang!" The neighbors looked upon him with a mixture of awe, admiration, and good will; and when any madcap prank, or rustic brawl, occurred in the vicinity, always shook their heads, and warranted Brom Bones was at the bottom of it.

This rantipole hero had for some time singled out the blooming Katrina for the object of his uncouth gallantries, and though his amorous toyings were something like the gentle caresses and endearments of a bear, yet it was whispered that she did not altogether discourage his hopes. Certain it is, his advances were signals for rival candidates to retire, who felt no inclination to cross a lion in his amours; insomuch, that when his horse was seen tied to Van Tassel's paling, on a Sunday night, a sure sign that his master was courting, or, as it is termed "sparking," within, all other suitors passed by in despair, and carried the war into other quarters.

Such was the formidable rival with whom Ichabod Crane had to contend, and, considering all things, a stouter man than he would have shrunk from the competition, and a wiser man would have despaired. He had, however, a happy mixture of pliability and perseverance in his nature; he was in form and spirit like a supple-jack—yielding, but tough; though he bent, he never broke; and though he bowed beneath the slightest pressure, yet, the moment it was away—jerk! he was as erect, and carried his head as high as ever.

To have taken the field openly against his rival would have been madness; for he was not a man to be thwarted in his amours, any more than that stormy lover, Achilles. Ichabod, therefore, made his advances in a quiet and gently-insinuating manner. Under cover of his character of singing-master, he made frequent visits at the farmhouse; not that he had any thing to apprehend from the meddlesome interference of parents, which is so often a stumbling-block in the path of lovers. Balt Van Tassel was an easy indulgent soul; he loved his daughter better even than his pipe, and, like a reasonable man and an excellent father, let her have her way in every thing. His notable little wife, too, had enough to do to attend to her housekeeping and manage her poultry; for, as she sagely observed, ducks and geese are foolish things, and must be looked after, but girls can take care of themselves. Thus while the busy dame bustled about the house, or plied her spinning-wheel at one end of the piazza, honest Balt would sit smoking his evening pipe at the other, watching the achievements of a little wooden warrior, who, armed with a sword in each hand, was most valiantly fighting the wind on the pinnacle of the barn. In the mean time, Ichabod would carry on his suit with the daughter by the side of the spring under the great elm, or sauntering along in the twilight, that hour so favorable to the lover's eloquence.

I profess not to know how women's hearts are wooed and won. To me they have always been matters of riddle and admiration. Some seem to have but one vulnerable point, or door of access; while others have a thousand avenues, and may be captured in a thousand different ways. It is a great triumph of skill to gain the former, but a still greater proof of generalship to maintain possession of the latter, for the man must battle for his fortress at every door and window. He who wins a thousand common hearts is therefore entitled to some renown; but he who keeps undisputed sway over the heart of a coquette, is indeed a hero. Certain it is, this was not the case with the redoubtable Brom Bones; and from the moment Ichabod Crane made his advances, the interests of the former evidently declined; his horse was no longer seen tied at the palings on Sunday nights, and a deadly feud gradually arose between him and the preceptor of Sleepy Hollow.

Brom, who had a degree of rough chivalry in his nature, would fain have carried matters to open warfare, and have settled their pretensions to the lady, according to the mode of those most concise and simple reasoners, the knights-errant of yore—by single combat; but Ichabod was too conscious of the superior might of his adversary to enter the lists against him: he had overheard a boast of Bones, that he would "double the schoolmaster up, and lay him on a shelf of his own school-house;" and he was too wary to give him an opportunity. There was something extremely provoking in this obstinately pacific system; it left Brom no alternative but to draw upon the funds of rustic waggery in his disposition, and to play off boorish practical jokes upon his rival. Ichabod became the object of whimsical persecution to Bones, and his gang of rough riders. They harried his hitherto peaceful domains; smoked out his singing school, by stopping up the chimney; broke into the schoolhouse at night, in spite of its formidable fastenings of withe and window stakes, and turned every thing topsy-turvy: so that the poor schoolmaster began to think all the witches in the country held their meetings there. But what was still more annoying, Brom took all opportunities of turning him into ridicule in presence of his mistress, and had a scoundrel dog whom he taught to whine in the most ludicrous manner, and introduced as a rival of Ichabod's to instruct her in psalmody.

In this way matters went on for some time, without producing any material effect on the relative situation of the contending powers. On a fine autumnal afternoon, Ichabod, in pensive mood, sat enthroned on the lofty stool whence he usually watched all the concerns of his little literary realm. In his hand he swayed a ferule, that sceptre of despotic power; the birch of justice reposed on three nails, behind the throne, a constant terror to evil doers; while on the desk before him might be seen sundry contraband articles and prohibited weapons, detected upon the persons of idle urchins; such as half-munched apples, popguns, whirligigs, fly-cages, and whole legions of rampant little paper gamecocks. Apparently there had been some appalling act of justice recently inflicted, for his scholars were all busily intent upon their books, or slyly whispering behind them with one eye kept upon the master; and a kind of buzzing stillness reigned throughout the school-room. It was suddenly interrupted by the appearance of a negro, in tow-cloth jacket and trowsers, a round-crowned fragment of a hat, like the cap of Mercury, and mounted on the back of a ragged, wild, half-broken colt, which he managed with a rope by way of halter. He came clattering up to the school door with an invitation to Ichabod to attend a merry-making or "quilting frolic," to be held that evening at Mynheer Van Tassel's; and having delivered his message with that air of importance, and effort at fine language, which a negro is apt to display on petty embassies of that kind, he dashed over the brook, and was seen scampering away up the hollow, full of the importance and hurry of his mission.

All was now bustle and hubbub in the late quiet schoolroom. The scholars were hurried through their lessons, without stopping at trifles; those who were nimble skipped over half with impunity, and those who were tardy, had a smart application now and then in the rear, to quicken their speed, or help them over a tall word. Books were flung aside without being put away on the shelves, inkstands were overturned, benches thrown down, and the whole school was turned loose an hour before the usual time, bursting forth like a legion of young imps, yelping and racketing about the green, in joy at their early emancipation.

The gallant Ichabod now spent at least an extra half hour at his toilet, brushing and furbishing up his best, and indeed only suit of rusty black, and arranging his looks by a bit of broken looking-glass, that hung up in the schoolhouse. That he might make his appearance before his mistress in the true style of a cavalier, he borrowed a horse from the farmer with whom he was domiciliated, a choleric old Dutchman, of the name of Hans Van Ripper, and, thus gallantly mounted, issued forth, like a knight-errant in quest of adventures. But it is meet I should, in the true spirit of romantic story, give some account of the looks and equipments of my hero and his steed. The animal he bestrode was a broken-down plough-horse, that had outlived almost every thing but his viciousness. He was gaunt and shagged, with a ewe neck and a head like a hammer; his rusty mane and tail were tangled and knotted with burrs; one eye had lost its pupil, and was glaring and spectral; but the other had the gleam of a genuine devil in it. Still he must have had fire and mettle in his day, if we may judge from the name he bore of Gunpowder. He had, in fact, been a favorite steed of his master's, the choleric Van Ripper, who was a furious rider, and had infused, very probably, some of his own spirit into the animal; for, old and broken-down as he looked, there was more of the lurking devil in him than in any young filly in the country.

Ichabod was a suitable figure for such a steed. He rode with short stirrups, which brought his knees nearly up to the pommel of the saddle; his sharp elbows stuck out like grasshoppers'; he carried his whip perpendicularly in his hand, like a sceptre, and, as his horse jogged on, the motion of his arms was not unlike the flapping of a pair of wings. A small wool hat rested on the top of his nose, for so his scanty strip of forehead might be called; and the skirts of his black coat fluttered out almost to the horse's tail. Such was the appearance of Ichabod and his steed, as they shambled out of the gate of Hans Van Ripper, and it was altogether such an apparition as is seldom to be met with in broad daylight.

It was, as I have said, a fine autumnal day, the sky was clear and serene, and nature wore that rich and golden livery which we always associate with the idea of abundance. The forests had put on their sober brown and yellow, while some trees of the tenderer kind had been nipped by the frosts into brilliant dyes of orange, purple, and scarlet. Streaming files of wild ducks began to make their appearance high in the air; the bark of the squirrel might be heard from the groves of beech and hickory nuts, and the pensive whistle of the quail at intervals from the neighboring stubble-field.

The small birds were taking their farewell banquets. In the fulness of their revelry, they fluttered, chirping and frolicking, from bush to bush, and tree to tree, capricious from the very profusion and variety around them. There was the honest cock-robin, the favorite game of stripling sportsmen, with its loud querulous note; and the twittering blackbirds flying in sable clouds; and the golden-winged woodpecker, with his crimson crest, his broad black gorget, and splendid plumage; and the cedar bird, with its red-tipt wings and yellow-tipt tail, and its little monteiro cap of feathers; and the blue-jay, that noisy coxcomb, in his gay light-blue coat and white under-clothes; screaming and chattering, nodding and bobbing and bowing, and pretending to be on good terms with every songster of the grove.

As Ichabod jogged slowly on his way, his eye, ever open to every symptom of culinary abundance, ranged with delight over the treasures of jolly autumn. On all sides he beheld vast store of apples; some hanging in oppressive opulence on the trees; some gathered into baskets and barrels for the market; others heaped up in rich piles for the cider-press. Farther on he beheld great fields of Indian corn, with its golden ears peeping from their leafy coverts, and holding out the promise of cakes and hasty pudding; and the yellow pumpkins lying beneath them, turning up their fair round bellies to the sun, and giving ample prospects of the most luxurious of pies; and anon he passed the fragrant buckwheat fields, breathing the odor of the beehive, and as he beheld them, soft anticipations stole over his mind of dainty slapjacks, well buttered, and garnished with honey or treacle, by the delicate little dimpled hand of Katrina Van Tassel.

Thus feeding his mind with many sweet thoughts and "sugared suppositions," he journeyed along the sides of a range of hills which look out upon some of the goodliest scenes of the mighty Hudson. The sun gradually wheeled his broad disk down into the west. The wide bosom of the Tappan Zee lay motionless and glassy, excepting that here and there a gentle undulation waved and prolonged the blue shadow of the distant mountain. A few amber clouds floated in the sky, without a breath of air to move them. The horizon was of a fine golden tint, changing gradually into a pure apple green, and from that into the deep blue of the mid-heaven. A slanting ray lingered on the woody crests of the precipices that overhung some parts of the river, giving greater depth to the dark-gray and purple of their rocky sides. A sloop was loitering in the distance, dropping slowly down with the tide, her sail hanging uselessly against the mast; and as the reflection of the sky gleamed along the still water, it seemed as if the vessel was suspended in the air.

It was toward evening that Ichabod arrived at the castle of the Heer Van Tassel, which he found thronged with the pride and flower of the adjacent country. Old farmers, a spare leathern-faced race, in homespun coats and breeches, blue stockings, huge shoes, and magnificent pewter buckles. Their brisk withered little dames, in close crimped caps, long-waisted short-gowns, home-spun petticoats, with scissors and pincushions, and gay calico pockets hanging on the outside. Buxom lasses, almost as antiquated as their mothers, excepting where a straw hat, a fine ribbon, or perhaps a white frock, gave symptoms of city innovation. The sons, in short square-skirted coats with rows of stupendous brass buttons, and their hair generally queued in the fashion of the times, especially if they could procure an eel-skin for the purpose, it being esteemed, throughout the country, as a potent nourisher and strengthener of the hair.

Brom Bones, however, was the hero of the scene, having come to the gathering on his favorite steed Daredevil, a creature, like himself, full of mettle and mischief, and which no one but himself could manage. He was, in fact, noted for preferring vicious animals, given to all kinds of tricks, which kept the rider in constant risk of his neck, for he held a tractable well-broken horse as unworthy of a lad of spirit.

Fain would I pause to dwell upon the world of charms that burst upon the enraptured gaze of my hero, as he entered the state parlor of Van Tassel's mansion. Not those of the bevy of buxom lasses, with their luxurious display of red and white; but the ample charms of a genuine Dutch country tea-table, in the sumptuous time of autumn. Such heaped-up platters of cakes of various and almost indescribable kinds, known only to experienced Dutch housewives! There was the doughty dough-nut, the tenderer oly koek, and the crisp and crumbling cruller; sweet cakes and short cakes, ginger cakes and honey cakes, and the whole family of cakes. And then there were apple pies and peach pies and pumpkin pies; besides slices of ham and smoked beef; and moreover delectable dishes of preserved plums, and peaches, and pears, and quinces; not to mention broiled shad and roasted chickens; together with bowls of milk and cream, all mingled higgledy-piggledly, pretty much as I have enumerated them, with the motherly tea-pot sending up its clouds of vapor from the midst— Heaven bless the mark! I want breath and time to discuss this banquet as it deserves, and am too eager to get on with my story. Happily, Ichabod Crane was not in so great a hurry as his historian, but did ample justice to every dainty.

He was a kind and thankful creature, whose heart dilated in proportion as his skin was filled with good cheer; and whose spirits rose with eating as some men's do with drink. He could not help, too, rolling his large eyes round him as he ate, and chuckling with the possibility that he might one day be lord of all this scene of almost unimaginable luxury and splendor. Then, he thought, how soon he'd turn his back upon the old school-house; snap his fingers in the face of Hans Van Ripper, and every other niggardly patron, and kick any itinerant pedagogue out of doors that should dare to call him comrade!

Old Baltus Van Tassel moved about among his guests with a face dilated with content and good humor, round and jolly as the harvest moon. His hospitable attentions were brief, but expressive, being confined to a shake of the hand, a slap on the shoulder, a loud laugh, and a pressing invitation to "fall to, and help themselves."

And now the sound of the music from the common room, or hall, summoned to the dance. The musician was an old grayheaded negro, who had been the itinerant orchestra of the neighborhood for more than half a century. His instrument was as old and battered as himself. The greater part of the time he scraped on two or three strings, accompanying every movement of the bow with a motion of the head; bowing almost to the ground, and stamping with his foot whenever a fresh couple were to start.

Ichabod prided himself upon his dancing as much as upon his vocal powers. Not a limb, not a fibre about him was idle; and to have seen his loosely hung frame in full motion, and clattering about the room, you would have thought Saint Vitus himself, that blessed patron of the dance, was figuring before you in person. He was the admiration of all the negroes; who, having gathered, of all ages and sizes, from the farm and the neighborhood, stood forming a pyramid of shining black faces at every door and window, gazing with delight at the scene, rolling their white eye-balls, and showing grinning rows of ivory from ear to ear. How could the flogger of urchins be otherwise than animated and joyous? the lady of his heart was his partner in the dance, and smiling graciously in reply to all his amorous oglings; while Brom Bones, sorely smitten with love and jealousy, sat brooding by himself in one corner.

When the dance was at an end, Ichabod was attracted to a knot of the sager folks, who, with old Van Tassel, sat smoking at one end of the piazza, gossiping over former times, and drawing out long stories about the war.

This neighborhood, at the time of which I am speaking, was one of those highly-favored places which abound with chronicle and great men. The British and American line had run near it during the war; it had, therefore, been the scene of marauding, and infested with refugees, cow-boys, and all kinds of border chivalry. Just sufficient time had elapsed to enable each story-teller to dress up his tale with a little becoming fiction, and, in the indistinctness of his recollection, to make himself the hero of every exploit.

There was the story of Doffue Martling, a large blue-bearded Dutchman, who had nearly taken a British frigate with an old iron nine-pounder from a mud breastwork, only that his gun burst at the sixth discharge. And there was an old gentleman who shall be nameless, being too rich a mynheer to be lightly mentioned, who, in the battle of White-plains, being an excellent master of defence, parried a musket ball with a small sword, insomuch that he absolutely felt it whiz round the blade, and glance off at the hilt: in proof of which, he was ready at any time to show the sword, with the hilt a little bent. There were several more that had been equally great in the field, not one of whom but was persuaded that he had a considerable hand in bringing the war to a happy termination.

But all these were nothing to the tales of ghosts and apparitions that succeeded. The neighborhood is rich in legendary treasures of the kind. Local tales and superstitions thrive best in these sheltered long-settled retreats; but are trampled under foot by the shifting throng that forms the populations of most of our country places. Besides, there is no encouragement for ghosts in most of our villages, for, they have scarcely had time to finish their first nap, and turn themselves in their graves, before their surviving friends have travelled away from the neighborhood; so that when they turn out at night to walk their rounds, they have no acquaintance left to call upon. This is perhaps the reason why we so seldom hear of ghosts except in our long-established Dutch communities.

The immediate cause, however, of the prevalence of supernatural stories in these parts, was doubtless owing to the vicinity of Sleepy Hollow. There was a contagion in the very air that blew from that haunted region; it breathed forth an atmosphere of dreams and fancies infecting all the land. Several of the Sleepy Hollow people were present at Van Tassel's, and, as usual, were doling out their wild and wonderful legends. Many dismal tales were told about funeral trains, and mourning cries and wailing heard and seen about the great tree where the unfortunate Major André was taken, and which stood in the neighborhood. Some mention was made also of the woman in white, that haunted the dark glen at Raven Rock, and was often heard to shriek on winter nights before a storm, having perished there in the snow. The chief part of the stories, however, turned upon the favorite spectre of Sleepy Hollow, the headless horseman, who had been heard several times of late, patrolling the country; and, it was said, tethered his horse nightly among the graves in the church-yard.

The sequestered situation of this church seems always to have made it a favorite haunt of troubled spirits. It stands on a knoll, surrounded by locust-trees and lofty elms, from among which its decent whitewashed walls shine modestly forth, like Christian purity beaming through the shades of retirement. A gentle slope descends from it to a silver sheet of water, bordered by high trees, between which, peeps may be caught at the blue hills of the Hudson. To look upon its grass-grown yard, where the sunbeams seem to sleep so quietly, one would think that there at least the dead might rest in peace. On one side of the church extends a wide woody dell, along which raves a large brook among broken rocks and trunks of fallen trees. Over a deep black part of the stream, not far from the church, was formerly thrown a wooden bridge; the road that led to it, and the bridge itself, were thickly shaded by overhanging trees, which cast a gloom about it, even in the daytime; but occasioned a fearful darkness at night. This was one of the favorite haunts of the headless horseman; and the place where he was most frequently encountered. The tale was told of old Brouwer, a most heretical disbeliever in ghosts, how he met the horseman returning from his foray into Sleepy Hollow, and was obliged to get up behind him; how they galloped over bush and brake, over hill and swamp, until they reached the bridge; when the horseman suddenly turned into a skeleton, threw old Brouwer into the brook, and sprang away over the tree-tops with a clap of thunder.

This story was immediately matched by a thrice marvellous adventure of Brom Bones, who made light of the galloping Hessian as an arrant jockey. He affirmed that, on returning one night from the neighboring village of Sing Sing, he had been overtaken by this midnight trooper; that he had offered to race with him for a bowl of punch, and should have won it too, for Dare-devil beat the goblin horse all hollow, but, just as they came to the church bridge, the Hessian bolted, and vanished in a flash of fire.

All these tales, told in that drowsy undertone with which men talk in the dark, the countenances of the listeners only now and then receiving a casual gleam from the glare of a pipe, sank deep in the mind of Ichabod. He repaid them in kind with large extracts from his invaluable author, Cotton Mather, and added many marvellous events that had taken place in his native State of Connecticut, and fearful sights which he had seen in his nightly walks about Sleepy Hollow.

The revel now gradually broke up. The old farmers gathered together their families in their wagons, and were heard for some time rattling along the hollow roads, and over the distant hills. Some of the damsels mounted on pillions behind their favorite swains, and their light-hearted laughter, mingling with the clatter of hoofs, echoed along the silent woodlands, sounding fainter and fainter until they gradually died away—and the late scene of noise and frolic was all silent and deserted. Ichabod only lingered behind, according to the custom of country lovers, to have a tête-à-tête with the heiress, fully convinced that he was now on the high road to success. What passed at this interview I will not pretend to say, for in fact I do not know. Something, however, I fear me, must have gone wrong, for he certainly sallied forth, after no very great interval, with an air quite desolate and chop-fallen.—Oh these women! these women! Could that girl have been playing off any of her coquettish tricks?—Was her encouragement of the poor pedagogue all a mere sham to secure her conquest of his rival?—Heaven only knows, not I!—Let it suffice to say, Ichabod stole forth with the air of one who had been sacking a hen-roost, rather than a fair lady's heart. Without looking to the right or left to notice the scene of rural wealth, on which he had so often gloated, he went straight to the stable, and with several hearty cuffs and kicks, roused his steed most uncourteously from the comfortable quarters in which he was soundly sleeping, dreaming of mountains of corn and oats, and whole valleys of timothy and clover.

It was the very witching time of night that Ichabod, heavy-hearted and crest-fallen, pursued his travel homewards, along the sides of the lofty hills which rise above Tarry Town, and which he had traversed so cheerily in the afternoon. The hour was dismal as himself. Far below him, the Tappan Zee spread its dusky and indistinct waste of waters, with here and there the tall mast of a sloop, riding quietly at anchor under the land. In the dead hush of midnight, he could even hear the barking of the watch dog from the opposite shore of the Hudson; but it was so vague and faint as only to give an idea of his distance from this faithful companion of man. Now and then, too, the long-drawn crowing of a cock, accidentally awakened, would sound far, far off from some farmhouse away among the hills—but it was like a dreaming sound in his ear. No signs of life occurred near him, but occasionally the melancholy chirp of a cricket, or perhaps the guttural twang of a bull-frog, from a neighboring marsh, as if sleeping uncomfortably, and turning suddenly in his bed.

All the stories of ghosts and goblins that he had heard in the afternoon, now came crowding upon his recollection. The night grew darker and darker; the stars seemed to sink deeper in the sky, and driving clouds occasionally hid them from his sight. He had never felt so lonely and dismal. He was, moreover, approaching the very place where many of the scenes of the ghost stories had been laid. In the centre of the road stood an enormous tulip-tree, which towered like a giant above all the other trees of the neighborhood, and formed a kind of landmark. Its limbs were gnarled, and fantastic, large enough to form trunks for ordinary trees, twisting down almost to the earth, and rising again into the air.

It was connected with the tragical story of the unfortunate André, who had been taken prisoner hard by; and was universally known by the name of Major André's tree. The common people regarded it with a mixture of respect and superstition, partly out of sympathy for the fate of its ill-starred namesake, and partly from the tales of strange sights and doleful lamentations told concerning it.

As Ichabod approached this fearful tree, he began to whistle: he thought his whistle was answered—it was but a blast sweeping sharply through the dry branches. As he approached a little nearer, he thought he saw something white, hanging in the midst of the tree—he paused and ceased whistling; but on looking more narrowly, perceived that it was a place where the tree had been scathed by lightning, and the white wood laid bare. Suddenly he heard a groan—his teeth chattered and his knees smote against the saddle: it was but the rubbing of one huge bough upon another, as they were swayed about by the breeze. He passed the tree in safety, but new perils lay before him.

About two hundred yards from the tree a small brook crossed the road, and ran into a marshy and thickly-wooded glen, known by the name of Wiley's swamp. A few rough logs, laid side by side, served for a bridge over this stream. On that side of the road where the brook entered the wood, a group of oaks and chestnuts, matted thick with wild grapevines, threw a cavernous gloom over it. To pass this bridge was the severest trial. It was at this identical spot that the unfortunate André was captured, and under the covert of those chestnuts and vines were the sturdy yeomen concealed who surprised him. This has ever since been considered a haunted stream, and fearful are the feelings of the schoolboy who has to pass it alone after dark.

As he approached the stream his heart began to thump; he summoned up, however, all his resolution, gave his horse half a score of kicks in the ribs, and attempted to dash briskly across the bridge; but instead of starting forward, the perverse old animal made a lateral movement, and ran broadside against the fence. Ichabod, whose fears increased with the delay, jerked the reins on the other side, and kicked lustily with the contrary foot: it was all in vain; his steed started, it is true, but it was only to plunge to the opposite side of the road into a thicket of brambles and alder bushes. The schoolmaster now bestowed both whip and heel upon the starveling ribs of old Gunpowder, who dashed forward, snuffling and snorting, but came to a stand just by the bridge, with a suddenness that had nearly sent his rider sprawling over his head. Just at this moment a plashy tramp by the side of the bridge caught the sensitive ear of Ichabod. In the dark shadow of the grove, on the margin of the brook, he beheld something huge, misshapen, black and towering. It stirred not, but seemed gathered up in the gloom, like some gigantic monster ready to spring upon the traveller.

The hair of the affrighted pedagogue rose upon his head with terror. What was to be done? To turn and fly was now too late; and besides, what chance was there of escaping ghost or goblin, if such it was, which could ride upon the wings of the wind? Summoning up, therefore, a show of courage, he demanded in stammering accents—"Who are you?" He received no reply. He repeated his demand in a still more agitated voice. Still there was no answer. Once more he cudgelled the sides of the inflexible Gunpowder, and, shutting his eyes, broke forth with involuntary fervor into a psalm tune. Just then the shadowy object of alarm put itself in motion, and, with a scramble and a bound, stood at once in the middle of the road. Though the night was dark and dismal, yet the form of the unknown might now in some degree be ascertained. He appeared to be a horseman of large dimensions, and mounted on a black horse of powerful frame. He made no offer of molestation or sociability, but kept aloof on one side of the road, jogging along on the blind side of old Gunpowder, who had now got over his fright and waywardness.

Ichabod, who had no relish for this strange midnight companion, and bethought himself of the adventure of Brom Bones with the Galloping Hessian, now quickened his steed, in hopes of leaving him behind. The stranger, however, quickened his horse to an equal pace. Ichabod pulled up, and fell into a walk, thinking to lag behind—the other did the same. His heart began to sink within him; he endeavored to resume his psalm tune, but his parched tongue clove to the roof of his mouth, and he could not utter a stave. There was something in the moody and dogged silence of this pertinacious companion, that was mysterious and appalling. It was soon fearfully accounted for. On mounting a rising ground, which brought the figure of his fellow-traveller in relief against the sky, gigantic in height, and muffled in a cloak, Ichabod was horror-struck, on perceiving that he was headless!—but his horror was still more increased, on observing that the head, which should have rested on his shoulders, was carried before him on the pommel of the saddle; his terror rose to desperation; he rained a shower of kicks and blows upon Gunpowder; hoping, by a sudden movement, to give his companion the slip—but the spectre started full jump with him. Away then they dashed, through thick and thin; stones flying, and sparks flashing at every bound. Ichabod's flimsy garments fluttered in the air, as he stretched his long lanky body away over his horse's head, in the eagerness of his flight.

They had now reached the road which turns off to Sleepy Hollow; but Gunpowder, who seemed possessed with a demon, instead of keeping up it, made an opposite turn, and plunged headlong down hill to the left. This road leads through a sandy hollow, shaded by trees for about a quarter of a mile, where it crosses the bridge famous in goblin story, and just beyond swells the green knoll on which stands the whitewashed church.

As yet the panic of the steed had given his unskilful rider an apparent advantage in the chase; but just as he had got half way through the hollow, the girths of the saddle gave way, and he felt it slipping from under him. He seized it by the pommel, and endeavored to hold it firm, but in vain; and had just time to save himself by clasping old Gunpowder round the neck, when the saddle fell to the earth, and he heard it trampled under foot by his pursuer. For a moment the terror of Hans Van Ripper's wrath passed across his mind—for it was his Sunday saddle; but this was no time for petty fears; the goblin was hard on his haunches; and (unskilful rider that he was!) he had much ado to maintain his seat; sometimes slipping on one side, sometimes on another, and sometimes jolted on the high ridge of his horse's backbone, with a violence that he verily feared would cleave him asunder.

An opening in the trees now cheered him with the hopes that the church bridge was at hand. The wavering reflection of a silver star in the bosom of the brook told him that he was not mistaken. He saw the walls of the church dimly glaring under the trees beyond. He recollected the place where Brom Bones's ghostly competitor had disappeared. "If I can but reach that bridge," thought Ichabod, "I am safe." Just then he heard the black steed panting and blowing close behind him; he even fancied that he felt his hot breath. Another convulsive kick in the ribs, and old Gunpowder sprang upon the bridge; he thundered over the resounding planks; he gained the opposite side; and now Ichabod cast a look behind to see if his pursuer should vanish, according to rule, in a flash of fire and brimstone. Just then he saw the goblin rising in his stirrups, and in the very act of hurling his head at him. Ichabod endeavored to dodge the horrible missile, but too late. It encountered his cranium with a tremendous crash—he was tumbled headlong into the dust, and Gunpowder, the black steed, and the goblin rider, passed by like a whirlwind.

The next morning the old horse was found without his saddle, and with the bridle under his feet, soberly cropping the grass at his master's gate. Ichabod did not make his appearance at breakfast—dinner-hour came, but no Ichabod. The boys assembled at the schoolhouse, and strolled idly about the banks of the brook; but no school-master. Hans Van Ripper now began to feel some uneasiness about the fate of poor Ichabod, and his saddle. An inquiry was set on foot, and after diligent investigation they came upon his traces. In one part of the road leading to the church was found the saddle trampled in the dirt; the tracks of horses' hoofs deeply dented in the road, and evidently at furious speed, were traced to the bridge, beyond which, on the bank of a broad part of the brook, where the water ran deep and black, was found the hat of the unfortunate Ichabod, and close beside it a shattered pumpkin.

The brook was searched, but the body of the school-master was not to be discovered. Hans Van Ripper, as executor of his estate, examined the bundle which contained all his worldly effects. They consisted of two shirts and a half; two stocks for the neck; a pair or two of worsted stockings; an old pair of corduroy small-clothes; a rusty razor; a book of psalm tunes, full of dogs' ears; and a broken pitchpipe. As to the books and furniture of the school-house, they belonged to the community, excepting Cotton Mather's History of Witchcraft, a New England Almanac, and a book of dreams and fortune-telling; in which last was a sheet of foolscap much scribbled and blotted in several fruitless attempts to make a copy of verses in honor of the heiress of Van Tassel. These magic books and the poetic scrawls were forthwith consigned to the flames by Hans Van Ripper; who from that time forward determined to send his children no more to school; observing, that he never knew any good come of this same reading and writing. Whatever money the schoolmaster possessed, and he had received his quarter's pay but a day or two before, he must have had about his person at the time of his disappearance.

The mysterious event caused much speculation at the church on the following Sunday. Knots of gazers and gossips were collected in the churchyard, at the bridge, and at the spot where the hat and pumpkin had been found. The stories of Brouwer, of Bones, and a whole budget of others, were called to mind; and when they had diligently considered them all, and compared them with the symptoms of the present case, they shook their heads, and came to the conclusion that Ichabod had been carried off by the galloping Hessian. As he was a bachelor, and in nobody's debt, nobody troubled his head any more about him. The school was removed to a different quarter of the hollow, and another pedagogue reigned in his stead.

It is true, an old farmer, who had been down to New York on a visit several years after, and from whom this account of the ghostly adventure was received, brought home the intelligence that Ichabod Crane was still alive; that he had left the neighborhood, partly through fear of the goblin and Hans Van Ripper, and partly in mortification at having been suddenly dismissed by the heiress; that he had changed his quarters to a distant part of the country; had kept school and studied law at the same time, had been admitted to the bar, turned politician, electioneered, written for the newspapers, and finally had been made a justice of the Ten Pound Court. Brom Bones too, who shortly after his rival's disappearance conducted the blooming Katrina in triumph to the altar, was observed to look exceedingly knowing whenever the story of Ichabod was related, and always burst into a hearty laugh at the mention of the pumpkin; which led some to suspect that he knew more about the matter than he chose to tell.

The old country wives, however, who are the best judges of these matters, maintain to this day that Ichabod was spirited away by supernatural means; and it is a favorite story often told about the neighborhood round the winter evening fire. The bridge became more than ever an object of superstitious awe, and that may be the reason why the road has been altered of late years, so as to approach the church by the border of the mill-pond. The school-house being deserted, soon fell to decay, and was reported to be haunted by the ghost of the unfortunate pedagogue; and the ploughboy, loitering homeward of a still summer evening, has often fancied his voice at a distance, chanting a melancholy psalm tune among the tranquil solitudes of Sleepy Hollow.